Don't Marry Me to a Plowman!

Don't Marry Me
to a Plowman!

Women's Everyday Lives
in Rural North India

Patricia Jeffery
and Roger Jeffery

WestviewPress
A Division of HarperCollinsPublishers

Copyright © 1996 by Westview Press, Inc., A Division of HarperCollins Publishers, Inc.

Published in 1996 in the United States of America by Westview Press, Inc., 5500 Central Avenue, Boulder, Colorado 80301-2877, and in the United Kingdom by Westview Press, 12 Hid's Copse Road, Cumnor Hill, Oxford OX2 9JJ

A CIP catalog record for this book is available from the Library of Congress.
    ISBN 0-8133-1994-3 (hc)—ISBN 0-8133-2621-4 (pbk.)

The paper used in this publication meets the requirements of the American National Standard for Permanence of Paper for Printed Library Materials Z39.48-1984.

10   9   8   7   6   5   4   3   2   1

Contents

Preface and Acknowledgments

Since the early 1980s, we have been working in Bijnor District in the north Indian state of Uttar Pradesh. People's lives there are being influenced by numerous interlinked changes: Whether in connection with agriculture, religious conflicts, or health, the Indian state plays a central role. Within this rapidly changing context, our research has primarily focused on aspects of domestic and gender politics, especially on issues surrounding women's autonomy and childbearing. During our research, our expectations concerning how we would write about our experiences in Bijnor followed well-trodden tracks. Our thanks, then, must go to Carolyn Elliott for prompting us to experiment with the storytelling genre that we have adopted here.

We are very grateful for the funding we have received over the years from the Economic and Social Research Council, the Overseas Development Administration, and the Hayter Fund at the University of Edinburgh. None of these, of course, bears any responsibility for what we have written here. During our research in Bijnor, we were helped by Radha Rani Sharma and Swaleha Begum in 1982-1983, 1985, and 1990-1991; by Savita Pandey in 1982; and by Zarin Ahmed, Chhaya Pandey, and Swatantra Tyagi in 1990-1991. The material in this book comes from just two of the villages where we have worked, Dharmnagri (a caste Hindu and Harijan village) and Jhakri (a Muslim village). Radha and Swaleha worked particularly in these two villages, and we are endlessly grateful for the care and enthusiasm that they both brought to their work. We are also greatly indebted to Khurshid Ahmed, from Jhakri. In 1982, he helped to dispel people's initial anxieties about us, and he prepared a map and a preliminary household census for Jhakri. From late 1990, he worked with Roger for some three months, smoothing our access to a nearby village, Qaziwala, where the combination of the Ayodhya crisis, the brewing Gulf War, and Muslims' worries about the implications of the national decennial census was threatening to derail our research.

While we were based in Bijnor we relied on many people in Delhi (and in 1990-1991, in Mussoorie) for hospitality and for intellectual and moral support. In particular, we thank Meera Chatterjee and her family,

vii

Bina Agarwal, Loki Madan, Walter Fernandez and others at the Indian Social Institute, Jennifer and Robert Chambers, Carolyn Elliott, Kamlesh and John Mackrell, James and Willi Barton, June Rollinson, and Kunwar Satya Vira and his family.

Since completing our fieldwork we have exploited the patience and good humor of friends and colleagues who have commented on all or some of the manuscript or discussed the general issues raised by our writing. In particular, we thank our editors Alison Auch and Susan McEachern at Westview, Colin Bell, Mary Buckley, Pat Caplan, Judith Fewell, Ann Gold, Paul Greenough, David Ludden, David McCrone, Ritu Menon, Pravina King, Judith Okely, Gloria Goodwin Raheja, Ursula Sharma, Peggy Duncan Shearer and Jennifer Shearer, Nandini Sundar, Sylvia Vatuk, Susan Wadley, and Shona Wynd. Toby Morris provided valuable page-setting assistance. Catherine Robin based her lovely line drawings on some of our own photographs, and we thank her for all her efforts, which far exceeded what we had a right to expect. As a two-year-old, our daughter Laura shared our first fieldwork in Bijnor. She, too, has commented on this text, and we thank both her and Kirin for their usual forbearance with our preoccupations.

As people in Dharmnagri and Jhakri often told us, our hearts are in two parts, one "at home" in Edinburgh and one "at home" in Bijnor. In no small measure this is because of the kindness and warmth so many people in the two villages extended to us while we lived among them. It would be impossible ever to convey our gratitude adequately and invidious to pick out just one or two people for special mention. We can only hope that something of our affection for them comes through in the stories that follow.

Patricia Jeffery and Roger Jeffery
Edinburgh

Introduction

O, mother, marry me to a man in service,
Don't marry me to a plowman!

When a plowman returns from his plowing,
A revolting stench comes from afar.
When an office worker returns from his office,
A sweet perfume comes from afar.
O, mother, marry me to a man in service,
Don't marry me to a plowman!

When a plowman returns from his plowing,
He eats a dozen or so pieces of thick griddle bread,
When an office worker returns from his office,
He eats just a couple of little puffed fried breads.
O, mother, marry me to a man in service,
Don't marry me to a plowman!

When a plowman returns from his plowing,
His goad shows up from afar.
When an office worker returns from his office,
Wads of hundred rupee bank notes show up from afar.
O, mother, marry me to a man in service,
Don't marry me to a plowman!

In north India, there are many occasions when special happiness is marked by women singing in groups of varying sizes, usually with one of their number taking the lead by beating out the rhythm on a drum. Often, women's songs touch ironically on important aspects of women's lives.[1] This wedding song—reflecting the bride's point of view—would be sung by women at the bride's house before a bride departed for her husband's house. The rural economy throughout the region is so dominated by agriculture that being married to a "man who plows" would be precisely what happened to most women, however. For many brides, indeed, the plowman would be just an agricultural laborer and not an independent farmer, as only the fortunate could hope to be married into a family that owned enough land to keep it in comfort. In the north Indian villages that figure in this book, then, very few women could seriously expect to be married to a man in "service," the local term for secure and preferably urban, white-collar employment. And even marriage to a man in service would not guarantee urban residence for his wife and family. Further, the singers' raucous and assertive demands are far from what the typical village bride would express: She would neither have been consulted nor have made suggestions about how her parents would settle her in marriage for fear that her family would be dishonored by her brazenness or that allegations would begin circulating that she was having a clandestine affair. The appeal to the mother provides another layer of irony. Although some mothers were indeed central in the decisions about their daughters' marriages, many were not consulted any more than their daughters were.

The social sciences tend to approach the analysis of women's lives, like other aspects of social life, by searching for patterns and generalizations, for sense and orderliness, within the complexity of daily interactions. In many ways, village women did share a social environment or "enclosing context" in which their lives exhibited some common influences.[2] We could describe—and have done so elsewhere—the "normal" trajectories for women's lives in this region, and village women and men in Bijnor readily discussed with us how domestic life ought to be organized.[3] Yet such accounts can easily become overly structured, and women's situations can thus become so homogenized and their responses so stereotyped that the picture distorts individual experiences.

In relation to studies of ex-colonies on the one hand and gender issues on the other, recent developments in the social sciences as well as other fields have indeed challenged the straitjacketing that conventional social science approaches have tended to entail. Moreover, portrayals of women's lives in South Asia (as in other parts of the developing world) have sometimes been accused of overstressing oppressive structural constraints on women and of representing women as passive and hapless victims of their fate rather than as agents taking charge of their lives.[4]

We need to explore not just the general patterns but also the diversities in people's lives and not only the power of cultures and social structures to constrain individuals but also how people use social arrangements creatively to carve out spaces for themselves. In rural Bijnor, for instance, similarities in women's experiences were crosscut by diversities, whether because of class, caste, or religious allegiances or because women's positions and interests changed throughout the life cycle. We want to convey this in what follows. Trying to write about women's agency in Bijnor, however, is not straightforward. There is little leverage to be made out of focusing on women's agency as visible activism, for village women in Bijnor have rarely been mobilized around gender issues, or even class or religious matters. An interest in women's agency, then, fixes our attention on the ways nonactivist women might try to influence (often covertly) the directions their lives took. Their agency was largely evidenced in the domestic realm, whether in the small-scale ways women collaborated with one another to deal with their problems or in the individualistic struggles that might set woman against woman.

These considerations suggested that a biographical approach to writing about our research might enable us to address both the range of women's differing experiences within a single locality and the interplay of social structure and individual agency. Hitherto, we have generally deployed our fieldwork data in somewhat abstracted form, detached from individual biographies, to illustrate common features and develop theoretical points. By contrast, here we try to make sense of people's lives in a way that illuminates the social contexts in which they were embedded in rural Bijnor.

Through the stories about eight women, four Muslim and four Hindu, we have portrayed something of the experiences of ordinary people in the area—not historical figures or people in the public eye, not women devoting their energies to political activism. Some of these lives contained quite enough drama for comfort; none was less important or interesting than the lives of activists. Overall, we want to convey both the uniqueness and the ordinariness of the experiences of the central characters. These stories are interleaved with thematically organized interludes containing brief dialogues, incidents, and women's songs that highlight some important aspects of domestic life in rural north India. We have tried to encompass the range of responses that women made to their situations—their ambivalences as well as their certainties, their anger as well as their acceptance, their hopes as well as their hopelessness—and to portray women as sometimes feisty, sometimes cruel, and sometimes vulnerable. In so doing, we want to provide new insights into the ups and downs of village life, the depressing and the cheering stories, through exploring themes that were crucial in the everyday lives of village women in north India. Although the details of other women's lives would certainly differ, many of the general parameters echo the day-to-day realities of village women in much of the Indo-Gangetic plain. But we do not claim any more than that. In particular, the women who feature in this account should not be read as ciphers for "the Third World woman."

Exploring how women are actors and agents in their own right is by no means an uncontroversial exercise. In the following pages, we want neither to emphasize social structure at the expense of the diversities and complexities of people's lives nor to portray people as free and unrestrained agents continually making choices from an infinite variety of possibilities. These women were tied to social structures, yet their lives were not completely determined by them. They were affected by global as well as local forces beyond their control, but they also tried to shape their own fate. Their options were not totally closed, nor were they completely open. The verbalization of an imaginary bride's desires for a "man in service" perhaps hints at alternative scenarios and unfulfilled dreams. But although expressing ironies and anger through songs may have lightened women's hearts, it could not remove them from the structures in which they were embedded except in their imagination. As elsewhere, women in rural north India could be agents only within the limits set by the context in which their lives unfolded.

Village Life in Bijnor District

The women we are writing about in this book lived in the middle of a zone stretching through the Indo-Gangetic plain from Punjab to Bihar. Since the early 1980s, we have researched aspects of women's lives in Bijnor District in western Uttar Pradesh, some 100 miles northeast of Delhi. Much of our time there was spent in two adjacent villages, Dharmnagri and Jhakri. We both lived in the compound of the government dispensary on the outskirts of Dharmnagri for over a year during 1982-1983, Patricia spent two months there in 1985, and we both lived there for a further year in 1990-1991.[5]

In Indian terms, Bijnor District was not poor. It had benefited from guaranteed water supplies since the mid-1960s, and high-yielding varieties of wheat, rice, and sugarcane were the main crops. There was little local manufacturing industry; but the cities of Delhi, Muzaffarnagar, and Meerut were easily accessible by bus, and some young men were working there. Basically, though, access to land was the most crucial determinant of a household's well-being, although it is extremely difficult to provide a clear picture of people's social class.[6] Over time, households expanded and divided and their access to land changed. Small children grew to become adult labor for their family, and the need to employ nonfamily members or to seek off-farm employment shifted over time.

Nevertheless, we distinguish four broad categories in the two villages. Rich peasants owned over five acres per adult man, and they did not work on other people's land. Generally, they hired labor to complete their work on a regular or seasonal basis. Alternatively, they would rent their land on a sharecropping basis to other villagers, who would take 50 percent of the crop in payment for their labor. Middle peasants owned between two and five acres per adult man; they rarely

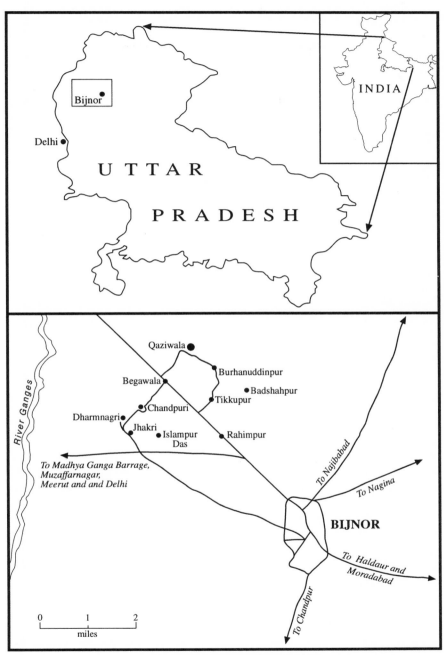

Map of Bijnor Town and Its Environs

worked for others or hired labor or had their land sharecropped for them unless by relatives. Poor peasants generally owned around one acre per adult man, and they had to rent or sharecrop additional land or seek an alternative source of income such as laboring on other people's land. Landless households relied entirely on obtaining employment from other people. In Bijnor District as a whole, about 20 percent of the villagers were landless and another 40 percent did not have enough land for subsistence, but the district had a less skewed pattern of landholding than many other parts of Uttar Pradesh.[7]

In 1990, Dharmnagri had a caste Hindu and Harijan [ex-untouchable] population of nearly 800 people. The caste Hindus composed over 60 percent of the population; over half of them were Sahnis, nearly 20 percent were Dhimars, and there were smaller numbers of Jats, Rajputs, and others. The Sahnis were split almost evenly between rich and middle peasants on the one hand and poor peasants and landless on the other. Dhimars were mainly middle peasants; the Jats and Rajputs were almost all rich and middle peasants. Over two-thirds of the Harijans were Chamars and most of the rest were Jatabs. About half the Chamars were middle peasants and the rest were poor peasants or landless. Three-quarters of the Jatabs were in poor-peasant or landless households. In 1990, Jhakri had a population of about 450, all Muslim. Of these, about 300 were Sheikhs, the most numerous Muslim group in the area. Almost all the rest were Telis [oil pressers] and Julahas [weavers]. The Sheikhs owned most of the village land. About three-quarters of them were rich and middle peasants. By contrast, around three-quarters of the Telis, Julahas, and others lived in landless households.[8]

Throughout a girl's childhood, her parents would prepare her for her inevitable marriage, for she was "someone else's property" [*parāyā dhān*], a temporary resident in her parents' house and destined to live elsewhere. Their love for her would be reflected in their concern that her upbringing ensured that she was sufficiently tamed and domesticated to become an acceptable bride and one who would fit in with her in-laws' ways. She would be trained to do housework and care for animals. She would be required to be demure and undemanding and to respect the decisions her elders made for her. Her activities would be monitored in an attempt to ensure that she had no sexual liaison before her marriage. She would learn to be circumspect in how she dressed and taught to cover her head to signal her bashfulness [*sharm*] and respect for her seniors. Her compliance was likely to be fragile, however, and it would have to be constantly constructed and enforced through her elders' strenuous discipline. She would be chastised for failures, rebuked for insubordination, and repeatedly reminded that her parents' leniency regarding her transgressions might not be replicated by her in-laws. Through constant reiterations about the demeanor of women who had been married into her natal village, through watching how young married women conducted themselves, she would come to understand the difference between being a "daughter of the village" and a "bride of the village."

As in most of Uttar Pradesh, illiteracy was high and school attendance was still sporadic for most children (especially for girls). In Dharmnagri, roughly half the girls aged between six and thirteen and two-thirds of the boys attended school in 1990. There was no specifically Hindu religious instruction at the local temple. Girls and boys alike either attended the state primary and secondary schools in Dharmnagri—schools that served Jhakri and several other surrounding villages as well—or they attended private schools, sometimes as far away as the town of Bijnor. About one-quarter of the Jhakri boys and one-third of the girls aged between six and thirteen were in school in 1990. But only five children from Jhakri—all of them boys—were attending the Dharmnagri primary school. The rest of the boys and all the girls attending school were studying at the *madrasā* [Islamic academy] at Begawala, a mile beyond Dharmnagri. The girls' schooling stopped when they reached puberty. In both villages, boys were far more encouraged to continue schooling than were girls. In wealthier families, certainly, girls were more likely to attend school, but no one expected schooling to prepare girls for employment. Rather, people hoped that an educated daughter could be married to an educated man and do household accounts and write letters to her relatives once married. Generally, though, girls' training for adult duties and for marriage was largely a domestic matter. A girl's parents were duty bound to make every effort to give her lifelong security through the prudent selection of a husband for her. But their responsibilities and concern for her well-being would not cease once she was married, as we discuss in more detail further on. They would expect to give her gifts throughout her life, welcome her into their home, and protect her in the event of marital crises.

Although members of all the local caste groups and religious communities regarded marriage as inevitable, there were differences in detail in how people went about settling their children's marriages. Among Muslims, marriage negotiations were initiated by the boy's family, which sent an offer of marriage [*paighām*, or message] to the girl's family. Among Hindus, the girl's relatives searched out a potential groom, initiated the marriage negotiations, and gave some cash (often only a token sum) to the boy "to bind" [*ghernā*] him to the match. Muslims commonly (though not universally) arranged marriages within a small geographical distance. The vast majority of marriages involving Sheikhs in Jhakri, for instance, took place within about five miles of the village. Those for Dharmnagri people were more farflung. Muslims are often stereotyped as marrying close relatives who would be prohibited marriage partners for caste Hindus and Harijans. Certainly, marriage between first cousins was acceptable to Muslims in Bijnor, but it was not the predominant form of marriage in the area. Among first-cousin matches, marriage to the mother's brother's daughter [MBD] was most popular, a marriage in which a woman's mother-in-law [HM] was also her father's sister [FZ]. We also found some examples of mother's sister's daughter [MZD] and father's brother's daughter [FBD] marriages. Marriage to the father's sister's daughter [FZD] was very uncommon.[9] It must be emphasized, though, that genealogical links between Muslim spouses were generally more complicated than that, and even those marriages that took place within a small radius were not necessarily between people who were closely related. The prohibition on certain matches among caste Hindus and Harijans probably reduced somewhat the density of their marriage and kinship networks, which were important routes through which news traveled, for instance, to a woman's parents about her situation in her husband's home. As with Muslims, though, caste Hindus and Harijans used their marriage networks to search out potential spouses for their children, and it was not uncommon for a caste Hindu or Harijan bride to be married into the same village (though not the same house) as her father's sister or for two sisters to be married to two brothers or paternal cousins if their ages were appropriate.

Among Hindus and Muslims alike, once the engagement was agreed upon, gift exchanges generally ensued. Some people could afford to spend lavishly; others could afford only modest celebrations. The wedding itself could be very expensive, especially for the bride's relatives. They should have provided a dowry [*dahez, jahez*] comprising items of clothing (for the bride's in-laws as well as the bride), jewelry for the bride and probably a watch for the bridegroom, household effects (utensils, bed and bedding, a stool, perhaps a table and chairs, a sewing machine, a cycle for the groom, and so forth), possibly a milch animal, and (among Hindus) cash that could amount to several thousand rupees among wealthier families.[10] Parents often felt that they could not afford to give as much as they wished, and people asserted that dowries had been escalating in recent years. Providing a dowry was a major cause of rural indebtedness.[11] The boy's family was expected to provide living quarters for their son and his bride, and many families scheduled their sons' marriages according to their ability to add new and preferably kiln-brick [*pukkā*] rooms to their homes. The groom's family should also have presented some jewelry to the bride, though many women reported that their mother-in-law reclaimed it with a view to presenting it to the next bride to marry into the family. Among Hindus and Muslims alike, the *bhāt* might also be presented. The *bhāt* would consist of items of jewelry and clothing for the bride and groom, foodstuffs for the wedding feasts, and cash, all of which were presented by the bride's uncles [MB] (if she was the first of her siblings to be married) or by the groom's uncles [MB] (if he was the oldest son).[12] Among Muslims, the groom should settle the *mahr* on his bride. The *mahr* was a sum of money specified in the marriage contract, but it was not in any sense a payment for the bride. Rather it was one facet of the husband's more general obligation to provide for his wife, who was entitled to receive it at the time of marriage or in the event of divorce and use it as and when she wished.[13]

Sometimes, among Muslims and Hindus alike, engagements were settled when the bride and groom were young children. In recent years, however, wedding ceremonies [*shādī, byāh*] for sexually immature children have become very rare. Even if such marriages did occur, the couple would not begin living together until they were sixteen or seventeen. Most wedding ceremonies, however, took place six months or even a year before the cohabitation [*gaunā*], which was a further occasion when the bride's parents would provide gifts for their daughter and her in-laws, normally clothing, jewelry, and foodstuffs.

The implications of marriage and the experiences of married life for women in rural Bijnor were very similar, whatever the bride's religion or her family's wealth. Normally, men expected to remain firmly rooted in their natal village throughout their lives. Women's life trajectories, however, usually entailed a shift in residence when they married. The bride might have seemed like a mere walk-on character in her own wedding arrangements and ceremonies, but her marriage was a crucial watershed for her, a point of rupture when she would leave her childhood home and migrate to her husband's village. She would be collected by the *barāt*, the party of men from her husband's village who had attended the wedding ceremonies. She would then become incorporated into her husband's household while yet retaining a foothold in her parents' home. Her arranged marriage—typically while still in her teens—would place the new bride in a position with little power in her in-laws' house. She would probably start her married life in a joint household with her husband's parents and under the tutelage of her mother-in-law. She would be required to be acquiescent and to subordinate her own wishes to those of her in-laws. She would signal her respect for her senior in-laws (including her husband) by refraining from addressing them by name and by practicing bodily concealment and seclusion [purdah] in relation to her husband's senior male relatives. Her work would be guided and corrected by her mother-in-law, her movements monitored, and her contacts with her parents and other relatives regulated.[14]

Moreover, a vital aspect of her marital career would revolve around bearing and raising children. Although people talked about the importance of sons in terms of "name and mark" [nām-nishān] after their death, they emphasized the need for sons (and daughters-in-law) to sustain them in old age. Such dependency was not considered demeaning. Rather, it was an entitlement that enabled sons to repay their parents for rearing them and settling them in marriage. Dependency on daughters, by contrast, would be a matter of profound shame. Without sons, then, the elderly faced a lonely and impoverished old age, for few people had savings or access to pensions. But people could not guarantee that their sons would survive. Rates of infant and child mortality in Bijnor District and in Uttar Pradesh as a whole were well above the all-India averages.[15] By the 1980s, despite dramatic improvements in the previous two decades, roughly 10 percent of children still died before their first birthday, and another 5 percent died before their fifth birthday. Death rates among girls were higher than among boys, and women in the childbearing ages also experienced high rates of mortality in and around childbirth. In combination, these factors have led to a very unbalanced sex ratio. At about 873 females for every 1,000 males in 1991, Bijnor District was very similar to Uttar Pradesh as a whole. Because of the high rates of child mortality and the need for sons, fertility rates in rural Uttar Pradesh remained high in the 1980s. Despite relatively rapid declines in fertility, women were still giving birth five or six times on average. Few couples were using "modern" contraceptives; the most common method—sterilization—was usually resorted to only after the survival of four or five children was ensured.[16]

Crucially, women's situations were further encoded by their lack of property rights, which obtained regardless of their household's financial standing. A woman would be unlikely to inherit land from her parents or to attain rights of ownership or effective control over the land owned by her husband's kin.[17] Nor would she have ownership rights in the houses where she lived, either as a child or as a married woman. Yet this was not generally regarded as problematic. In rural Bijnor, men were expected to provide for their womenfolk, their daughters, their wives, and their elderly mothers. Most did so. Only when this support broke down—if a woman's marriage failed, if she was widowed, or if her husband's income was inadequate—did she experience the far-reaching implications of her economic powerlessness. Still, few women considered it desirable to be employed. With their low levels of education, they could expect to obtain only poorly paid and demeaning employment. Only a poor man was likely to swallow his pride and face accusations of living off his wife's "immoral earnings." Only women in very poor households were likely to be employed outside their family enterprise, generally as workers in the fields or homes of more wealthy farmers. Some elderly widows without support resorted to work as traditional birth attendants [*dāīs*]. Even then, their income probably did not provide economic independence. The major "incomes" of the women we knew were the goods and cash presented by their parents when they married and throughout their lives thereafter. And control over these resources was by no means guaranteed, particularly for a new bride.[18]

In other words, the young married woman would have to deal with life in her husband's village on a day-to-day basis with little economic power and without the ready availability of the support networks established during her childhood. Over time, she would move up the domestic hierarchy and become a more powerful mother and mother-in-law, provided she bore sons. Especially in the early years of her marriage, though, her scope would be severely constrained by the everyday living arrangements within her husband's village. She would find it quite difficult—but not impossible—to exercise her will. The challenge for us as social scientists is to find ways to describe women's situations that neither deny this potential and victimize women nor overrate these women's capacity to alter the conditions under which they lived. Perhaps the techniques of biographers offer a way forward.

The General and the Particular

If social science portrayals tend to obscure the individual within patterns and generalities, conventional biographies and autobiographies tend to concentrate unashamedly on individuals. Yet if they often present their subjects as the makers of their own destiny, as agents determining their own life's trajectory, there is also generally some attempt to locate them in their family networks and the wider society of their time. Within the social sciences, indeed, a style of biographical writing more deeply informed by sociological perspectives has recently come to be seen as a way of addressing the interplay of social structure and individual agency. In this book, we are taking our lead from these discussions.[19]

There are many parallels in the stories and incidents that we present. We are not dealing with isolated individuals but with people responding to the expectations of others around them, expectations that reflect commonly held assumptions about the rights and obligations of people to one another and about the proper way of organizing social life. An individual's story or a brief episode can highlight some common features of village life in north India. But this approach also gives us some leeway to indicate how people's lives were neither identical nor solely dictated by social forces. It also enables us to focus on the ambiguities that surrounded women's views of their situations.

Women themselves expected to be married and said "marriage is essential" [*shādī majbūrī hai*]. Yet many also complained about their married lives, and some went so far as to say that "marriage is a calamity" [*shādī hai barbādī*]—and not just financially for their parents. Parents knew they must get their daughter married, yet their relief at having done so was tinged with sadness and anxiety when their daughter departed. Some husbands were kindly and generous; others were prone to beat their wives at the slightest provocation. Some mothers tried to prevent their sons from moving out of their ambit and into that of their wife; others delighted in having a daughter-in-law in the house. Some brides found their in-laws authoritarian or grasping or prone to favor one daughter-in-law over the others. Some women found that their parents became inaccessibly distant, others that interference from their parents provoked their in-laws' hostility. Parents knew that whether a girl was born into a wealthy or an impoverished home had ramifications for her entire life. But they also knew that much might happen that could not be predicted on their daughter's wedding day. There might be untimely deaths or serious ailments. She might fail to bear children who survived or might give birth to girls but no boys. There might be "sadness and happiness" [*dukh-sukh*] in her future. Even from apparently similar beginnings, women's lives could take different trajectories.

Through the voices of the women who figure in this book, we can hear strident assertions as well as doubt, ambivalence, and differences of opinion.[20] We can grasp something of their zest for life even when they portrayed themselves as the victims of a thieving mother-in-law or a violent husband. There were women who wholeheartedly embraced the expectations placed on them and who criticized women who dared to rebel. Some women bemoaned their fate, and some simply endured the difficult circumstances in which they found themselves. Yet others resisted what life had dealt them. Maybe they appeared submissive in their actions but critiqued their situations through their speech and their ironical songs. Maybe they resisted in deed as well.

It is difficult to render the complexities of village women's lives in north India, not least because conducting fieldwork is an intensely interactive process. The material in this book has been drawn from our conversations with people in Dharmnagri and Jhakri. Inevitably, this results in a partial and limited picture of life there. Before embarking on the main body of the book, then, we must address some important issues connected with trying to strike a balance between structure and agency and with how we went about the research and writing on which these stories and episodes are based.

Personhood and Agency

Some would argue that grappling with individual agency in India is an inappropriate and misguided exercise, for "the investigator who seeks ways of asking in rural India about equivalents of Western 'individuals' . . . risks imposing an alien ontology and an alien epistemology on those who attempt to answer."[21] If Indian people are so locked into relationships that the very notion of the individual actor is problematic, would this not pose insuperable difficulties for using a biographical approach? What sort of narrative would the unbounded "fluid person" of India visualize and construct for her (own, individual) life?[22]

By contrast, we believe that the stark dichotomy between the Westerner's "hard individualism" and the connected person of India needs to be challenged. On the one hand, it represents the West with an image of very debatable applicability. The hermetically sealed room of one's own is available only to the select few (mainly white elite men). Ordinary people—women and men—generally experience their lives as bound up with the concerns of other people in the home and the workplace, and with the obligations and demands, joys and benefits, of social life.[23] Indeed, a central tenet of the sociological perspective is that individuals are formed and molded through their interactions and connections with other people. On the other hand, people in India have a notion of their own individuality even while being closely connected to others and embedded in wide-ranging social networks.[24] An overdrawn dichotomy between India and the West tends to "other" people in India by suggesting that their social contexts are so "other" that radically different types of personhood are created within them.[25] Clearly, there are differences between the daily livelihood concerns of rural Indian women and the readers of this book. The locally specific preoccupations generated within an agrarian economy gave a distinctive flavor to people's lives, yet (we would argue) not to such a degree that they remain completely opaque to readers who try to imagine themselves in that context.

Drawing a rigid contrast tends to deny the potentialities for Indian people's individuality, whether in their practices or in their imaginations, and could easily lead to portrayals of rule-bound automata. People everywhere engage in attempts to balance the often conflicting obligations they have to other people, to enhance their reputation among relatives and neighbors, and to prevent others from undermining their well-being. Certainly, in recounting incidents in which they figured, people in Dharmnagri and Jhakri portrayed themselves and other people as thinking agents, to some degree making an impact on their own lives or those of others. They would also express their uniqueness by contrasting themselves with other people they knew. A sense of the individual agent and of personal autonomy is not evidenced solely in Western models of the individual and personal rights; nor was something like it utterly meaningless to Indian villagers.

Moreover, as elsewhere, personhood is not monolithic in India. People's social locations are various. Their connections to other people are different, and the spaces available to them for individual agency are diverse. In rural Bijnor, people were differentiated by wealth, by religious community, and by caste. And most crucially for us here, personhood was also gendered. A woman would normally experience her connectedness to other people and her capacity to exercise agency quite differently from a man. Her marriage would loosen (but not normally destroy) her connections with her natal kin. Then the process of incorporating her into her husband's household and village would begin. Her husband would never expect to be disconnected from his natal kin, and he would never become as connected to her natal kin as she did to his. In addition, unlike his wife, a young man could anticipate a degree of economic independence from his father and brothers and the capacity to make decisions on behalf of his family even if he was unlikely to do so at the time of his marriage. Further, people's experiences of personhood would change. Some connections were lifelong, others were dissolved and faded away, yet others were created in adulthood. A girl in her natal village would have little say over the decisions that affected her future. As a young married woman, she would have much less space for individual agency than would be available to her when she was in her thirties and forties. And an elderly widow might find her position of domestic power usurped by her juniors. In other words, gendered personhood was intertwined with biography and the passage of time. There are, then, good reasons—both academic and political— for not abandoning a search for women's agency.

Women's Agency and Women's Resistance

In recent years, considerable attention has been paid to the "weapons of the weak" and the forms of everyday resistance that subordinated sectors (such as the poor peasantry) use to challenge the structures that oppress them.[26] Typically, such forms of resistance are spontaneous and individual rather than highly organized social rebellions. They are generally mundane rather than spectacular challenges to the status quo, avoiding open confrontation rather than being revolutionary. They often entail subterfuge and secrecy. They might seem devious and underhanded to the powers that be. They are also likely to be rather elusive for the transient researcher. Incontrovertibly, however, this is important material to document, for portraying subordinates simply as passive and obedient can provide only a seriously lopsided account of social order.

In similar vein, historians associated with the *Subaltern Studies* approach to Indian history have departed from the tendency to see history "from the top down" and have begun to explore and applaud the willfulness evidenced in the various forms of resistance of rebellious "subalterns" such as peasants and factory workers.[27] And partly because of a desire to counter the passive-victim stereotype of the South Asian woman, some feminist historians and social scientists have emphasized women's resistance, whether in word or deed, and described the alternative discourses through which women create definitions of autonomy and power that enable them to justify their attempts to direct and shape their lives. Such approaches certainly make more sense of our experiences of doing research than one that sidelines women's complaints and critiques.[28]

Women in rural Bijnor did sometimes struggle against their situations. In their husbands' homes, they sometimes answered back and refused to cooperate. They put too much salt in the food or refused to cook at all. They also sang derisive and obscene songs, mocking their menfolk, slandering their in-laws. Sometimes their songs relied on irony for effect, inverting social hierarchies by elevating juniors over their elders, parodying social superiors who should be respected not ridiculed, and giving a window on women's imagined alternatives to the normal patterns of everyday life. Sometimes they alluded to the sadness of parting when the bride goes to her husband's home or to her vulnerability in her in-law's home. Some men in Jhakri opposed their wives' and daughters' singing and dancing, saying that the vulgar lyrics and lewd gestures were not permissible for Muslims. But, as in Dharmnagri, there were women in Jhakri famed for their skills in song. Women might also act in cautious and undramatic ways that rested on concealment rather than open confrontation, such as selling small quantities of grain to raise cash. Further, mobilizing natal kin was one of the most promising avenues of support for a young married woman. Her parents would normally continue to provide gifts on a regular basis, so she usually maintained some degree of contact with them and her siblings. When she visited her natal village, she could don a much more independent persona than in her husband's village. She could also achieve a degree of privacy to do things without the knowledge of her in-laws, but often with the complicity of her mother. And it might be through actively requesting her parents' interventions that some of the more severe constrictions of her married life could be relaxed.[29]

Citing such evidence of women's resistance is one thing. In reacting against accounts that emphasize constraining and oppressive structural forces, however, we could easily tip the scales in the other direction and seem to imply that women were not subordinate at all. The twin tendencies of romanticizing women's resistance and seeing it as coterminous with agency contain their own difficulties.[30] It is important neither to exaggerate the potential of women's everyday resistance to alter the terms under which they lived nor to render invisible the ways women were co-opted by the protective and maybe comforting certainties of the structures in which they were embedded.

People have to deal with the social structures within which they live. They cannot ignore them. Thus, women's resistance was conditioned and limited by the power structures to which it was a response. It was channeled by women's understanding that they acted within largely unalterable structures. Often, as women knew all too well, their acts of resistance might be self-defeating and self-destructive. Indeed, women tempted to resist might have second thoughts. A woman who complained to us about being beaten might hesitate to "move her tongue" and "give answers" to her husband for fear of a further beating. Satirical sentiments expressed in song could not safely be verbalized in normal speech outside the circumscribed contexts of songfests associated with weddings and births. The woman who refused to cook went hungry too.[31] The full force of "social structure" was exposed by the punishment aimed at the person who stepped too far out of line. Fear of shaming, of gossip and ostracism, even of the loss of home and children could all deter the resentful woman from open defiance. It was not something a woman was likely to undertake unless pushed to the limits of her endurance.

Subaltern groups, such as agricultural laborers or the urban working classes, generally have much greater opportunities than women to escape the controls over them and develop a forceful counterculture. The normal residential patterns of family life seriously reduce women's scope in this regard. Minimal privacy and dense information networks restricted women's opportunities even for subterfuge and cheating. A young man's visits to town, his attendance at weddings in other villages or his time spent on "guesting" at the homes of his mother's brothers, his married sisters, or his wife's parents all provided some opportunities for developing personal space outside other people's gaze. His wife, by contrast, would probably leave his village only to visit her own parents or in search of medical treatment, and she would rarely do so alone.

Moreover, we must keep in mind the limitations of the support provided by a woman's natal kin. Precisely because her in-laws would understand the potential for insubordination, they would control her contacts with her parents and brothers. In any case, she would have to be circumspect in obtaining their support. Her parents could not intervene without fear of being reminded that their daughter was now "someone else's property." If she told them all about her marital difficulties, the argument went, they would needlessly suffer. Thus, a woman might remain silent until her situation was unbearable rather than upset her parents. Many parents did indeed help in a crisis. Many mothers were willing allies of their daughters. But women also knew there was no certainty of this. Parents might say it was not their business. They might refuse to let their daughter return to live in their home, saying her presence would dishonor the whole family. Often, they simply advised her to bear her troubles silently. Thus, although a woman's natal kin could be a crucial resource, she herself was not in a very strong negotiating position in relation to them. What is more, this individualistic and often covert reliance of married women on their parents scattered women's struggles rather than concentrating them within their in-laws' villages.[32]

If women resisted, then, it was often against considerable odds and with little guarantee that their resistance could be very effective. It might not always seem the most sensible of responses—and women were not in a constant state of rebellion. But in any case, conflating women's agency with resistance would be to misconstrue the nature of women's agency within structures of domination. Women handled and perceived their situations in diverse ways. Their agency was evidenced in different guises, including ones that upheld the status quo rather than challenged and undermined it.

For one thing, women made only partial critiques of their situations.[33] Certainly, women complained and resisted, but they did not complain about everything; nor did they complain all the time. If women's songs sometimes provided glimmerings of an alternative world of inverted hierarchies, the resistance seemingly implied by them was often "unthinkable" because it would be shameless or undesirable rather than incautiously risky. We have, for instance, found it difficult to unearth satisfactory translations for the ideas bound up in "agency" and "autonomy." Several words of Arabic or Persian origin were used

by Muslims and Hindus alike in Bijnor, among them the related terms
ikhtiyār [power, right, authority], *ikhtiyārī* [optional, voluntary], *mukhtār*
[free agent, empowered] and *mukhtārī* [authority, freedom of action]. A
more common word, but rather less close in meaning, was *āzādī*
[freedom, independence]. There was also *zimmedār* [responsible] and
zimmedārī [responsibility]. When we discussed these words with
women, it became clear that a term such as "agency" was not
necessarily positively valued when translated as *ikhtiyār* or *zimmedār*,
especially not when applied to women. It was not that women could not
visualize having these qualities. Rather, being in control or having
responsibility was problematic for them in various ways. Being required
to accept responsibility might be a frightening rather than an attractive
prospect for those without much power, who would be blamed and
punished if their initiatives failed. And young married women who
tried to wrest some freedom of action for themselves might face
accusations of acting shamelessly or inappropriately. A daughter-in-
law's agency might be construed as bad agency if she did not veil
herself properly or if she initiated conversation with her father-in-law,
that is, as agency with the capacity to bring havoc and disorder.[34]

Further, it would be a serious mistake to see women as unrelentingly
pitted against their situations. We need to explore not only "the ways in
which women evade subordination" but also "how they are
'apprenticed' in these conditions."[35] Crucially, women generally differ
from other subalterns in having rather greater stakes in the system, at
least in the long term. The very structures through which women in
Dharmnagri and Jhakri were controlled and which they might be
tempted to resist also provided the only means by which their well-
being could be sustained. Short-term resistance might jeopardize long-
term well-being.[36] And the transformations that would occur during the
course of a woman's life offered promotional chances of sorts. Not
surprisingly, women generally preferred to make "patriarchal
bargains," trading off resistance and acquiescence.[37] The obedient wife
could usually expect her husband to fulfill his obligations to provide her
with lifelong economic support. The compliant young daughter-in-law
could anticipate changes in her domestic situation. The marriages of her
husband's brothers, the deaths of her parents-in-law, or arguments
about work or property could all result in the creation of separate
households. With time, her movements would no longer be so
controlled by others and nor would her responsibilities be allocated by
her mother-in-law. Some personal space might be won, although she
would remain subject to her husband's requirements and effectively
tied to her work unless she had a daughter capable of helping.
Gradually, too, a woman might accumulate more social support in her

husband's village. During her middle years, at any rate, a woman could expect to reap rewards even though by old age she might have become beholden to her sons and their wives.

Women in Bijnor would probably not admire the daring (and maybe foolhardy) resister. Are such women, then, really more worthy of our respect and attention than the women who (maybe prudently) opted for damage limitation, who quietly and patiently endured their situations and staked out a few modest claims? Might they not have correctly gauged that alternative paths would be counterproductive and unpalatable? Might they not have considered their capacity to fulfill their duties as wives and mothers a worthy and positive form of agency? Yet clearly, it would not be a use of agency that would topple the status quo. What of the initiative of the young woman who (rather than engaging in open combat) called on her father or brothers to protect her? Would not her very reliance on them to wield power on her behalf underscore her vulnerability in her husband's village? And in any case, her father would probably consent to this mediated agency only in the interests of bringing a miscreant husband or grasping in-laws into line, not to create a totally new vision of domestic life.

Moreover, if an older woman gained somewhat greater control over her own life, she would also have greater capacity to enforce her will on her juniors. She would expect to be obeyed rather than to obey. The same woman who once resented her parents' power over her marital destiny might yet demand her own daughter's obedience in the interests of protecting family honor. The same woman who complained about her oppressive mother-in-law might yet point to an obstinate or lazy daughter-in-law's failure to provide her with the respite to which she felt entitled. How could we—and women in Bijnor—draw the line between the acceptable use and the illegitimate abuse of power, between "good" agency and "bad" agency? Could we applaud the mother-in-law who incited her son to beat his wife or the mother who told her daughter to endure her lot? Could we approve of the woman who stole her daughter-in-law's jewelry or who demanded more from her daughter-in-law's parents? And how should we respond to the woman who, in the fullness of time, took revenge on her widowed mother-in-law by making her life a misery?

Over time, women's locations in domestic structures altered, their interests shifted, and the opportunities to exercise power over their own lives and those of others changed. Thus, women did not experience their daily lives from the same vantage point. One implication is that women's divergent interests tended to set women in the same or closely related households apart from one another.[38] For reasons such as these, we want to avoid either stereotyping women as the virtuous victims of oppressive structures or romanticizing their capacity to resist. Their lives were far more complex than that. Women did not speak with a single voice. If they sometimes talked about themselves as victims, they also portrayed themselves in ways that suggested either critique or acceptance. Often, their resistance coexisted with a subservience that took account of both the balance of power and the balance of long-term benefits.[39] We should perhaps expect a "complex mixture of deep-rooted commitment and reluctant compliance, of accepting things as they are and of undermining them through their questions and evasions" or, in slightly different terms, "omnipresent tension and contradictions between the hegemony and autonomy of consciousness, between submission and resistance in practice."[40]

If we see women simply as innocent victims, we can be seduced into believing in their inherent goodness. That goodness, however, is a feature of their relative powerlessness.[41] Yet even the most apparently powerless had some means of strategizing and carving out space for themselves from among the realistic and thinkable options presented to them. There were opportunities for women's agency. And if we see women as agents and concede that women had some power, then we must also admit that they sometimes used their power not just in locally unacceptable ways—many of which might cause us little or no offense—but also in ways that might trouble us when we think through the implications for mobilizing women around gender issues.[42] Certainly, women's agency by no means always took the form of resistance. Women also had many stakes in the system. Their agency might entail endurance as well as acquiescence. It might also entail coercing other women. In brief, women's agency was rather more complex and rather less rosy-tinted than it is sometimes portrayed.

Our Agency as Researchers

In the midst of trying to grasp such issues, we also have to address our own agency. What sort of agency could (or should) we as outsiders have, whether during the research or while writing about it? How should we have handled the numerous and perplexing decisions about responding to people in our own daily lives in Dharmnagri and Jhakri, or the vexing dilemmas about how to write about them for an audience that would probably be predominantly non-Indian?

During our research, we were constantly confronted by the complexity of the experience. Just as people in Dharmnagri and Jhakri had differing vantage points and ambivalent stances, so too have we faced our own uncertainties about the mixed messages we were receiving. There were contrasts as well as parallels between locally defined parameters for reading what we saw and heard and the nonlocal readings that we inevitably brought to bear. Often we empathized with women's assessments of their situations; sometimes we felt at odds with their views. Aligning ourselves with one person's critique would almost inevitably put us out of alignment with other people's. Something obvious to local eyes might suggest irresolvable dilemmas to us.

Frequently, we felt constrained by circumstances and by local expectations. Sometimes, we obeyed the demands of the situation, whether by Patricia's joining in songfests to celebrate a boy's birth (while inwardly both uplifted by the women's exuberance and saddened by the lack of comparable celebrations for a girl's birth) or by Roger's willingness to transport wedding parties in our jeep (while feeling both pleased by helping the bridegroom's party to stage an impressive performance and disconcerted by the weeping bride squeezed onto the backseat). Through choices such as these, our agency helped to sustain practices about which we felt ambivalent.

Sometimes, though, we dared to be openly defiant, directly challenging people's behavior and assumptions about social distinctions and appealing rather to their alternative but generally muted rhetorics about common humanity. We listened to people's pejorative stereotypes of people regarded as inferiors but we refused to endorse them. We insisted on eating in any home to which we were invited, whether Muslim or Harijan, much to the chagrin of some caste Hindus. Sometimes, we contested local views of birth pollution by picking up a newborn baby or by displaying an unseemly interest in local obstetric practice by talking to *dāīs*. Or we questioned people's views of wife beating or the value placed on women's work. Unwittingly, too, we violated local, taken-for-granted assumptions about proper behavior only to be taken to task and asked to explain our bizarre actions. But, however much we disapproved of casteism, communal prejudice, and sexism, we could hardly expect to convert people to our views.

We were also perturbed about the ethics of intervention. Using our jeep for medical emergencies was the only decent thing to do, but we were more uncertain about other medical matters. What should we do about local medical treatments that we believed to be dangerous, such as the practice of swaddling a feverish baby in layers of clothing and blankets, or the excessive use of injections, generally given with unsterile syringes? What if we foresaw an obstetric calamity as yet unrecognized by local medical staff? And given women's complaints about the burdens of childbearing, their views of the government family-planning program, and our own awareness of the ethical and political issues connected with contraception and women's reproductive rights, how should we respond to requests for family-planning advice?

Every day, we had to examine our role in Dharmnagri and Jhakri, living, researching, and at some level tampering. Yet even though our relatively brief presence was certainly felt in several ways, our impact should not be overestimated. We could not make a deep impression on the wider social setting in which people's households were embedded, nor could our presence alter the terms on which women would negotiate their everyday domestic lives. But was our agency then limited to giving people lifts in our jeep or providing family-planning advice and so forth?

In thinking about such issues, we have come to see some correspondences between therapy and social research. Therapy can enable people to express a sense of themselves and their lives. Indeed, the ability to formulate a coherent personal narrative is considered a key to mental health and self-esteem. The therapist's facilitating agency is akin to that of the researcher who asks people to talk about their lives, listens intently, and (generally) refrains from making overt judgments, and who takes the whole exercise seriously and carefully registers what people say. After initial suspicions, almost all the women we talked to became willing narrators, appearing to value constructing their accounts for us. Perhaps we inspired them to give their testimony because we had time to pay attention to the detail of their daily lives. By not gossiping about people's confidences, maybe we offered a novel space for women to bring issues into the open and talk through the problems confronting them. Possibly, through our responses to their questions, we sparked off discussions that continued even after we had left. But did encouraging women to construct their own narratives enhance their self-esteem? Maybe the catharsis simply contained their critiques and enabled them to cope and endure rather than protest and organize. Or maybe it heightened their frustrations. We can only speculate about the longer-term impact, for good or bad, of our research practice.

Beyond the politics of research, we have also lived with the politics of writing and representation on a daily basis. We are constantly daunted by the danger of being entrapped in different forms of ethnocentrism. At one extreme, non-Indian authors have sometimes used Indian women as a foil for the (supposedly) liberated Western woman and have emphasized difference, whether romanticizing the "Indian woman" as alien and fascinatingly exotic, or stereotyping her as the oppressed victim of a more or less explicitly criticized other culture. At the other extreme, a universalizing tendency generalizes the demands of Western feminism and ignores the locally specific impact of global processes on women's daily lives—on work patterns and consumption possibilities, on health and reproductive rights, on the household and the state, and thus on women's hopes and dreams. Could we avoid all these pitfalls and present specific structures of opportunity and constraint without othering the women located in them? We are continually mindful that polarized debates have left us with very little space to understand, let alone convey to others, the ambiguities and complexities of social life in rural Bijnor.

Women's Accounts

These concerns imply that the business of presenting people's stories is by no means straightforward. So does adopting a biographical approach open up a space that might bring us substantially closer to "real" people? Or do people constantly form and re-form in response to crucial life events? Does oral history unproblematically retrieve the "truth" about people's pasts and about local history more generally or are we in the domain of accounts rather than true stories? Does our writing seem to provide a clear glass through which to view women's lives? Or is it a prism that directs the reader's gaze and distorts the women's lives to the point that they would no longer recognize themselves? Would they have encapsulated their lives in the same way? In using quotations from our fieldnotes, do we perhaps give the impression that there are no authorial interventions in the reporting? Have we framed the stories too much or provided an appearance of order and closure on events that are not tidy, clear-cut, or finished? And in what ways have our interventions and interpretations been influenced by our own biographies?

Precisely such issues have taxed social scientists using biography and autobiography in their work. A central theme is the need to present life stories not as unmediated and true histories but as accounts in which the subject and the author alike constantly interpret and reinterpret, order and reorder, past events to make sense of both the past and the present.[43] Such considerations necessitate some discussion of our procedures. How did we go about our research? How do we think we know what were the common features of social life in rural Bijnor or the preoccupations of village women? And how did we try to turn a mass of reportage into (what we hope are) readable and informative accounts without overdetermining them?

During our initial research in Jhakri and Dharmnagri, much of our fieldwork material came from forty-one couples, half of them caste Hindu or Harijan and half Muslim. We had selected them to give a range of caste and class positions and, crucially, because the wife was either pregnant or had recently given birth when we first arrived in 1982. At that time, most of these women were in their twenties or early thirties, and none was employed outside the family enterprise. These couples have continued to be central to our subsequent research in the area. By 1990, some of the women were still preoccupied with childbearing; others were becoming more concerned with arranging their children's marriages.

Often, the formal interview both hinges on the assumption that the individual is an appropriate focus and tends to reinforce images of individuals separable from other people. We have now talked in depth to the original wives and husbands, more or less formally and separately and together on numerous occasions. We have also talked to their relatives and others such as birth attendants. Frequently, we were unable to talk to people alone even when we wanted to, and our "interviews" often spiraled off at tangents when bystanders contributed to the discussion of some topic we had raised. Such material is supplemented by observation and by the conversations these and other women initiated when they visited us. Simply living in the villages also meant that numerous incidents came to our notice concerning family disputes, marriage arrangements, illnesses, and so forth. Further, every time a woman told us something about herself, she also gave biographical details about kin and neighbors, who in turn often added their own detailed commentaries on events. Thus, we have been able to tap into people's interrelationships, watch them in their dealings with other people, and look at issues from more than one person's perspective. Gradually, we have built up quite a complex picture of village life, though of course a rather discontinuous and fragmentary one.

We did not directly ask women to recount their life stories.[44] Rather, many of the issues that we delved into concerned women's networks and their connectedness to other people—their sources of help during pregnancy and after childbirth, the links they sustained with their natal kin, and the changing profiles of their households as people were born or died, or as women married in or out.[45] We looked broadly at gender politics in domestic life, at issues such as preferences for sons, arranged marriage, and the "husband's rule" (as women described it), as well as a range of issues connected with agriculture. These were all topics of tremendous local interest and importance, although of course there were many others with which people were also preoccupied. Our interviewing style was open-ended, actively encouraging people to expand on points that particularly interested them. And concerns with births, marriages, and deaths framed a great deal of what they talked about among themselves. Women's commentaries about domestic organization and power often featured judgments about good and bad practice among their relatives and neighbors or their analyses of the implications of wider political and economic changes for their own daily lives. Thus, whereas our own particular (and necessarily blinkered) research interests certainly channeled many of our conversations and much of the material that we accumulated, we also tried to respond to their interests. Indeed, long-term research could scarcely be sustained (let alone be justified) if researchers doggedly persisted in asking about topics that were supremely boring to local people.[46]

Further, people in Dharmnagri and Jhakri were not, of course, operating merely in reactive mode in relation to us. We were engaged in dialogues with them, processes of two-way questioning and mutual attempts to make sense of our various lives.[47] Their interest in quizzing us and in pointing to differences between their expectations and our own acted as a foil for their own social theorizing as much as for our own. People sometimes found us bemusing. They wanted to find out how we ticked and how our puzzling behavior squared with their ideas about Westerners.[48] Conversations were often initiated with us about how we had met, how we had come to be married, and what gift exchanges had taken place. People wanted to know why we had never lived in a joint household with Roger's parents or why our daughter was born several years after marriage. All these discussions were interwoven with their commentaries about life in rural Bijnor, about dowry, about the cost of marrying girls and the importance of having sons, about the problems of living jointly with relatives, and about the conflicts that arise between mothers- and daughters-in-law.

In some measure, then, we were engaged in a collaborative activity with people in Dharmnagri and Jhakri. Often they adopted an active role and initiated conversations with us, trying to ensure that we understood what was happening. Gradually, many people became patient and enthusiastic providers of their perspectives on particular incidents, arguing their cases, showing us how their views differed from other people's. With time, some were so insistent that we "got it right" that they made us take verbatim notes of their personal testimonies.

Our "raw" material from these encounters should not, of course, be read as "right" but as selective accounts that have been touched up and colored by the speaker in various ways and for various purposes. Women's different interests and involvements might mean they glossed the same event in different ways, judging a mother-in-law's punishments and her daughter-in-law's insubordination in starkly contrasting lights. One woman might represent her own initiative as justifiable revenge against someone else's alleged misdeeds. Another woman's self-portrait of injured innocence might aim to absolve her of responsibility for a crisis largely sparked off by her own actions. Even single individuals' accounts were not set in stone. Women often voluntarily returned to topics of previous conversations, or we ourselves followed up on issues that had been germane during a previous visit. Generally, the differences in accounts amplified rather than directly contradicted previous ones. Occasionally, though, there were nuanced shifts in emphasis, more rarely glaring contradictions, that we could pinpoint because we tried to select out as little as possible in recording our fieldnotes. Such inconsistencies highlight the importance of people's shifting positions in relation to the events being discussed and further underscore that these tales, often told with great verve and finesse, cannot be read straight. They are accounts, not "true stories."

In trying to grasp what we were hearing and seeing, we were also engaged in dialogues with the various female research assistants who worked for us over the years. Generally, Patricia was accompanied by one of them, partly because they felt unable to go alone into the villages and partly because teamwork permitted a conversational style of "interviewing" that accommodated taking notes. We did not use tape recorders, but the detailed notes taken at the time by the research assistants were always written in Hindi as soon as possible afterward. Meanwhile, Patricia would go elsewhere with another assistant. As Radha and Swaleha became more attuned to what we wanted, they sometimes went to the villages with another assistant and then worked together on the writing. In the evenings and early mornings, Patricia checked the assistants' records and embarked on the lengthy task of rendering their reports in English. Roger focused his work among the men, as did Andrew Lyon, our doctoral student who lived in Dharmnagri with us in 1982-1983 and during Patricia's stay in 1985. They both did most of their work without formal research assistants, though both relied greatly on Khurshid Ahmed from Jhakri.

Our female research assistants were not merely note takers, however. We spent a lot of time asking them to amplify material they had not covered in sufficient detail in their notes or to provide exegeses of points that remained unclear. Conversations over lunch or the discussions arising from their notes all provided opportunities to check our impressions and explore our hunches or reflect on the inconsistencies and puzzles that our work was revealing. Frequently, of course, we were alerted to the limitations of the understandings we had built up since our first research in South Asia in 1970. But we also became aware of how much our locally born assistants, some Muslim and some Hindu, were learning from one another as well as from their experiences in Dharmnagri and Jhakri. Often their understandings of village life were partial, often they were startled by what they were finding, and often they made divergent interpretations of events. If we were outsiders in the villages, so too, in some senses, were they. Their differing readings of village life underscored the difficulty of finding a single "insider" for all the diverse groupings and categories of women in rural north India.[49]

In addition to these notes from daytime interviews, both Patricia and Roger recorded "after-hours" material when the research assistants had gone home: material on births and weddings that took place at night, on patients brought to the dispensary in the early morning, on chats with men who sat with us on our veranda after dusk, or on our discussions with our assistants. All these procedures took time, but they also meant that we recorded details and snatches of conversation rather than generalities. Perhaps the most labor-intensive project was recording Zebunnisa's story. She arrived one day just as we were all settling down for writing up after lunch. Five research assistants plus Patricia and Roger listened agog to her story, prompted her to proceed, and then reconstructed her story from the notes that Zarin and Radha had taken by turns during the telling.[50]

Telling It How It Was?

It was not our initial intention to collect "life stories" and to write in biographical mode about the everyday lives of women in Dharmnagri and Jhakri. That agenda has evolved since returning to Edinburgh. And even if our data collection entailed some collaboration with the people in the two villages and with our research assistants, the data analysis and the decisions about what to include and exclude in our writing was not done in Bijnor. We have spent many hours in our Edinburgh study reliving and rethinking our experiences of our Bijnor fieldwork, visualizing conversations and replaying incidents, with our notes and discussions with colleagues and friends in India and beyond as prompts.

We have tried to reflect the concerns of people in Dharmnagri and Jhakri. Yet our decisions have also been crucially influenced by the priorities of the social sciences. We—rather than the women about whom we write—have set the agenda for producing the text even though the style in which we recount the stories and episodes may seem to minimize our involvement in how the material is presented. At the end of the day, an author's power cannot be denied, for all that we have struggled to use that power sympathetically.[51] Moreover, all our squirreling of material has resulted in several thousand pages of single-spaced typed fieldnotes, supplemented by information in our village census schedules, in the maternity histories and time-use forms, and in forms focusing on agricultural work and cropping decisions and so forth that has accumulated over the years. Clearly no publisher would take all that as it is, nor would any reader have the stamina to sift through it. Our material clearly had to be abridged. We must, then, briefly indicate how we arrived at our selections.

Real lives rarely follow a straight path or have a clear agenda, yet there is a tendency in biographical writing, as in fiction, to constrain people's life stories. There is usually a plot and maybe a few subplots, but not so many that the reader will be confused. There may be events that, with the wisdom of hindsight, can be read as decisive in changing the course of a person's life. Equally, there may be events that seemed important at the time, but that seem irrelevant sideshows in retrospect. A heavy authorial hand acting in the interests of readability can create an excessive sense of closure and order.

We have tried not to overstructure the longer stories or create the impression that they have reached their final scene. These are the unfinished lives, still unfolding, of women in their middle years. Their futures are not absolutely determined; the plots could take courses that might astonish us.[52] At the same time, however, it was we, not the women in question, for whom considerations of themes and plots came into play in our decisions to include or excise material in our fieldnotes about particular individuals. While trying to hold on to some of the richness of people's lives, we have cut out some details to reduce the complexity and unwieldiness. Moreover, the particulars of women's lives in the following chapters were not recorded at single sittings but were fragments gleaned on numerous occasions over the years and subsequently woven together. The locations ranged from women's houses to the patches where they made dung cakes for cooking fuel, from the dispensary where we lived to a village pathway. Sometimes women talked to us alone; sometimes bystanders threw their views into the ring. And Patricia or Roger might listen to a tale or attend an event with or without the various research assistants. We have excluded such contextual details unless we felt that they were salient.

All this, of course, begs a further series of questions. If we cut out some conversations and information because we decreed them to be a distraction from the main "point" of the story, how had we decided what the "point" itself was? How did we alight upon one story rather than another? How did we arrive at a final listing of what to include?

Many of the topics touched on could have been addressed many times over by drawing on different women and on other incidents. Issues connected with childbearing, with dowry and marriage arrangement, with the ways a mother-in-law controls a woman's contacts with her parents, or with the belittling of a woman's work by her husband all feature on many pages of our fieldnotes. We have, for instance, parallel sets of interview notes from the forty-one women who have been central to our research in Dharmnagri and Jhakri, in addition to material from our less-directed fieldwork with them. In our selection, we have been mindful of many commonalities while also wanting to avoid excessive repetition.

We had other criteria as well. We wanted to use individual cases to illustrate some general parameters of domestic and sexual politics in rural north India. In the wake of Hindu-Muslim communal disturbances associated with the Ayodhya affair and shifting political allegiances around class and caste, there has been a marked tendency to essentialize differences between members of different social groupings. In such a climate, it is important to highlight some common elements of village women's lives without, of course, essentializing gender differences. This is a key part of our project here, and it influenced our decision to select four Hindu and four Muslim women in different class positions for the main stories and to provide a rough balance on these counts in the thematic interludes.

In highlighting some commonalities in domestic organization, of course, we are not denying the importance of social class and religious community in people's everyday lives in rural Bijnor. A family's location in the class system would certainly affect its ability to meet the financial demands of marriages and illnesses. Although rich and poor alike might articulate very similar hopes, they were not equally well placed to realize them. For the poor, an illness might become fatal for want of resources to pay for medical treatment—and a death would have a long-term impact on the surviving relatives' unfolding stories. By the same token, a family that was comfortably placed could make choices about the marital destinations of its daughters that would be unthinkable for a family in which even feeding its members was a constant and worrying struggle.[53] Similarly, communal politics, both local and on the national stage, affected everyone whether Hindu or Muslim. People's identities, their hopes and fears for their futures, their approach to family building and contraception or to children's schooling, for instance, might all be colored in complex ways by community membership. We have foregrounded these questions elsewhere.[54] Here, such concerns weave through the following accounts in muted fashion rather than constituting their central theme.

Beyond these considerations, we wanted to include tales of everyday life that were well told. Admittedly, supportive relationships or harmonious households were rarely subjects of conversation except to set the unsatisfactory into relief. References to such positive relationships were often difficult to craft into interesting accounts, whether for village women or for ourselves. Nevertheless, examples—of kindly mothers-in-law and loving daughters-in-law, supportive sisters-in-law and affectionate spouses—do feature in the following pages. But some people's conversational style was regarded as particularly "tasty" [*mazedār*], and such a raconteur could easily be spurred to pepper her account with the amusing or apparently trivial incidents that punctuated everyday lives. In capable hands, small yet commonplace crises of family life became riveting with pithy turns of phrase or pungent commentaries on relatives' or neighbors' behavior. Arguments about the division of family land and the sharing of jewelry among a family's daughters-in-law could give insight into women's struggles and family dynamics. The way women organized their work together and the tensions between mothers-in-law and their daughters-in-law could generate spirited accounts told with feeling and gusto. Dowry demands or wife beating might result in a sad tale of victimization, told with verve nonetheless. And negotiations over a woman's visits to her natal kin, contestations over their involvement in her marital problems, or her in-laws' scathing comments on the gifts they sent all gave drama to people's lives.

If many features of life in Dharmnagri and Jhakri were reflected in parallel experiences and in issues that kept recurring, people's lives were not identical, nor were their interpretations of them. Most women's marriages had been arranged by their parents, and most were married outside their natal village. Generally, exceptions provided illuminating commentaries on the normal and the expected. Some women's accounts yielded far more elaborate sketches than others. Sometimes, the good yarn spun when a woman had something to complain about could highlight the hopes and expectations that many more people entertained for their lives. Sometimes a woman might energetically justify her own actions during an argument while accusing the other party of all manner of misdemeanors. A special twist might give extra piquancy and sometimes poignancy. Some accounts concerned issues of as much interest to relatives and neighbors as to us.[55] In others, the implications of something relatively commonplace, for instance having no sons or no brothers, had left its traces throughout a woman's life.[56] Sometimes, there were dramatic events in which the "normal" was a backdrop that helped women to put their difficulties into perspective.[57] Yet we have not selected stories and episodes that diverged from the normal to the point of being bizarre either to the women themselves or to their relatives and neighbors. The events we have recounted were not daily experiences for all the women in Dharmnagri and Jhakri, yet they were everyday enough and sufficiently echoed in our fieldnotes to warrant inclusion. In other words, all the accounts are unique in their details, but they also resonate with many other women's experiences and responses.

Moreover, many accounts and incidents left themselves open to multiple readings. Events that seemed positive from one angle could look bittersweet from another. The celebrated birth of a son needed to be juxtaposed with the lack of celebration when a girl was born. The joy of being able to give generously to one's daughter had to be framed within a context in which many parents could not do so and in which dowry was central to married women's vulnerability. Support provided by a woman's natal kin might be a direct response to her difficulties in her husband's village. A woman who took the initiative might have to listen to backbiting even if she weathered the storm. A woman who spoke out might find her husband's venom turned against her. A mother-in-law who got her way might cause misery to her daughter-in-law.

In the midst of this, women theorized about their own lives in relation to the wider context in which they were located. They (as well as we) tried to make sense of their experiences and in so doing often provided a story line, repeating threads that they could trace through the plot, ordering their present situations in relation to their past, pointing out ironies and echoes, and reiterating comments on different occasions. Over the years, women repeatedly drew our attention to patterns in their lives by referring to earlier conversations with us or to incidents of which they knew we were aware. Whether talking retrospectively or trying to put current events into perspective, women constructed accounts that created levels of coherence that sometimes proved difficult to sustain in changing circumstances. And sometimes neighbors and relatives set these accounts into relief with their own alternative ones. All these have been important prompts and guidelines for us in framing our somewhat simplified accounts.[58]

We have, then, tried to steer clear of the spectacular or of events that seemed to accentuate the "otherness" of women and their lives in rural north India. In culling variations and nuances, we have also tried to avoid inventing a single reality out of the complex and ambiguous realities of women's daily lives. Thus, we specify women's social locations in class, caste, and community terms, as well as their household situations. Moreover, timing is important, for people's experiences altered during their life cycle and in relation to longer-term secular change. Thus, we also include the dates of conversations and episodes in which we participated. Although people could readily specify the order of marriages, births, and so forth, they could rarely attach firm dates. Thus dating events that took place before 1982 has proved rather difficult. In the absence of written family records, we have cross-checked the maternity history material we collected, collating our information about older women with that about their daughters-in-law and daughters to arrive at dates that are probably correct within a couple of years. We have, then, sometimes violated people's accounts in the hope of enabling the reader to keep track of the unfolding accounts or people's perceptions of social change.

Our research assistants appear with their own names, as does Khurshid Ahmed from Jhakri. All the other Jhakri and Dharmnagri residents, however, have pseudonyms, Muslim names for those from Jhakri and Hindu names for those from Dharmnagri. These names are unique to each person throughout this book.[59]

Our Own Narrative

A sociologically informed approach to everyday lives and life stories should not detach individuals from their social moorings. People's lives are socially embedded. They are closely interwoven with those of others in complex ways. They also reflect commonalities in the experiences of people living in a particular social context. Yet people in Dharmnagri and Jhakri also sensed their own uniqueness and individuality and had personal interests that were played out within the constraints of their social environment. This is reflected in the accounts that follow, whether in the odd-numbered chapters that are thematically organized or in the even-numbered ones that focus on particular people.

Each thematic chapter begins with a summary of the chapter's central topic. These eight chapters comprise several sorts of material. There are brief monologues and discussions as well as short episodes of the kind that are sprinkled through any research effort, some involving people who have been our key informants since 1982, others featuring people whom we came to know quite well for some other reason. We have used direct speech from our fieldnotes, often including comments from close relatives and neighbors. Linking these statements and conversations are abridged extracts from our notes, as well as our own commentaries putting the details into perspective. And we have included songs that highlight relationships between relatives—giving and receiving gifts, the balance of power between husband and wife or mother-in-law and daughter-in-law, the separation of a woman from her natal kin. The remaining chapters each focus on one woman and relate to the thematic chapters preceding and following them; they also raise issues that ripple through the book as a whole. All eight women in these chapters have been our key informants since 1982.

Personhood both is gendered and changes throughout the course of an individual's life. The ordering of the chapters reflects this by constructing an overarching narrative out of the narratives of people in the two villages. In the first two chapters we explore the significance of childbearing in Bijnor, highlighting the crucial differences between daughters and sons that will echo through the rest of the book and hinting at the problems faced by women whose childbearing careers go awry in some way. In childhood, a girl is connected to people from whom she—unlike her brothers—will be detached when she is married. The following four chapters (Chapters 3-6) feature marriage arrangement, centering on people's concerns about dowry and with ensuring that their children are well settled in marriage. Once married, a woman will live in her husband's village. Thus, the next four chapters (Chapters 7-10) focus on women's marital careers, particularly the relationships that married women build with their husbands and with other women in their marital villages. Married women, however, have feet in two camps in ways that their husbands do not. The four succeeding chapters (Chapters 11-14) look at the relationships that married women sustain with their natal kin, relationships that include gift giving, visiting, and helping in times of crisis. The last two chapters are about widowhood, an experience most women can expect at some stage in their lives. The final chapter brings us full circle, since it also touches on the importance of sons and people's concerns with getting their daughters married.

Notes

1. Although women's songs are not an area on which we claim expertise, we have nevertheless included some songs here because they highlight the issues with which this book is concerned. Women sing at various points in the activities associated with weddings, en route to collect the gifts called *bhāt* from the bride or groom's uncle [MB], when preparations are being made for the bride's departure for her husband's home, at the groom's home when the new bride arrives, and so on. Songs are also sung when a boy is born and during other events in the annual calendar. All the songs in this book are wedding or birth songs. For more extended discussions of the significance of women's songs (and other performance genres) in India, see, for example, Appadorai, Korom, and Mills (1994); Narayan (1986); Raheja and Gold (1994); and Wadley (1994). Ann Gold recorded a song similar to this in Rajasthan in 1993 and was told that it was very new in the area (personal communication).

2. See Humphrey (1993) for a discussion of the many parallels in the biographies of people living in the same place and experiencing similar events.

3. This book represents only part of our writing about our work in Dharmnagri and Jhakri. See especially Jeffery, Jeffery, and Lyon (1989) and the

other references to our work in the bibliography. We were also academic consultants for a television program made by the Open University for their course U208 Third World Development. See Jeffery, Jeffery, and Johnson (1994).

4. See Mohanty (1988); Mohanty, Russo, and Torres (1991); and Marchand and Parpart (1995).

5. In the 1980s, our research focused on women's experiences as childbearers and workers in their in-laws' villages. More recently, we have been exploring the issue of female autonomy, particularly in relation to education, fertility, and the daily lives of young, married women. One reason for locating our work in Bijnor District was its relatively high Muslim population. Some villages in the district are mixed Hindu-Muslim villages with various balances of the different communities and caste groups, but Dharmnagri and Jhakri were not.

6. See Jeffery, Jeffery, and Lyon (1989), chapter 2, for more details on the two villages and the difficulties in assigning class position to households.

7. Bijnor District compares favorably on most conventional indices of development with eastern Uttar Pradesh and also Bihar. Indicators of social and economic development are, however, lower than in Punjab and Haryana to the west, as well as those Uttar Pradesh districts to the west of the river Ganges.

8. Terminology is a problem. "Caste Hindu" refers to "clean" caste Hindus as distinct from "Scheduled Castes" or Harijans, who are usually also considered to be Hindus. Jatab is a caste name adopted by some Chamars in the 1930s to downplay the occupation of leatherworking associated with Chamars. Some neo-Buddhist followers of Dr. Ambedkar, the main leader of Harijans in the nationalist movement, have gone back to calling themselves Chamars. They also reject the title Harijan, which was given to the ex-untouchables by Mahatma Gandhi, and prefer a term such as Dalit [oppressed]. But we never heard the term Dalit in Bijnor and so use Harijan in its place. Respecting the views of our respondents, we have also decided to treat Chamars and Jatabs as separate castes. No Chamars in Dharmnagri were leatherworkers. Muslims in South Asia have caste-like divisions that are sometimes associated with caste occupations. In Bijnor, some Telis worked as mustard oil pressers or at sugarcane crushers and many Julahas earned their living through weaving. But in both cases, agriculture was also an important source of livelihood.

9. See the glossary for an explanation of kinship abbreviations. In passing, we can note that we are (reluctantly) following the convention by which such marriages are described from the man's and not the woman's point of view. See Jeffery, Jeffery, and Lyon (1989:26-39) for more detail on close-kin marriage and the implications for women of dense marriage networks.

10. The official exchange rate for the rupee in 1995 was in the region of Rs 30 per US$1. This, however, can give little insight into purchasing power and living standards. For instance, the salary for a senior lecturer (associate professor) in a government college was about Rs 5,000 per month. The comparisons are made more complex because rural people in particular were often less fully absorbed into the cash economy. As an indication, however, an agricultural laborer in rural Bijnor could expect to earn in the region of Rs 600 per month, though not necessarily throughout the year.

11. For more on the anxiety that this generates, see Chapters 3 and 11.

12. For examples of *bhāt* and other presentations that are made to the out-married daughter, see Chapters 4 and 11.

13. For more on *mahr* in Jhakri, see Chapter 7. See Chapters 3 and 14 for a discussion of "bought brides."

14. There are several other recent sources dealing with the lives of women in other parts of north India. See, for instance, Bardhan (1993); Dube (1988); Gold (1988); Jacobson and Wadley (1977); Mandelbaum (1988); Raheja (1988); Raheja and Gold (1994); Sharma and Vanjani (1993); Sharma (1978a, 1978b, 1980); Thompson (1984); and Wadley (1994). For urban women see Sharma (1986); and Vatuk (1972).

15. For more details on the demography of India, see Visaria and Visaria (1994); for the position of Bijnor, see R. Jeffery and P. Jeffery (1996).

16. We address some of the implications for women of the Indian government's family-planning program in Chapters 1 and 2.

17. For further on this, see Agarwal (1994a).

18. See Jeffery, Jeffery, and Lyon (1989), chapter 3, for a general discussion of women's work and their access to economic resources. In some caste groups, women have an independent income from sweeping and cleaning latrines, but these are considered especially polluting and demeaning jobs. For an extended discussion of the ambiguous position of traditional birth attendants, see R. Jeffery and P. Jeffery (1993).

19. Considerations of space prevent us from presenting a literature review. There is now a considerable corpus of material discussing the use of biographical and autobiographical materials in social science, derived at least in part from the work of C. Wright Mills (1959). One particularly useful recent source is the entire volume of *Sociology*, vol. 27, no. 1, February 1993, given over to papers on this topic. Those papers and the references contained within them have been particularly valuable in developing our ideas here. Tonkin (1992) is another important contribution to this literature. Also pertinent are the discussions in Okely and Callaway (1992) of the bearing that researchers' own biographies have on their work. For life stories of women in north Africa, Iran, and north India, see, for instance, Abu-Lughod (1993); Atiya (1982); Friedl (1989); and Wadley (1994). Geiger (1986) has a good general discussion of issues in writing women's life histories.

20. The dangers of imposing a unity on these women are well expressed in Nicholson (1990); and Marchand and Parpart (1995).

21. Marriott (1990:2).

22. See, for instance, Daniel (1984); and Parry (1989).

23. Some feminists have argued that women are more attuned to their connections to other people than men are.

24. Mines (1994).

25. We are not suggesting that this tendency reflects any notion of genetic or psychological determinism, but one of social determinism. See also Brah (1992) for a discussion of issues of difference, universalism, and identification as alternatives to essentialism.

26. See Scott (1985, 1990).

27. See especially the various volumes of *Subaltern Studies* (Guha, 1982-1994); see also Chatterjee (1989); Hardiman (1987); and Spivak (1987, 1988). Masselos (1994) has criticized the *Subaltern Studies* school for writing in such a way as to deindividualize the very subalterns they are attempting to recover from the dustbins of history.

28. See, for instance, Raheja and Gold (1994); Jeffery (1979); P. Jeffery and R. Jeffery (1994); Kumar (1994); and Wadley (1994).

29. We have discussed this in more detail in Jeffery, Jeffery, and Lyon (1989: 31ff.). See also Mandelbaum (1988:45-46); and Raheja and Gold (1994:73-120).

30. This point is made by Mani in her discussion of *sat$\bar{\imath}$* [widow immolation]. See Mani (1990), and also Abu-Lughod (1990), and Rajan (1993).

31. For another instance of this type of resistance, see Thompson (1985).

32. Proximity to one's parents or marriage to a close relative, such as experienced by many Muslim women in Bijnor, was sometimes viewed not as an advantage that protected women but as a source of problems, since it was very hard to prevent the parents from learning about marital difficulties.

33. Willis (1979).

34. P. Jeffery and R. Jeffery (1994; forthcoming) have further discussions of this point; for some examples from central India, see Thompson (1981, 1985).

35. Okely (1991:8).

36. Sen (1990).

37. Kandiyoti (1988).

38. Sharma (1978b) provides a particularly useful account of the differing interests of women as mothers and daughters, mothers-in-law and daughters-in-law. Wadley (1994) lays out the significance of class and caste variations.

39. See Okely (1991) for a discussion of subservience.

40. Jeffery (1979:161); and Haynes and Prakash (1991:13).

41. See Segal (1987) for a useful elaboration of this point.

42. Sarkar (1991) discusses the difficulty for feminists of equating agency (in her case, the effect on women of their involvement in the women's wing of the Hindu nationalist movement) with empowerment.

43. See note 19.

44. See Abu-Lughod (1993:31).

45. For more details on our research strategy, see Jeffery, Jeffery, and Lyon (1989), appendix 1.

46. We ourselves tried to collect time-use data, but people found the task boring and we discontinued that work after a few months in the villages.

47. Dwyer (1982) discusses further the possibility of research being collaborative.

48. On this point, see Okely and Callaway (1992).

49. For further consideration of this issue in India, see Agarwal (1994b); and Narayan (1993). See also Mascia-Lees, Sharpe, and Cohen (1989). Aside from such issues of positionality, low rural female literacy rates would also compromise any attempts to do comparable research with village research assistants in the foreseeable future.

50. See Chapter 13.

51. In contrast to the way in which ethnographic monographs have usually been written to appear definitive and timeless, many recent discussions note that they should not disguise, through the style in which they are written, how they are inevitably selective and historically contingent. Mintz (1989) analyzes how authorial interventions are unavoidable in life histories as much as in any other form of ethnography. Hastrup (1992:121) concurs: "However many the direct quotations, the informants' voices cannot penetrate the discursive speech of the ethnographer." There remain, however, considerable difficulties in writing ethnographies. These entail acknowledging the interplay of auto-biography and fieldwork without losing the purpose of ethnography by continual reference to the conditions under which it was created.

52. As indeed is the case in Chapters 2 and 16.

53. Social class in the sense of class relationships (such as between employers and employees) is muted in what follows. Issues connected with the capacity to pay for medical treatment or to cover wedding expenses, however, do feature in several of the stories and briefer incidents.

54. See R. Jeffery and P. Jeffery (1994, 1996); and P. Jeffery and R. Jeffery (forthcoming). In general, too, people in Dharmnagri and Jhakri were not greatly preoccupied with spiritual matters and religious practice, although their conversations were often spiced with idioms to do with "sin" [*pāp* or *gunāh* for Hindus and Muslims, respectively] or destiny and fate [*qismat, nasīb, taqdīr, bhāg*, all used by Muslims and Hindus alike].

55. The accounts contained in Chapters 8 and 14 are cases in point.

56. This is reflected in Chapters 4, 6 and 12.

57. This is the case in Chapters 2 and 16.

58. Chapters 6 and 12 are clear examples of this.

59. Our key informants, who were in our earlier book about Dharmnagri and Jhakri, keep their original pseudonyms. See Jeffery, Jeffery, and Lyon (1989), appendix 2 for more details.

1

Queen Today in a Red *Sārī!*

One day in 1991, the wife of Roger's assistant, Khurshid Ahmed—herself heavily pregnant at the time—was leading her goat into her courtyard in Jhakri. Firdausi began laughing and instructed us to fill out one of our maternity-history forms for the goat, because it too was about to kid. When we first arrived in 1982, however, our interests in childbearing were scarcely ever met with such lightheartedness.

Above all else, it was as childbearers that women were brought into direct contact with the Indian state, in the guise of the auxiliary nurse-midwife [ANM]. Sterilization had long been the family-planning method most favored by the Indian government, in the early years of the program mainly male sterilization but since 1978 generally female sterilization.[1] For many years, ANMs and other workers in the health services (as well as other branches of the state) had been given targets for the numbers of people they should "motivate" to become family-planning "acceptors" or "cases." Such sterilization targets were a crucial ingredient in the relationships between local people and the ANM, especially as the coercive tactics used in the family-planning program during the Emergency (from 1975 to 1977) were still fresh in people's minds. Indeed, health workers posted at the government dispensary in Dharmnagri, especially the ANM, were still regarded with suspicion and cynicism. People commonly asserted that the ANM was so concerned about meeting the sterilization targets set by her superiors that she would help only those who complied. The health services, people felt, were a ruse to persuade them to be "motivated for sterilization." But sterilization was unacceptable to many people. Some feared the operation itself. Others were anxious about the finality of sterilization: What would happen to them in old age if their children were to die? Yet others—mainly Muslims—believed that the operation was contrary to their religion.[2]

People's initial surmise that we were associated with the family-planning program nearly caused the downfall of our research.[3] With time, though, such fears evaporated, and women began asking how we were planning our own family. Even though the ANM supposedly had supplies of contraceptive pills that she could provide free, women mistrusted her. Women asked us for advice on contraception, especially about spacing methods, and for help with obtaining abortions.[4] *Gradually, women became more voluble, whether about the government's provision of services or about their own ambivalent responses to childbearing.*

In poking fun at our enthusiasm to complete maternity histories for the married women in Jhakri and Dharmnagri, Firdausi was not suggesting that childbearing was a trivial matter in rural Bijnor District. Because levels of fertility and child mortality were high in the district, the adult lives of married women in both Jhakri and Dharmnagri generally entailed lengthy periods devoted to childbearing and -rearing that had to be dovetailed with their other activities. As women themselves were aware, this was often achieved at great cost to the health of women and their children alike. Yet they also considered childbearing an essential part of an adult woman's life. As married women and mothers, their interests lay in bearing sons to care for them in old age.[5] *As daughters, however, they were also sensitized to the different value attached to boys and girls. The "son preferences" characteristic of the region as a whole were evidenced in both villages in several ways, including higher rates of female than male child mortality.*[6]

"Queen Today in a Red Sārī!" addresses some of the varied meanings of childbearing. Of these, whether a woman's children were boys or girls echoed through our fieldnotes. The themes elaborated in later chapters indicate why people placed so much store on having sons and greeted their arrival with celebration and giftgiving (which they sometimes found oppressive). By contrast, the response to a girl's birth was often ambivalent. Girls were loved and cherished, and they would become key players in kinship networks and life-cycle rituals—yet parents would readily admit to the costs and difficulties of having daughters. In addition, many women were deeply concerned about child deaths or infertility and feared a lonely and maybe destitute old age. Equally, though, unlimited childbearing raised issues about women's health or their ability to care for their children, about their children's prospects when they grew up, or about their own access to contraception.

A Song Marking a Boy's Birth

Lying on her bed alone, the clever new mother is thinking,
"Now who will play the flute?"

Sweetly, sweetly she says to her mother-in-law,
"Listen to my voice, revered mother-in-law, listen to my voice.
Bring me drinking water in a water pot.
Finish your work for your honorarium.
It's getting late.
Now who will play the flute?"

Sweetly, sweetly she says to her sister-in-law [HeBW],
"Listen to my voice, revered sister-in-law, listen to my voice.
Perform the *chath ī* prayers.
Finish your work for your honorarium.
It's getting late.
Now who will play the flute?"

Sweetly, sweetly she says to her husband's sister,
"Listen to my voice, revered husband's sister, listen to my voice.
Prepare the *sathīyā* motif.
Finish your work for your honorarium.
It's getting late.
Now who will play the flute?"

Sweetly, sweetly she says to her husband's younger brother,
"Listen to my voice, revered brother-in-law, listen to my voice.
Perform the taking outside and make me stare at the stars.
It's getting late.
Now who will play the flute?"
Lying on her bed alone, the clever new mother is thinking.[7]

Khadija's Anger and Mehbuba's Grief

Mehbuba's seven-year-old son became seriously ill in late 1982. He had had a difficult birth and had been prone to fits ever since. Now he was suffering from a high fever. After another fit he became unconscious. Fortunately, his father was a middle peasant and could contemplate getting treatment for the boy. Our jeep was commissioned to take him and his parents to obtain various remedies: prayers and an amulet from a *maulvī* [Muslim holy man], massage from a *hakīm* [Muslim traditional healer], and a glucose drip at the local general hospital. After some twenty-seven glucose bottles, the boy regained consciousness, and he was allowed home a few days later. But he was paralyzed on one side, he could not speak, and his chest was constantly soaked with saliva.

Mehbuba—a Sheikh woman of nearly forty—was beside herself. The boy had to be fed soft foods. He could not dress or wash himself, and Mehbuba spent hours each day massaging him, cleaning him up, and carrying him around the village astride her hip. Her oldest daughter, Rabia, had not been married long, and Mehbuba decided to call her back to Jhakri to help with the additional work the boy's illness had caused. Mehbuba was despairing: "I'm exhausted with all this work. All five of my girls are fine, but this boy was born with difficulty and he's never been right. It's a question of destiny. My destiny is weak. There's only one son and he's sick."

Mehbuba's mother-in-law, Khadija, was very bitter about it all. Mehbuba's husband was the oldest of her three sons, and his only surviving son now had no prospect of marrying or being able to work the farm and look after his parents when they became elderly. As it happened, Khadija's youngest daughter-in-law, Imrana, gave birth to a girl a couple of weeks before the boy became ill. Khadija was angry. "Allah has sent us bad fate. My oldest son's five daughters are all fine; but one son died of smallpox, and three other boys were stillborn. And the one remaining boy is useless now that he's paralyzed after having fever. And look, now Imrana has had yet another girl."

The point was brought home after Khadija's second daughter-in-law, Hashmi, also had another girl a couple of months later. "Hashmi's had another girl," complained Khadija. "First a girl, then two boys, and now another girl! Nine granddaughters but only four grandsons!" Khadija paid no attention when Hashmi pointed out that she had also had two other girls who had died. "What can anyone predict?" Hashmi asked her.

Even before her grandson's illness, though, the old woman had been seething over her bad luck. Her near neighbor Fatima claimed that Khadija's evil eye had afflicted her after she gave birth to a son: "I vomited when I drank sugar water, for Khadija is burning with evil eye because I had a son. She will not even pick him up. But the giving of boys or girls is Allah's work, so what is the benefit of burning with jealousy about other people's descendants? My husband is one of five brothers and now he has had a son too."

In light of all this, it was perhaps not surprising that Khadija was displeased when the *dāī* [traditional birth attendant] who delivered her granddaughter Rabia's first baby in 1985 brought the news that Rabia had given birth to a girl. Indeed, when Patricia tried congratulating Khadija on the birth of her first great-grandchild, she began crying. The *dāī* also told Mehbuba what she had been paid by Rabia's mother-in-law: "Only two rupees and a tiny dishful of grain! I attended the delivery only because of my relationship with you. Otherwise, I wouldn't have gone."

Mehbuba promised to give the *dāī* some more grain. A few days later, Mehbuba decided to visit Rabia in her in-laws' house: "I've heard that Rabia is tearful because she's had a girl. I'm going to reason with her. Our fate is no good. If my one son were fine or if we had another one, we'd feel that our work and responsibilities could be completed.

Now Rabia has a girl. If she'd had a boy, my heart could have been happy. At least Rabia would have had a son even if I myself did not have one who was healthy."

After she had visited Rabia, Mehbuba told us how Rabia had burst into tears as soon as she arrived and had begun pleading to be brought home to Jhakri. Rabia's mother-in-law was not proposing to hold a *chathī* ceremony [to celebrate the birth and remove the birth pollution], and Rabia was feeling wretched about having given birth to a girl. To Khadija, there seemed no hope in view:

> We have a shortage of good fortune. I'm very worried about my son, Rabia's father. He has no healthy son, and people are tormenting him because of that. My other two sons both have sons of their own, but he has just the one who is not right. My daughter—the one who is also Rabia's mother-in-law—is no good. One day she quarreled with Rabia's father and she put a curse on him. Since then, he's always behaved well to his sister for fear of making her angry. Rabia could have been married into a good house, but my son married Rabia to his sister's son so that the sister could be kept happy. Now I'm telling Rabia's mother not to send things to Rabia but to wait until Rabia herself comes to Jhakri for a visit.

Somewhat ironically, Rabia's own birth was marked by a splendid *chathī* ceremony with a feast for all their relatives. According to Khadija, they had cooked some eighty pounds of rice for the guests: "But that was because there had been a stillborn boy before Rabia. That's why there was so much celebration when she was born. It was much more than usual for a girl. After that, we did the *chathī* only for the boys. There were no *chathīs* when the other girls were born."

Hiran Weighs the Costs of Children

When we returned to Dharmnagri in 1990, we learned that Hiran had been sterilized some four years earlier, when she was in her late twenties, after having been married for about ten years. There had been no pressure from the medical staff at the dispensary in Dharmnagri to agree to the "operation." Hiran's husband, Harwan, had organized the sterilization through the land records officer, who was able to allocate Harwan just under an acre of land, which he would farm until he inherited from his father; Harwan's father was a Dhimar middle peasant and all his land was still under his control. According to Hiran's account, the decision had been difficult for her: "It was my husband's wish. His mother was totally against it. I didn't want to have the operation either. I was afraid of having it. I was also hoping that we might have just one girl. But he kept saying that we weren't going to get a daughter. He insisted there was no girl in our destiny and it was useless for us to have more children. 'How will we benefit from having more children?' he kept saying."

Reluctantly, Hiran gave in to her husband. With hindsight, however, Hiran conceded that it had been the right decision:

> For one thing, I had no aftereffects from the operation. For another, we've been able to feed and water our three sons properly. And all three boys are attending school. I'm keen for them to study as long as they wish. We're educating them because then they may be able to get employment—although where do people like us find jobs? But education is a good thing in any case. We'll send them to college in Bijnor if they want to go. And what's more, my oldest son had measles shortly after I had the operation. Then he developed a cough and began spitting up blood. We were dreadfully worried. A relative told us to take him to a doctor, which we did. That doctor charged a lot of money—500 rupees every time we visited him. As a result, all my dowry jewelry was sold, apart from one piece. But our son didn't seem to be recovering, so my husband took him to the TB [tuberculosis] hospital in Bijnor. Then he began to get better. That treatment is still going on. If we'd had more children, where would the money for all that treatment have come from?

Qudsia Wants No More Children

Qudsia was a Sheikh woman in Jhakri. Ever since we had known her, she had been anxious about her children. Her fourth child was born in late 1984 when her oldest child was still only six years old and Qudsia herself was about twenty-four. Then, shortly before Patricia returned for further fieldwork in 1985, Qudsia became pregnant again. Her baby was less than a year old. She was desperate: "I can get no peace when surrounded by little children. Small children cause endless worries. My own health was being damaged and we couldn't afford to eat properly. Then my period was two months overdue. I was terribly upset. I didn't want any more children. Khurshida was also pregnant then and we went together to the Dharmnagri dispensary."

The ANM told them that their pregnancies were too advanced and nothing could be done. They would simply have to be sterilized after having their babies—not the most appropriate advice for Muslim women. The compounder [pharmacist] tried to be more helpful: He gave them injections and capsules to take daily for three days.[8]

> But nothing happened. So I went back and he wrote a prescription for some tablets and said we'd see after that. My husband fetched the tablets

and gave them to me. Again nothing happened. I was dreadfully worried. At that very time, Imrana was also pregnant. Together, we went to a doctor in Bijnor. I'd never taken his treatment before. He gave us both an injection and the same tablets as the compounder had prescribed and some others as well. Even after all that, nothing happened. I was furious and vowed I wouldn't go back to him. Imrana did, though. She complained to him that she had taken his medicine but nothing had happened. He said her pregnancy was now too advanced and it would be dangerous for her to take more medicines. Then he asked about me and Imrana explained why I hadn't gone back to him. He said I should have gone to see him again, and he gave Imrana another medicine for me to take. He said that something would surely happen within ten days. Nine days later, in the middle of the night, the bleeding began. Then I went back to him and he has given me some pills [oral contraceptives] and I am taking one every evening. Please will you tell me some way to stop having children? I don't want any more. These four are a lot.

When we returned in 1990, Qudsia was still troubled. After the abortion in 1985, she had managed to obtain free contraceptive pills from the ANM posted at the Dharmnagri dispensary. Qudsia continued taking the pills for a couple of years until she was ill with a fever one time and her supply of pills ran out. Her husband, Qadir, refused to fetch more pills from the dispensary: "He said he'd be too embarrassed. So I became pregnant again. I've had another two children since you were here last, both of them girls. We don't have enough income for them now, let alone for the future. We shall have to provide four dowries now. The two girls we had before were quite enough to provide for. Please, get me a prescription for pills again."

Why had she stopped taking the pills? Had they given her bad side effects? "No, it wasn't like that. I went back to the ANM and she said I could have more pills if I paid for them. The ANM keeps all the government medicines herself and sells them. What can poor people be expected to do? The ANM said the only way to stop having children is to be sterilized."

Had Qudsia not thought about having a Copper-T [an intrauterine contraceptive device] in that case?

Oh, yes. I had one put inside me at that very time. But it caused me a lot of pain all the time and especially during my period. There was a lot of bleeding. I have a great deal of heavy work and I couldn't manage it feeling like that. Village women have heavy work, lifting headloads of cattle dung and fodder and so on. A woman can't do all that when her body's not right. So I had the Copper-T taken out after a couple of months. Now you must get me the names of those pills again. I used to feel heat when I took the pills, but I'm prepared to tolerate that to prevent having more children.[9] I can't consider being sterilized. That's against Islam, and my funeral prayers couldn't be said if I were sterilized.[10]

And was Qadir in agreement with all this? "Yes, indeed. I didn't take the pills secretly. He knew about it and the abortion, too. He said that if I was troubled, he would be too. He said it's better that I take the pills. Many of the men in Jhakri don't think that way, though."

Qudsia was adamant that we obtain contraceptive pills for her, which we did. Her oldest daughter was twelve and soon they would have to think about getting her married. Yet they had little income of their own. Qadir's father was a middle peasant. All the land was still in his name and would remain so until all three of Qadir's young brothers had been married.

> Many families do it that way. The land is divided into equal shares only after the children have all been married. If the oldest sons get their shares when they're married, they wouldn't contribute to the marriage expenses for their younger brothers and sisters. They'd be thinking about their own children's expenses. Also, by the time the youngest brothers are married, there might be less land for them if the father had to sell some to meet the wedding expenses for his younger sons and daughters. That's why we're still living in an adobe house even though my parents-in-law have a kiln-brick house. We don't have the money to build a better one. So what will happen if we have even more children? How could we feed and clothe them properly?

Shakuntala Wants a Daughter

Shakuntala had always said that her husband, Shankar, did not want a big family. Like other Chamars [Harijans] in Dharmnagri, Shankar owned very little land. "Two sons will be quite enough," he had said. "We won't be able to feed more, let alone pay for their education." By 1990, however, Shakuntala had had a third son. She was then in her mid-twenties. "Our third son was born because of our search for a girl. If we have a girl next time, we won't have any more. I'll have the operation."

We were perplexed. Our assistant Radha asked Shakuntala why she wanted a girl, since there was so much expense in providing a dowry that no one else these days said they wanted a girl. Shakuntala was clear: "It's essential to have a girl. I myself would get some peace. Whenever we have festivals or weddings, I could call her back. Only a daughter can be useful like that. You can call her home to help."

Further, at present, Shakuntala had no one in Dharmnagri to call upon. Shankar's brothers' daughters were still too young to manage

Shakuntala's work. If Shakuntala was sick or there was a lot of work during the harvest season, she asked her parents to let one of her unmarried sisters come to Dharmnagri. "If one of my sisters comes, she stays for two or three months and helps with all my work, in the house, caring for the animals, doing the dungwork, cooking, working in the fields, and collecting fodder. I get lots of peace then! When I go away, I have to send flour to my sister-in-law [HeBW] so that she'll cook for my husband. That's another reason why we certainly need a girl."

Shakuntala paused briefly, marshaling her thoughts. After a few moments, she continued.

> Then again, when our sons are married, their sisters would receive honoraria. When our sons have children, their sisters would get honoraria again. To give to one's own and to call one's own gives a different kind of happiness. A man without any real sister may call his cousin, but he'll return home feeling hopeless if her in-laws refuse to send her. He can't compel them to send her like he could for a real sister. At times like that, a man remembers that real sisters are real. He'll know that you can persuade their in-laws to let them come. If he's calling his cousin, her in-laws might think they don't need to agree to her going, since it's not a real brother who's calling her. They'd reckon that only a real brother would think badly of them if they refused to send her. If you don't have a daughter of your own, you understand the difference when you see the face of someone else's girl instead. There is joy in the house only when you have your own girl. Your own is your own and you don't have rights over anyone else's daughter. That's why a daughter is necessary for the giving and taking. If I'd had a girl after the first boy, we'd have had just two children. That was also my husband's wish. He wants a girl too.

Hanifa's Sick Daughter

During our first research in 1982, Hanifa—herself from Jhakri—had been married within Jhakri, to the son of one of the wealthiest Sheikh farmers in the village. One day in 1990, Patricia and our assistant Swaleha arrived in her courtyard to find her asking her sister-in-law [HeBW] Ghazala for advice about her daughter's diarrhea. As their discussion came to a close, Ghazala motioned us to sit down. She began complaining about her health. "I have lots of pain in my lower back and pelvis," she explained. "Standing up and sitting down are very painful, and my children are troubling me a lot. I'm very worried about my own health too. Swaleha, you're right not to have married. You can have some peace!"

Hanifa agreed. "That's right," she commented as she stroked her daughter sitting on her lap. "Swaleha has no children crying or waking her up in the night. Look at our youngest sister-in-law. She still sleeps peacefully while the two of us are tied up with our children."

"Our sister-in-law doesn't have any children yet," Ghazala added. "And the days are not so long at this time of year that she has lots of work to do. She just remains in bed sleeping!"

At this point, the little girl climbed off Hanifa's lap and announced that she wanted something to eat. Hanifa served some food into a dish and the girl went inside to ask her grandmother for some clarified butter to spread on top. From inside the house, we could hear her grandfather's voice, chiding her for asking for clarified butter for herself. "I can't think where you came from," he commented gruffly.

Hanifa hung her head sadly and became silent.

"Our father-in-law shouldn't have said that," Ghazala said in lowered tones. "If someone says bad things to a girl, Allah will give more girls. People shouldn't say bad things to a girl."

The Difficulties of Afrozi and Nusrat

Afrozi and Nusrat were distant cousins from middle-peasant Sheikh households in Jhakri. They were both married in nearby Begawala, Afrozi in the mid-1970s and Nusrat to Afrozi's husband's nephew during our first fieldwork in 1982. Nusrat's wedding had been the talk of the village, for her dowry was regarded as extremely generous and the feasts associated with her marriage—in both Jhakri and Begawala— had been sumptuous.

Over the years, we would meet Afrozi and Nusrat when they visited their families in Jhakri, and we often picked up news of them from their relatives who had been to Begawala, buying vegetables in the weekly market or taking a sick child to one of the private medical practitioners in the village. Both marriages were difficult and tempestuous.

Afrozi's mother often talked about trying to give Afrozi some peace by letting her visit Jhakri frequently: "Afrozi's mother-in-law insists that Afrozi do all the work for the dozen or so cattle. She fetches their fodder and chops it, she waters them, milks them, and cleans up the dung, as well as cooking for the family and sewing all their clothes. She's exhausted the whole time."

In addition, Afrozi was in a difficult position for several years because her husband and his father often argued. Once, when Afrozi was in Jhakri, her husband separated from his father. Afrozi's father refused to send her back until the father and son had reestablished a joint household. Then, after Afrozi had her first child, she was wrongly accused of stealing money from her mother-in-law and giving it to her mother. She visited her parents a month later, but she told them nothing. After she returned to her in-laws' house, her husband whipped her so hard with coarse rope that her body and limbs were blue. Her parents-in-law secretly got a message to another Jhakri man, who told Afrozi's parents that she was in danger of being killed. Her mother took up the story:

> When we fetched her, she was very weak. We didn't send her back to Begawala for over two years. Even then, our son-in-law didn't forget about the money. My husband was planning to do the Haj pilgrimage but Afrozi's husband said that he wouldn't let him go because he needed 3,500 rupees. We gave him the money and Afrozi has been fine since then. Her husband says nothing against her now. It was because of that row that our son-in-law's younger brother couldn't get married. Whenever Afrozi's in-laws sent a marriage offer for a girl, the parents said that they didn't have enough money to satisfy them and they didn't want to see their daughter beaten up too. Eventually, our son-in-law's brother was married to his cousin [FZD]. She's a cripple and was hard to marry off.

Within a few months of Nusrat's marriage, Afrozi's mother also told us of Nusrat's troubles. Apparently, Nusrat's husband was furious that there had been no radio in the dowry: "His parents told him that he could buy one with his own money. He retorted that either they should buy one or else Nusrat must bring one from her parents' home. He was so angry that he broke all the utensils in Nusrat's dowry."

In Nusrat's case, too, rows between her husband and his parents had resulted in the separation of households—while Nusrat was visiting Jhakri just a few months after the wedding. Similarly, Nusrat's parents refused to send her back when her husband demanded that she return home. Later stories included accusations that Nusrat's husband had pawned her dowry jewelry to raise spending money. His father redeemed all the jewelry but said he would not return it to Nusrat until her husband had begun to do some work, for otherwise it would probably be pawned again.

But there the parallels stopped. Shortly after we arrived in summer 1990, Afrozi and Nusrat made the first of several trips to the Dharmnagri dispensary together. They came across the compound from the doctor's house to see us. Afrozi was annoyed: "The doctor doesn't give medicines without payment. Enough, the only thing he needs is money. I can't ask my husband for money for medicines to stop having children. I'd have to take them behind his back. If he ever found out, he'd be furious. But I don't want any more children. I already have four and the fifth will soon be born."

Nusrat's problem was rather different: "I've been married for eight years but haven't had a single child. That's why my husband beats me a lot. Sometimes I stay with my parents in Jhakri for a year at a time just because of that. I've had plenty of treatment but there's been no benefit from any of it. I went to the private lady doctor in Bijnor. She charged 100 rupees one time, 200 rupees the next time, and another 200 rupees the third time I went. But it did no good."

Some months later, Afrozi and Nusrat returned again. Afrozi had a new baby and was worried that she would soon be pregnant again. The doctor's wife, herself a trained doctor, told her to obtain pills from the ANM, but Afrozi was unwilling. Afrozi was convinced that the ANM was only in search of people willing to be sterilized. The doctor's wife said the ANM had already met her annual target for sterilization cases and would be prepared to give out pills. Nevertheless, the doctor's wife gave Afrozi a cycle of pills and a prescription for more. Afrozi looked at the packet. "I've already taken pills like these before and even then I had another baby. My problem is that three of my children were *lamra* [conceived during postpartum amenorrhea]. This baby is now six months and my periods haven't begun again. Are you sure there's no problem taking the pills while the baby is still breast-feeding?"

The doctor's wife reassured her. Then Afrozi laughed, saying, "Nusrat's worried about having no children. My worry is having children too quickly!"

Recently, however, Nusrat had thought she might be pregnant. As had happened several times before, her periods stopped for three months and she had gone to the ANM for a checkup. Then her periods began again. She went to a *dāī* in another village, who assured her that there was no pregnancy. Now, Nusrat told us, she had come to the dispensary to complain to the ANM: "The ANM told me wrongly that I was pregnant, and she was also demanding payment from me. How can I go places for treatment? My husband doesn't look after me at all. Only he could take me for treatment. Where could I go alone? If my husband cared for me at all, would he leave me languishing in my parents' home for a year or two at a time? His parents are good. It's he alone who doesn't call me back to Begawala."

Overhearing this, the doctor's wife suggested that Nusrat should have a urine test if her periods stopped again. She also advised Nusrat to have treatment for lymphatic tuberculosis, which might have caused her fallopian tubes to block. Nusrat and her husband should both be tested for infertility, since it might not be a problem with Nusrat at all. Afrozi commented that Nusrat's husband was very cruel: "He beats her a lot and leaves her standing outside all day long. He doesn't even let her into the house to escape."

The doctor's wife said Nusrat should adopt a child to make her husband happier, but Afrozi said this would not work: "Nusrat could love another person's child. But her husband wouldn't receive someone else's child hospitably, so who would give their child to them? Nusrat's husband is not right. He doesn't look after Nusrat properly. Nusrat thinks that if she has her own child, she'll begin to be treated with consideration because of the child."

A Song Marking a Boy's Birth

Beautiful new mother, Queen today in a red *sārī*!

The mother-in-law will come, yes indeed,
She'll demand her honorarium, yes indeed.
The new mother will take a stave and rain blows down on her head.
Mother-in-law-queen will flee, hoisting her *sārī* up her legs.
Beautiful new mother, Queen today in a red *sārī*!

The sister-in-law [HZ] will come, yes indeed,
She'll demand her honorarium, yes indeed.
The new mother will take a stave and rain blows down on her head.
Sister-in-law-queen will flee, hoisting her *sārī* up her legs.
Beautiful new mother, Queen today in a red *sārī*![11]

Notes

1. The Indian government favors sterilization because it requires only one action and is highly reliable, unlike most of the alternatives. From the mid-1960s to 1977 vasectomy (male sterilization) was the preferred method, being a simple operation. In 1975, however, the Indian prime minister, Indira Gandhi, suspended democratic procedures and declared a state of emergency. During the next two years, the family-planning program was characterized by such coercion—especially in the northern states, including Uttar Pradesh—that the government became very unpopular and was ousted in the general election of 1977. As a result of men's hostility to vasectomy, the family-planning program has now switched to tubectomy (female sterilization). Like vasectomy, the laparoscopic tubectomy or "one-stitch operation" is technically simple and can be done on an out-patient basis. From the government's point of view, one of the main advantages of both kinds of sterilization is that they cannot easily be reversed. This, though, is precisely the reason for opposition from couples fearful about their children dying and wanting a safety route in case they needed more children. Pressure on health staff to reach their sterilization "targets" creates major distortions in their work. Several English words

connected with the family-planning program have come into common Hindi usage, among them operation, family planning, target, case, and motivate, as in comments such as "*main ne do* case operation *ke lie* motivate *kar diyā hai*" [I have motivated two cases for the operation]. For more discussions of the Indian family-planning program, see Cassen (1978); Narayana and Kantner (1992); Ravindran (1993); Gupta (1993); and Vishwanath (1994).

2. This view of Islam's position on sterilization is discussed in more detail in R. Jeffery and P. Jeffery (1996). See also Chapter 2.

3. For more details on our research on childbearing in the two villages, see Jeffery, Jeffery, and Lyon (1989).

4. We were uncomfortable about dealing with such requests. Concerns about "contaminating" our research or encouraging women in acts of deception in relation to their in-laws were only part of it. Contraceptive pills can be bought over the counter, and even women who obtained them from medical practitioners would probably have no medical checkup. Aside from the usual concerns about the safety of hormonal contraceptive techniques, the hormone levels are calculated for women of much greater body mass than most women in Dharmnagri and Jhakri. Similarly, although legal abortions can supposedly be obtained very easily through the government health services, they are often performed in seriously unhygienic conditions along with pressure to be sterilized.

5. Kabeer (1985) discusses how women might gain from high fertility; for discussions of the importance of sons in old age see Vlassoff and Vlassoff (1980); Datta and Nugent (1984); Vlassoff (1984); Vlassoff (1990); Jeffery, Jeffery, and Lyon (1989).

6. Miller (1980, 1981) is a classic source on son preference in India. Anxieties about dowry have recently become linked with sex-determination testing (by amniocentesis or ultrasound) for babies in utero and with the selective abortion of any female fetus. Such facilities have been established in large cities such as Bombay and Delhi, and spread to smaller towns; but they were not available in Bijnor in 1991. For further details on the use of amniocentesis, see Ramanamma and Bhambawala (1980); Kumar (1983); Dube (1983); Balakrishnan (1994). Son preference is closely linked to the demands made of the parents of girls for dowry when they are married and for continuing help afterward. For more on this see Chapter 3.

7. The two songs in this chapter are birth songs [*janam gīt*], sung at the house where a woman has given birth to a son. Groups of women and girls from among the new mother's in-laws and their neighbors—but not her own natal kin—would gather at the house for several evenings following the birth and hold songfests, sometimes with dancing. Songs were not sung to mark a girl's birth. We have included another birth song in Chapter 11. Most birth songs and wedding songs have several more verses than we have included here. Generally, the verses refer in turn to the various relatives of the new mother or the bride and groom, either singly or as married couples (such as the bride's paternal grandparents). This birth song is sung to the tune of a film song and the final line of the chorus, "Now who will play the flute?" [*ab kaun bajāī*

bānsuriyā?], comes from the original song. The verses hinge on the tasks performed by the new mother's in-laws and the honoraria [*neg*] she is expected to present to them (normally cash, jewelry, or clothing). For other examples of birth songs in Bijnor, see Jeffery, Jeffery, and Lyon (1989), chapter 6.

8. Abortion was widely regarded as sinful by Muslims in Bijnor, but the willingness of Qudsia (and several other women in Jhakri) to consider abortion reflected their problems in obtaining suitable contraception when medical staff prioritized sterilization and often refused to provide other means of family planning. See also Chapter 16.

9. Local ideas of health drew heavily on the contrasting humors of "heat" and "cold." If these are not in balance, a person is likely to become ill. Foodstuffs and medicines have effects that are considered either "heating" or "cooling" and can be used to bring the body back into balance. Symptoms of "heat" include boils, skin rashes, giddiness, nausea, and diarrhea. For more details, see Jeffery, Jeffery, and Lyon (1989:24-5).

10. For more on this, see Chapter 2.

11. This birth song (see note 7) introduces another theme, the resentment that people often expressed about the financial difficulties created by people's demands for honoraria.

2

Just Because I Was Angry

Some months after our arrival in 1982, Nisar and his wife, Najma, were among those Jhakri couples we selected to be the focus of our research. They were Sheikhs, the dominant Muslim landowning community in the area. Nisar's paternal great-grandfather had had two sons, who each had four sons, one of whom had already died before we arrived. These "cousin-brothers" and their wives and children lived in houses around two linked courtyards in the center of Jhakri. Altogether, they were about one-eighth of Jhakri's population, and they farmed somewhat over thirty acres. They were one of the most powerful and prominent extended families in the village.

Najma was shy and rather self-deprecating, apparently not a very assertive young woman. She was very fond of her mother-in-law, a woman with a gentle manner and considerable charm. When we returned in 1990, we were saddened to learn that Najma's mother-in-law had died a couple of years earlier. For Najma, the death had been a watershed: A once bearable situation had become intolerable. In early 1991, Khurshid Ahmed—Nisar's paternal second cousin— was helping Roger with his work in Qaziwala, some two miles away from Jhakri and Najma's birthplace. One day, while they were cycling there together, Khurshid Ahmed casually remarked that Najma had gone to Bijnor a few days previously and had had the "operation." We were astonished.

It was not simply out of character for Najma to have acted so independently and seemingly precipitantly, for her decision went against the views of Jhakri people, including (as we had thought) her own. In north India, the most widespread—but not uncontested—reading of Islam was that limiting the number of children was contrary to Allah's will. The "operation" was usually regarded as particularly sinful.[1] Moreover, the first major assault on the Babri Masjid in Ayodhya had occurred in November 1990, only a couple of months earlier. There were serious communal problems in the town of Bijnor (and, to a lesser extent, in the rural hinterland), just as in many cities throughout northern India. In the looting, arson, and attacks on persons, Muslims had suffered disproportionately. Among other things, Muslims' fears often translated into assertions that the government family-planning program specifically targeted

Spinning Yarn in Jhakri

*Muslims and was essentially a form of ethnic genocide. For that very reason,
indeed, we were relying on Khurshid Ahmed to smooth our work in Qaziwala.*[2]

* * * * * *

The ANM posted at the Dharmnagri dispensary had often
complained that her work in Jhakri was much harder than in other
villages, and that "only three or four people there have the manners" to
ask her to sit down and to talk properly to her. People in Jhakri, for their
part, said that the ANM was solely interested in meeting the
sterilization targets set by her superiors. They believed that Muslims
should not have the operation. Some said that sterilized people could
not make the Haj pilgrimage to Mecca. Others said that such people's
daily prayers would be invalidated or their fasts during Ramzān would
no longer be acceptable to Allah, their funeral processions could not be
performed or their souls would not be allowed into Paradise. Not
surprisingly, the number of men and women in Jhakri who had been
sterilized could be counted on one hand. One man had undergone
vasectomy under compulsion during the Emergency of 1975-1977. This
man's brother (whose first wife had died in childbirth and whose
second wife nearly met the same fate) also had a vasectomy. One
woman had been sterilized after an obstructed labor and cesarean
section that nearly killed her. Only the two others—one man, one
woman—could be said to have opted for sterilization without the severe
pressure of circumstances. In 1985, when we had asked Najma's
husband, Nisar, about contraception, he said he had never used any
contraception and he never would: "Don't bother asking anyone else in
Jhakri, you'll be wasting your time! All the men will give you the same
answer. My wife's a Muslim, she'll say the same."

We did ask Najma. Like most of her neighbors, she said her string of
pregnancies was getting her down.

* * * * * *

Najma was born in the mid-1950s in Qaziwala, a much larger village
than Jhakri. Najma's father was relatively wealthy with over twenty
acres of land. When Najma was growing up, there was no government
school or *madrasā* [Islamic academy] in Qaziwala. Although there was a
madrasā in nearby Begawala, Najma's parents would not send her that
far to study:

> There was a woman in Qaziwala itself who knew the Qur'ān Sharīf by
> heart. She used to teach children to read it. That's where I went. Both my

parents wanted me to study, but I wasn't interested. I used to spend my time playing five stones! So I read just the first Arabic primer and one section of the Qur'ān Sharīf. Then I didn't go anymore. When I was about eight or nine, I began learning to spin cotton thread. And then, because I was getting big, my mother wouldn't let me study any more. In those days, people didn't send girls outside the house.

During Najma's adolescence, several offers of marriage came for her from within Qaziwala, though she could not remember how many. One of Najma's sisters was married in Jhakri, however, and her father-in-law worked hard to persuade both sides to arrange Najma's marriage to Nisar [his yBS]. The match was almost a foregone conclusion in any case, for Nisar's mother was also Najma's aunt [FZ]; for years she had been saying she would take Najma as her daughter-in-law. So when Najma was about seventeen, she was married to Nisar in Jhakri: "And my parents and my father's brothers were all happy to agree. For one thing, I'd be going to my father's sister's house. Also, the two families were on a par economically. In every way, they were the equals of my family. And the boy himself was strong."

Najma's aunt was born in the early 1930s, and she too had followed her father's sister in marriage to Jhakri. In her thirty years of marriage, Najma's aunt had borne ten children. One son died at age six from an unknown fever. All six live-born girls had died from unspecified fevers and vomiting. A seventh daughter was stillborn in 1973, around the time Najma and Nisar were married. Of the ten children, only Nisar and his younger brother remained. When Najma overheard her aunt telling us this grim tale in 1982, she commented: "Three boys and seven girls! But just two boys remain. Not one girl stayed alive. If just one was alive, what would be the matter with that? Why, I could sometimes call my husband's sister!"

*   *   *   *   *   *

From the start, Najma got on well with her aunt. In 1982, Najma was full of praise for her. There had been no demands for any items in Najma's dowry, nor was she ever pressured to bring things from her parents when she went to visit them. Her aunt never requisitioned the items that Najma's parents gave her—unlike many a mother-in-law— nor did she check up on what jewelry and clothing Najma was wearing:

And she's never beaten me or shouted at me. I'd never want to make my cooking hearth separate from my mother-in-law's. There are no definite decisions about which chores we do, but my daily work usually entails sweeping the house, grinding spices and preparing food, and washing dishes—with my mother-in-law's help—as well as collecting the cattle dung, making it into dung cakes, taking food to the men in the fields, and cutting fodder for the cattle. Periodically, I also spread diluted cattle dung on the ground inside the house and immediately outside, build a new cooking hearth, load the grain store with wheat and rice that I've previously dried in the sun, and collect wood fuel from the scrubland around the fields.

While she was telling us this, Khurshid Ahmed began teasing her. "She doesn't do any work at all! She's very *sīdhī*![3] She doesn't know how to do anything!" he said, laughing.

Najma grinned at him—and then turned to us: "I'm just right being *sīdhī*! My mother-in-law is like my mother. I'm the only daughter-in-law and I've never had a fight with my mother-in-law. She's very *sīdhī* and if she ever criticizes me I just listen silently. But my mother-in-law doesn't create fights."

At the same time, Najma was very conscious of the difference that marriage brings:

I have to observe *purdah* [veiling] from all the men in my marital village— apart from my husband's younger brother and cousins, and the boys. Otherwise I must keep *purdah* from everyone. There's no *purdah* in one's parents' village. And then you must do your work in your marital village. In your parents' place, you can do some or leave some. Before I was married, I didn't have to do everything. Now my brother's wife does everything. That's the difference between a daughter and a daughter-in-law. If I didn't do my work here, the neighboring women would start gossiping, and my husband would ask why I hadn't done my work.

Nevertheless, she believed that marriage was inevitable and that she could not have led a different life even if she had been educated:

After studying, what benefit do you get? What service jobs do Muslims get? Once you've studied, you still have to be a farmer. A few women in this courtyard studied the Qur'ān Sharīf but now they only read it during Ramzān.[4] The rest of the year it isn't read—there's no free time with all the work in the fields. And with the dung and midden work, our clothes are always dirty and we can neither pray nor read the Qur'ān Sharīf. If I were educated, I'd still have to do this same work. Village girls can't go away as you can to get jobs. And since it's like that in our destiny, what can I do? Whether someone is educated or not, they'll get what's written in their fate. And that's unknown.

In any case, Najma was in a comparatively enviable position. She was married into a household that could support its members comfortably. She had known the place and the people since her childhood. Nisar was a steady worker and no more prone to fight with her than his mother was. And she was still within easy walking distance of her parents: "Very distant marriage isn't good, but neither is marriage within the village. Distant marriage is no good because it's hard to come and go. Marriage within the village is no good because the parents get to hear all their daughter's troubles. A nearby village is best of all."

*　*　*　*　*　*

Yet all was not well. Najma's childbearing career soon began to resemble her mother-in-law's. In 1974, her first-born son died when he was seventeen days old. In 1983 her third child (a girl) died from diarrhea at age four. The following year, she had twin girls. They developed diarrhea from the cow's milk that they were fed after Najma's milk dried up because she had malaria. They both died at about three months of age. Only her second and fourth children, a boy and a girl, remained.

Our fieldnotes are littered with references to Najma's children's illnesses—malaria, fevers, boils, conjunctivitis. Once, when her daughter was ill with vomiting and diarrhea, the dispensary doctor chased her away without prescribing any medicines because the child had diarrhea in his consulting room. Najma herself had several unsolved health problems. She had severe menstrual pains but sought no treatment because she was too embarrassed. Occasionally she suffered fits, for which a *maulvī* had once given her an amulet. She had also gone to the Sufi shrine in Badayun with one of her sister's brothers-in-law [ZHB].[5] Khurshid Ahmed butted in to say that Najma was taunted when she returned, though she was so *sīdhī* that no one had seriously imagined that anything scandalous had happened.

During our visit in 1985, Najma gave birth to another boy. She was three days in labor and had severe afterpains, migraine, and fever after the delivery. She became exhausted from taking care of the baby. She believed he had been afflicted by the shadow of a menstruating woman because he would not sleep at night, his navel became septic, and his skin erupted with boils.

During the pregnancy, Najma's mother-in-law had been very supportive. Although Najma normally continued with much of her work during her pregnancies, she did not go beyond the domestic area once the delivery drew close: "Women without someone to take over their work usually just have to carry on, but I'm fortunate. I stopped doing outside work after the eighth month and my mother-in-law did it for me. What, does it look nice for a woman to go out with a drum strapped to her belly?" And after her deliveries, Najma was not required to do any work around the house for about a week. Nor did she do her outside work for over a month: "My mother-in-law is very good," she commented.

By 1985, Najma had had seven children, but just two boys and a girl remained alive. When we asked how she had felt about being pregnant again, she was caustic: "Ha! I was very happy! What happens as a result of being happy? It was a calamity. If it were within my control I wouldn't have had a single child, but what should I have done? Children are not within my control. Whatever God gives will have to be accepted."

Swaleha asked if she wanted any more children in that case. "Another fifty girls and fifty boys! No, really, I don't need either a girl or a boy," Najma retorted scornfully.

She had never, however, done anything to prevent further pregnancies. She had neither discussed the question with her mother nor spoken to her mother-in-law, who was too unworldly to raise the issue with her. Najma felt it was up to her husband. "I can't go anywhere or take any medicine without his permission. But he's too naive about such things to talk sensibly about pills to the dispensary compounder, so I've said nothing to him either. My husband isn't the sort of man who would bring pills. He's very *sīdhā* and doesn't know anything about such matters."

During our brief visit in late 1986, we found Najma's name entered along with the names of several other Jhakri women in the ANM's register of women who had accepted a Copper-T. We had no chance then to ask Najma or the others about this. When we did so in 1990, they said the ANM must have made false entries. The women's own accounts, indeed, were more plausible than the ANM's records: Najma, for instance, had given birth twice more since 1986. Seemingly, the ANM's need to meet family-planning targets had got the better of her.

* * * * * *

Meanwhile, several events had had a dramatic impact on Najma's everyday life. In early 1988 while Najma was milking the buffalo, its tail flicked and struck her left eye, badly irritating the cornea. Shortly after this, when Najma was due to give birth again, Nisar's mother got a severe chest infection and died: "And she loved me greatly," said

Najma. "When she died, I grieved terribly. I cried all the time." The weeping exacerbated the eye injury, and Najma could no longer see clearly. Nevertheless, she had to continue her work. In the same year, too, she finalized the arrangements for Nisar's younger brother's marriage to Furqana from nearby Rahimpur. The cohabitation was in July. A couple of months later, Najma's baby died, and Najma was soon pregnant again. This next child—born in October 1989—was the first of her children to receive polio and triple vaccine inoculations. Of the nine children born to her in about fifteen years, just three boys and one girl were alive when we returned to Bijnor in July 1990.

There seemed to be no money problems in the family. Nisar's father had a substantial sum in the bank (reputedly about Rs 80,000-90,000). And although Nisar's father still operated his inherited land jointly with his brothers, he also farmed a further one and a half acres that he had bought separately from his savings. "Just think about all the sugarcane he can grow," Khurshid Ahmed commented. Yet, as Najma explained, her baby born in early 1988 had died: "He was suffering from cholera.[6] But he got no treatment at first, as there was no one else at home who could go with me to see a doctor. Only when his condition became very serious was he taken to Bijnor. He was given a glucose drip, but he didn't survive."

Maqsood—Khurshid Ahmed's father and Nisar's father's cousin—did not stint on his criticism:

> My cousin-brother has been like this ever since his wife died. His character has come into the open. In his wife's lifetime he was constrained. Najma's oldest son has been suffering from a liver complaint for the past three years. He gets diarrhea repeatedly and his blood isn't being made. He's become yellow. But does his grandfather or his father see what state he's in and ask themselves why the boy is drying out? The moment the boy gets a bit better, he's put straight to work again. If he isn't treated, his liver will become infected and any treatment will be difficult. Neither the father cares for his son nor the grandfather for his grandson.

Maqsood told us how he had spent hundreds of rupees on medical treatments when his grandson—the son of his older son, Khalil—had chickenpox and his eye became badly infected. "Money is for spending. We alone will watch over our children and grandchildren," Maqsood concluded. According to Khurshid Ahmed, though, Nisar's father would never spend money like that: "He's just a miser! One time, I asked him why he isn't prepared to pay for treatments for his children and grandchildren when he is feeding and clothing them. He got furious with me and said, 'You're very wealthy—why don't you pay for it!'"

There was little chance that Najma could remedy the situation. Nisar still worked the land jointly with his father, and the land was in his father's name. His father would not pay for medical treatment until the last minute—and Nisar was afraid to ask before that. Najma commented:

> My father-in-law controls all the money and my husband doesn't have any himself. If I had money of my own, I wouldn't be blind. I have so much trouble with my eye. I get some income from spinning and that stays with me—but that money is so little. I keep that money aside to spend on medicines for myself and the children, as I can't be sure any other money for treatment will be forthcoming. I had cholera last year and again a few months ago. I had lots of pain. The whole night I had stomach pains that troubled me a great deal. But my father-in-law didn't even ask if I needed medicines. From the very beginning, even while my mother-in-law was alive, all the money has been with my father-in-law. And my husband never asks him for anything.

Nor did Najma obtain help from other quarters. Her sister, married into the adjacent house, was preoccupied with the needs of her own small children and with the marital problems of her two oldest daughters. Najma's parents provided some clothing and small gifts of money occasionally, but she could not expect more: "Why would my parents give me land or money? They too have offspring. They have sons and daughters-in-law who need the land and the money. Enough, when I have a baby or when my children are to be married, then they'll send some money and cloth and some other things."

* * * * * *

With her mother-in-law alive, Najma had been protected from the worst excesses of her father-in-law's miserliness. How different things had become. By early 1990, she was desperate. She decided to obtain contraceptive pills. The doctor told her to take a pill each evening with milk.

> But the day my buffalo stopped giving milk, I didn't take a pill. The next day, I took two with water. That very night, I had severe stomach pains and diarrhea. I became so sick that I thought I wasn't going to survive. Even then my father-in-law didn't give any money for medicine. And my husband is like this—he says nothing. That's why I took the pills for only

one and a half months. You must tell me more about medicines to stop
having children. What about this Copper-T? And I've heard there's an
injection that stops a woman having a child for two or three years. But the
operation isn't permitted in our religion. Medicines or injections alone are
acceptable for us.

In February 1991, however, Najma was again sick with diarrhea and
fever. That was evidently the final straw. She later recounted how she
had decided to tell the ANM at the Dharmnagri dispensary that she
wanted to be sterilized:

I finally had the operation just because I was angry. My own health was
very bad. And how could I get medicines for the children when I have no
money? I went to see the ANM and she was ready to take me. When my
mother-in-law was alive, she used to attend to my needs with great
consideration. She'd get money for treatment for me. It's very difficult to
find such a good mother-in-law. Now I'm angry. And since my father-in-
law does things like that to me, I'll also pay just so much attention to him.
Can't he notice when his daughter-in-law's health is bad or her children
are sick or she can't see properly? But he didn't give any money. Children
died because there was no medicine. That's why, in anger, I was sterilized. My husband never speaks up in front of his father. That's the whole
problem. He's afraid of his father. I cried a lot after my mother-in-law
died. My eye began hurting and it watered all the time. At that time I
could still see a bit, but now I can't see at all with it. I was ill and there
was this problem with money. And children kept dying, too, without
medicine. What could I do about them? So I had the operation. I asked no
one's advice, not even my husband's. That day, my husband's aunts and
my sister had all gone to another village together to pay a condolence
visit. They alone could have prevented me, that's all. I saw the occasion
was good. So I lifted the dung quickly in the early morning. I gave
Furqana [her HBW] fifty paisa [half a rupee] in case the children cried so
that she could buy them biscuits, and I left the food prepared. I myself
didn't eat because the ANM had told me not to. That's it. I just went.

After the operation, Najma spent some of the "compensation money"
of Rs 155 on apples for herself (though her children ate all but one).[7] The
ANM brought her back from Bijnor on a cycle rickshaw. The ANM
wanted the rickshaw driven right up to the village, but Najma refused:
"Everyone would hear about it, so I asked her to leave me at the main
road. But my husband's aunts and my sister had returned earlier.
They'd already heard all about it from Furqana. They all said I should
have told them."

Several of the women in her courtyard told her she should not have
gone for the operation alone: "If I'd gone with my husband, we'd have

been given some land, they said. But I hadn't gone to get land. My own health had become bad because of having so many children. That's why I had the operation. If there are few children, I can look after them properly. Now I have eye problems and I'm very troubled. Without eyesight, I'd have to rely on others just to look after myself. And my children are small. Who'd look after them?"

* * * * * *

Najma thought she had acted with good reason, but she was virtually alone in that. The reverberations rippled among her relatives. Najma's mother arrived from Qaziwala, demanding to know why Najma had done such a thing. When she wanted to return home, we gave her a lift along with our research assistants. Najma's mother briefly joined in our chatting and laughing, but then she stopped:

> When people are laughing among themselves, then I laugh too. But I feel as if my heart has an axe chopping it. Najma's been sterilized and I'm furious. I've been arguing with her. And with the doctor. I asked why they'd sterilized her. I wept the whole night. When Najma was coming back from the operation, the rickshaw tipped over and she fell out and was hurt. The ANM wasn't hurt at all. It would have been good if she had been! Najma didn't tell me anything beforehand. I'd have forbidden her if I'd known.

A few days later, our assistant Radha asked Najma how she was feeling. Najma put her finger to her mouth and laughed. "What's happened to me that you need to ask about my health?" Patricia pointed to Najma's midriff. "Be quiet! I've done nothing!" Najma hissed. When Radha told Najma about her mother's anger, Najma laughed. "My mother's crazy!" retorted Najma. "She's just worrying senselessly."

Nisar's father was also angry about not being consulted, but his anger cooled within a couple of days when he realized nothing could reverse Najma's action. Nisar kept a low profile, neither joining his elders in criticizing Najma nor openly supporting her.

In other courtyards in Jhakri, Najma's action became a matter of controversy. One day Hashmi was telling us that she and her husband, Haroon, did not want any more children. Haroon had apparently said that they would have more than enough children even if one of them died. Ahmed's mother was on a cot nearby: "Then have the operation like that one in the big people's courtyard!" she butted in acidly. Hashmi said she would not, for sterilization was not permitted. "Everything's permitted for the big people!" retorted Ahmed's mother.

But Hashmi was not prepared to condemn Najma: "What can I say about Najma? I can understand only my own business. My husband's sister also had the operation when her health was very bad and it was hard for her to survive. But our prayer is this, that Allah himself will stop more children coming."

Another woman from a neighboring courtyard also commented unfavorably on Najma's decision: "She's had the operation, but that's wrong. I too find it hard to rear children!" Ghazala (who, unbeknownst to her neighbor, had had an abortion and was currently using condoms) rallied to Najma's defense: "Najma's alone and weak," she said. "There's no one to help her. That's why she had the operation."

*   *   *   *   *   *

It proved particularly hard to throw off the disapproval of her sister-in-law [HyBW], Furqana. Najma could reasonably have expected Furqana to help for a few days after the operation, but she did nothing. Najma felt particularly aggrieved about this. She had arranged Nisar's brother's marriage after her mother-in-law died, and she had helped Furqana for a few days after she had her baby. But the two women cooked separately and they had a rota—two days on, two days off—for collecting dung from the jointly owned cattle and making dung cakes. These were stacked separately too. Perhaps, Najma thought, Furqana could have done the cooking for a couple of days or helped muck out the cattle. "I did everything connected with her marriage properly. But two days after the operation I had to lift dung again—she hadn't even touched it." Najma asked us to persuade Khurshid Ahmed to intercede on her behalf. Could he ask Furqana to do the cooking for a while, as sitting by a smoky cooking hearth was making her eye more troublesome? But Furqana refused to help.

Zebunnisa—Najma's niece [ZD], back in Jhakri after her marriage had broken down—told us that Najma was having trouble getting treatment for her eye:

> Najma would get lost if she tried to find the hospital by herself, but no one will take her. Who'd go with her? They're all angry with her. When her father-in-law didn't give enough food for the children, she got distressed and had the operation done. And now everyone's angry. Who will leave their work and go with her to the hospital? After the operation, when her eye began going bad again, her sister-in-law [Furqana] said, "Just look at the consequence of being sterilized! Now she's immobilized because of her eye. Whoever sins like that gets what they deserve."

Relations between Najma and Furqana had been tense for a while. Najma now had to compete for her father-in-law's favors. The two women were regularly accusing one another of getting things at the other's expense. According to Khurshid Ahmed, Nisar's father would forbid Najma—but not Furqana—to take her children for treatment. And now, a new house was being built. Najma's operation served as a convenient excuse for Furqana's antagonism. One day, Khurshid Ahmed told us the two women had been quarreling the previous day: "There was lots of swearing. Some building is going on and each is trying to get the new house. That sort of thing often happens. When it's finished, the two couples' expenses will be separate. That's good because you then have to take responsibility for your own expenditures. Otherwise people compete to see who can spend the most money."

Najma felt that Furqana was being favored by Nisar's father. Najma was to move into the new house with Nisar and their children, but it was so small (she claimed) that there would be room for only two beds once the grain store had been installed; and there was no hand pump or latrine, so she would be constantly running to and fro with buckets of water. Khurshida was listening to Najma's complaints. She pointed out that her husband, Khalil, and his brother, Khurshid Ahmed, had told Najma that she could have had a bigger house: Khalil had offered to exchange some land with Nisar so that they would each have larger house sites. But Nisar's father had offered too little money for the deal to make sense to Khalil and Khurshid Ahmed. After Najma went away, Khurshida said she was not convinced by Najma's complaints. She lowered her voice:

An especially excellent house has been built. You just take a look at it. Najma's telling you it's small, but it isn't. She's in the habit of saving money for herself. She doesn't want to share with Furqana. But a sister-in-law will demand her rights. She's also entitled to an equal share. Previously, everything came into Najma's hands, but now Furqana is getting her share. Anyway, Najma sells grain secretly, so why can't she pay for her own treatment herself? I can't tolerate being ill. I always take medicines quickly and tell my husband that I'm ill. But Najma just lies on her bed and does nothing. She gets medicines only when the trouble is serious. Najma always says, "Women dash off to Bijnor when they're sick, but illnesses are always coming." If Najma had told Nisar about her troubles when they were first married and had got them treated, he'd pay attention to her illnesses and her medicines now. But he doesn't take any care. Previously, to make her mother-in-law think she was good, Najma used to ask her husband for nothing. The man's developed a bad habit. And now Najma's crying about it.

Nevertheless, Khurshida was not wholly unsympathetic. She felt for Najma, who was suffering the criticism of other people in their courtyard. Indeed, Khurshida confided, she had been considering being sterilized herself because she too did not want any more children. Now, the repercussions that Najma's action had provoked made Khurshida too fearful to go ahead. Instead, she would take pills—but she would tell nobody, "for people create tales."

*   *   *   *   *   *

By now, Najma was desperate to have her eye treated: "My eyes can cope with making bread and stews. But I can't see the lice in my kids' hair. I'd be embarrassed to wear glasses. How could I conceal my face when I need to?"

Najma was getting no support from her neighbors. Moreover, she felt let down by the ANM, who had promised to get her eye treated after the operation. But the ANM had not been back even once to see her. We were not in the least surprised. As usual, the ANM was more concerned with new sterilization cases than with sorting out problems for women who had already contributed to her sterilization target.

At our suggestion, Najma asked the dispensary doctor to check her eye, and he referred her to the ophthalmologist at Bijnor government hospital. None of Najma's relatives would go with her, so she wanted us to steer her through the hospital bureaucracy. Like many people, she believed she would otherwise be treated both roughly and tardily. As we anticipated, our presence had its effect. A few weeks before, the ophthalmologist had worked in an eye camp—a mobile operating facility dealing with cataracts—held in Dharmnagri. He recognized Patricia—and Najma was moved to the head of the queue forthwith.

Najma detailed the history of her problem. Even before the doctor began his tests, he asked how many children she had. When Najma told him she had four, he straightaway asked if she had had "the operation." "Yes," Najma told him, "precisely because I'm troubled with this eye." He tested her vision using a screen with patterns of dots, since she could not read the Hindi script. The mirror reflecting the dots was so rippled that the images were badly distorted. She managed to decipher them with one eye but not the other. When the doctor examined her eye, he found a corneal ulcer, which could be cured fairly quickly, but also corneal opacity, which would require longer treatment and would never be fully rectified.

The drops and ointments prescribed for the first few days cost about Rs 25. Najma did not have enough cash with her. We lent her the money and she promised to repay it very soon. Meanwhile, she asked, would we rehearse the instructions for their use with Khurshid Ahmed, since he could read Hindi? And were there any dietary restrictions connected with the drugs? And now that it was Ramzãn, could she use the medicines during the hours of darkness so that her fast would not be broken?

Nisar's father was loath to repay us. Najma wanted Khurshid Ahmed to reason with her father-in-law, but he refused: "Neither Najma nor Nisar is prepared to ask. What business do I have to be a go-between for Najma and her father-in-law? I don't want Nisar's father to be in debt to you, but I'd rather repay you myself than confront my uncle's anger." Roger offered to intervene: "I'll ask him why he won't pay. I'll ask if he has no shame! It won't matter if he gets angry with me!" In response, Nisar's father grudgingly repaid the money.

Over the following days, Najma visited the Dharmnagri dispensary several times to have the dressings changed. The first time, they had come completely undone. Her youngest son had been so terrified when he saw her bandages that he hit her face and tore the dressings. Another time when Najma had called on us after having the dressings changed again, Khurshid Ahmed's father, Maqsood, also dropped in for a chat. Najma swiftly hid her face from him. Maqsood began chiding her: "You should have got yourself treated earlier, when the trouble first began. Even now you're having to meet your own expenses. If you'd done so before you wouldn't be having so many worries now." She retorted: "But what should I have done, since the old man never pays attention to me?"

By now, Najma's eye was badly irritated. Bright sunlight bothered her, but she would not wear sunglasses. She found it hard to work with the dressings in place. And the itching was so intolerable that she often rubbed her eye vigorously with her shawl. With hindsight, Najma now blamed all her woes on her inability to control her life, starting with the decision about getting married: "Who asks a girl about her marriage? Nobody ever asks. If they'd asked me I'd never have married. Seeing all these calamities—children, household worries, bad health, whatever else—I'd never have married. But the decision is for the parents alone."

Notes

1. This interpretation of Islamic doctrine is not universally accepted among Muslims, and there is considerable debate within Islam about family planning. For many Muslims, the finality of sterilization was the key to its sinfulness. As we indicate at various points here, however, spacing methods were not necessarily considered in the same league, and some Jhakri women resorted to intrauterine devices, hormonal pills, and abortions. The Bangladesh

government has stressed parental responsibility to ensure the high "quality" of children as part of their campaign to persuade people to limit their families. In some measure, this position probably reflects the weak position of Bangladesh in relation to aid donors who prioritize population control. Nevertheless, Muslim theologians there have developed interpretations that legitimize family planning on the basis of Islamic scripture. In Pakistan, there has been little hostility to sterilization from Islamic theologians on Islamic grounds per se.

2. For more details on communal issues in Bijnor see R. Jeffery and P. Jeffery (1994, 1996); P. Jeffery and R. Jeffery (forthcoming); and Basu (1994). For more general discussions of communalism in north India in the early 1990s, see Basu et al. (1993). The Indian national census was about to be conducted (in April 1991) and the Gulf War was brewing: These, too, were considered threatening by people in Qaziwala.

3. The word *sīdhī* (masculine *sīdhā*) is a polyvalent word and thus difficult to translate satisfactorily. About things, it means "straight," and when applied to people it carries connotations of straightforwardness, innocence, or simpleness; but this is positively valued in comparison with deviousness and cunning (as implied by a word such as *chalāk*, for instance).

4. During the Islamic month of Ramzān, particular emphasis is placed on religious observance: prayer and reading the Qur'ān Sharīf, and fasting between sunrise and sunset.

5. Sufi shrines generally mark the places where Muslim mystic saints worked and died. Many shrines—including the one at Badayun about 100 miles south of Bijnor—are places of pilgrimage where people in distress seek solutions to their problems.

6. The word "cholera" is widely used to describe severe diarrhea, but it is unlikely that it would have been diagnosed as cholera by a physician.

7. This money is supposed to compensate women for any loss of earnings and for costs incurred because of the operation—but it is usually regarded as an incentive, particularly for the very poor.

3

She's Brought Plenty of Wealth

Many conversations in Dharmnagri and Jhakri that began with women's childbearing experiences spiraled off into discussions about the differences between daughters and sons. From there, it was a small step for people to quiz us about marriage arrangements in Britain. And men and women alike often drew explicit contrasts between our situation (and our apparent complacency about having two daughters) and the anxieties that beset the parents of girls in north India. Many lamented the evils of dowry and asserted that the Indian government should ban it. Yet there is legislation ostensibly intended to do just that: The Dowry Prohibition Act was passed in 1961 and an Anti-Dowry Amendment Act in 1984.[1]

Nevertheless, people in Dharmnagri and Jhakri claimed that parents these days were far more worried about dowry than previously. In the "old days," we were assured, parents simply gave what they could afford and their daughter's in-laws would accept it without question. Now, things were very different. More commercialized agriculture had affected family life. Children's survival chances had improved dramatically. Consumerism had made its inroads into rural life. And the families of boys had also begun making demands about what should be provided in a dowry. Parents felt themselves enmeshed in an increasingly competitive and materialistic marriage market in which the stakes were constantly shifting. A dowry that would have been acceptable just a few years ago now seemed inadequate. More utensils were expected; the bed and bedding should be of better quality; the items of clothing should be more numerous and of finer cloth; more jewelry should be given, and more of it should be gold rather than silver. In the rural areas, television sets and motorcycles would have been unheard of in the 1970s, but they were not uncommon among the wealthy by the 1990s. In real terms, dowries have been increasing.

In large measure, these increases were responses to "dowry demands." And even if a groom's family did not stipulate what should be in the dowry, the bride's parents might feel compelled to give as much as possible to protect their daughter from mistreatment by dissatisfied in-laws. Dowry murder, in which a young married woman is killed by her in-laws (usually by being burned to

69

death with kerosene from a cooking stove), seems a mainly urban phenomenon and instances were not unknown in the town of Bijnor.[2] *Indeed, the younger sister of our assistant Radha narrowly escaped such a fate: With her clothes on fire, she rushed from her husband's home to Radha's house a few hundred yards away and recovered after hospital treatment. In Dharmnagri and Jhakri, though, people told us about young women who were seriously beaten by their in-laws or who were told to ask their parents to supply further items for the groom and his family. Some talked poignantly about the married daughter as a potential "hostage," the "looting" perpetrated by some families with sons, or the difficulty of fulfilling the daughter's dowry needs without sacrificing the well-being of her parents and siblings. No one could predict what would happen when they married their daughter.*

Aside from raising parents' anxieties, such issues undermined the notion of the dowry as female property, that is, as inherited property in the form of movable goods over which the woman retained control. Certainly, dowries contained items specifically intended for the bride. Equally, though, in-laws expected to receive things too—cash, clothes, and maybe a cycle or a watch at the time of the wedding. Mothers-in-law sometimes tried to take control over dowry items, though this was usually regarded as an illegitimate use of their position. And when the young woman gave birth, especially if the baby was a boy, her husband's sisters might insist on being given jewelry and clothing from the original dowry.[3]

As critical as people's commentaries about dowry often were, however, it would be inconceivable not to try to give one. And if there was more pressure to give, many people had a greater capacity to do so. Rural incomes in Bijnor had been rising (though not for everyone), and consumer goods were increasingly available. Efforts to dissuade people from giving and taking dowries, such as those made by a local Jat leader, Tikait, had little impact. Indeed, parents generally wanted to do their best for their daughter, and they would try to avoid a match with a family whose income was precarious. If they provided her with security and protection, they could feel they had discharged their parental duties properly. Other people, too, viewed their generosity with approval. Only the miserly would fail to give as elaborate a dowry as they could afford. Those unfortunates who could not give much and had to marry their daughter into a poor household would be the object of pity. Sometimes, among the poorest families, a woman's parents or brothers would accept a cash payment for her, but this was certainly not a favored way of arranging a marriage. For a man, too, buying a bride was usually a last resort.[4]

The out-married daughter—costly as providing for her could be—was a crucial means through which rural society was cemented. A man's mother and paternal aunts born in other villages and his sisters, female cousins, and daughters who married in yet others were vital for establishing and sustaining links between families. The gifts associated with marriages were the first major instance of patterns of giving that would continue through the years.[5]

A Wedding Song

Generous wedding gifts have been presented, the dowry was given,
But the boy's people were still scowling.

The bride's grandfather [FF] was compelled to hear the swearing,
Her grandmother [FM] was forced to hear the oaths.
Generous wedding gifts have been presented, the dowry was given,
But the boy's people were still scowling.

The bride's uncle [FeB] was compelled to hear the swearing,
Her aunt [FeBW] was forced to hear the oaths.
Generous wedding gifts have been presented, the dowry was given,
But the boy's people were still scowling.[6]

Khatun's Commentary on Dowry

Khatun reckoned there had been a great change in the dowry and jewelry given when a daughter married. When she herself was married into a rich-peasant household in Jhakri in the mid-1940s, there were just five kitchen utensils, five shawls and four suits for herself and five *dupattās* [lightweight shawls] for sharing among her husband's female relatives.[7] Her in-laws presented her with ten suits and a lot of silver jewelry—sets for her ankles, wrists, and upper arms, as well as necklaces and a headpiece. There was less jewelry from her parents, just three sets for her ears, some hair clips, and a ring, all of them silver. Hardly any of this jewelry was left now, as Khatun had much of it remade when her sons and daughters were married.

These days, more people are giving gold things. That began happening ten or fifteen years ago [about 1970]. There is more in the dowry, too. People with girls are worried about how they'll get them married. Among us Muslims, the girl's people have to wait until an offer comes from a boy's family. And these days, people with sons look for places where they can get things in the dowry. People with girls just have to wait for a message offering an engagement. That's the situation we're in with our second daughter. She's of an age to be married, but no offers are coming. In the old days, people with boys would come begging and ask for an "offering." They'd be begging for a wife for their son. And they'd take her honorably. In those days, no one said anything if the bride arrived with hardly any dowry. Nor would she be troubled by her in-laws if the dowry was small. But now the bride's asked what she's brought. "Look, she has nothing! Send her back! Throw her out of the house! Let's do another marriage!" That's the way people talk these days.

One of Khatun's daughters-in-law was sitting there too. "People these days don't want a bride. They want wealth," she interjected. Khatun continued: "Neither rich nor poor used to ask for anything in the dowry in the old days. Among us Muslims, it's not that people ask directly. But they look at the girl's house carefully before they send a marriage offer. Some people still think it's important to have a good-looking bride. But some people are saying, 'Let's get lots of things, no matter what the bride's like!' Nowadays, people are very greedy. There wasn't this greed in the old days."

Swati's Views on Giving and Receiving Dowry

By 1985, Swati's two oldest daughters were married and only the youngest remained at home. Swati felt it was time her oldest son was married, for his wife would help with the housework and the animals. Our assistant Radha asked if they would be specifying anything in the bride's dowry. "Since we did 'one rupee' marriages for our two daughters, I'll do the same for my son. What's the point of doing anything else? Today the girl's people may give and tomorrow a thief may steal the lot! If it's in our destiny, we'll get enough from our own fields. What, will we become rich with someone else's money? Anyway, what business do we have with the things that the girl's people give to their daughter and son-in-law?"

Swati herself was married to Brijpal in about 1954, when she was eleven years old. There were no demands, yet fifty-one utensils and fifty-one *dhotīs* [cotton *sārīs*] were given at the time of the marriage. She remained in her parents' home for two years, during which time her father died. If her father had still been alive when she returned to Dharmnagri for the cohabitation, she explained, there would probably have been ten suits for her, clothing for the children in her husband's family, and a couple of suits for her husband. Both her married daughters had taken dowries to their in-laws' villages. The older one had eleven cooking utensils, eleven suits, and Rs 800, and the younger one a watch, a cycle, a radio, a bed, and a table and chairs. Both girls received jewelry from their parents and their in-laws, but they were both married without demands, she said. The younger daughter's husband still refused to take anything from them. The older one's mother-in-law had once commented about the dowry, but Swati had responded promptly, and there had never been any more trouble: "I told her that she'd asked for one rupee for her own four annas [one-quarter of a rupee] when the marriage was being finalized. That meant she'd left my husband to give twelve annas [three-quarters of a rupee]. So why was she now asking for more? She should have said at the time that she wanted not one but five rupees. If it had been possible to give that much, my husband would have done so. And if not, we wouldn't have made the match with her son."

When we returned to Bijnor in 1990, Swati's son had been married for four years and he had a baby daughter. At the time of his wedding, the bride's parents had intended to invite 150 people in the *barāt* [party of men who go with the groom], but Tikait, a Jat peasant leader, was trying to persuade Jat farmers like Brijpal to curb their spending on wedding feasts and dowries.[8] Just eleven utensils, eleven suits and Rs 51 could be given in the *bhāt* presented by the bride's mother's brother. Tikait had said that there should be only five men in a *barāt* and that no one should either give or receive a dowry. Twenty of Tikait's men attended Swati's son's wedding to check, and Swati's husband, Brijpal, did not even go, for he did not want other relatives to be offended that he had failed to invite them. And the groom and the *barāt* did not stay overnight in the bride's village, as they would have needed another meal.

When the marriage was being arranged, Brijpal had visited the bride's home with four men from Dharmnagri. The bride had served them food and they had all seen her face. When they returned home, they reported that the girl was very beautiful, fair skinned and healthy. She was more beautiful than any of Swati's three daughters. What was more, she had passed the eighth class examinations. But when the *barāt* returned to Dharmnagri with the bride, it seemed they had been deceived. The bride was very thin, and she was neither fair nor educated. Nevertheless, Swati's unmarried daughter said, her father would allow no one to criticize or blame his daughter-in-law: "He says he brought her here as his daughter-in-law whether she's the same girl or a different one. If my sisters or I ever cook something badly, my father tells us off. But whether our brother's wife cooks well or badly, he doesn't criticize her."

Yet for all this rhetoric about dowry, some giving was still in order. And this bride did not always live up to her in-laws' expectations. After a pause, Swati's daughter continued:

> We didn't ask for anything in the dowry. Nor did the bride's people send very much. There was a table and chairs. The bed they sent broke after a week. And when our brother's baby was born, we three sisters could have no jewelry from his in-laws, as there had been none in the dowry. We told our brother's wife to look through her *sārīs*, and she said there were no

special ones. But even so, we looked at them all, and we each selected one. Later on, our mother gave us each five *sārīs*. Foodstuffs and some clothes did come from her parents for the *jasthawn* [naming and cleansing ceremony]. Our brother's wife is at her parents' house just now. It's her first visit since the baby was born. When she returns here, she'll bring us gifts of clothing and jewelry presented by her parents. If we try to call her back quickly, she gets cross and asks how she can possibly bring a lot of things with her. So this time, she has gone for six months and she'll bring lots of things then.

Mehbuba's Satisfaction About Her Daughters' Dowries

Mehbuba's second and third daughters were married shortly before we arrived in 1990. Several offers of marriage had come for both girls, from Sheikh families in Jhakri and from other villages in the locality—some from relatives and some from unrelated people. Mehbuba and her husband had eventually decided to accept an offer for the second daughter to be married to his sister's son, the very house into which their oldest daughter, Rabia, had been married some years previously. The third daughter was married to nonrelatives in another nearby village. In poor families, two daughters are often married simultaneously in order to cut expenditures, particularly by rolling two wedding feasts into one. That had clearly not been a consideration in this case. Mehbuba seated Patricia and our assistant Swaleha on a cot in her courtyard and proudly recounted the details of the dowries:

> I gave a good dowry for each of the girls, the same to them both. There were twenty suits (ten men's and ten women's) for the brides' mothers-in-law to distribute. Each girl had seventeen suits for herself. There were also suits for all the people in the grooms' immediate households. Then there were seventy utensils each. I gave them each nine items of jewelry, five gold and four silver. There was a table, chair, bed, and stool. For each groom, there was a watch and a gold ring. And in both cases, we gave nine sets of bedding, nine mirrors, and nine breadbaskets for the women of the families. I also gave the girls steel trunks costing 200 rupees each. And there were a couple of hundredweights of grain apiece. And there was more grain when the cohabitations took place. And more suits for the girls and their mothers-in-law, too.

Her daughters had also received things from their in-laws at the time of their marriages, thirteen suits or so each and about a dozen pieces of jewelry. The two newlywed sisters and their mother were bubbling with excitement. "My husband's sister bought a very expensive suit in Arabia when she went on Haj, and she presented it to me," the older sister told us. She rushed inside to fetch it.

"We presented a gold ring to my husband," said the younger sister, laughing. "But my in-laws consider that it's unlawful in Islam for a man to wear a gold ring. My husband has read the Qur'ān Sharīf and he never wears gold."

"I still have all the money that my in-laws presented during the *munh dykhāī* [the showing of the bride's face to her in-laws the day after the marriage]," the older sister told us. "Neither of our mothers-in-law took the money themselves. We both got to keep it!"

"And when we come here, our mothers-in-law still give us two or three new suits each," added the younger sister.

"When the marriages were taking place, the older girl's father-in-law gave 500 rupees and an electric ceiling fan to the mosque here in Jhakri. The younger one's father-in-law gave 500 rupees as well," exclaimed Mehbuba.

All three were clearly well pleased with the matches. Both girls had been married into homes with generous parents-in-law. And Mehbuba and her husband had provided showy dowries that reflected well on their generosity and their capacity to give: "About 19,000 rupees was spent on the jewelry alone. Altogether, the two weddings cost about 70,000-80,000 rupees. We gave so much in the dowries that we had to get tractors with trailers to take everything to the girls' in-laws' homes!"

Prabha and the Problems Poor People Face

Prabha was first married in the late 1930s near Nehtaur, some fifteen miles east of the town of Bijnor. Her husband and mother-in-law beat her, and she was never given enough to eat. After just a couple of years, she returned to her parents with her baby son. From there she was married to a poor Sahni man in Dharmnagri whose first wife had died leaving no children.[9] Prabha's parents were very poor, so when she was married this second time, they could give just a few utensils (seven or eight, she thought) and four narrow-legged *pājāmas* without any tunics. Nevertheless, she told us, her father and uncles did the farewell ceremony when she went to her second husband's home just as generously as they would have done if it had been her first marriage. Prabha's new in-laws gave her two *dhotīs* and some jewelry, though the jewelry was later taken back by her mother-in-law and presented to her husband's brother's bride. Of the things Prabha's father had given her, her mother-in-law took the clothes but gave her the utensils: "In those days, no one asked for anything from the girl's people. People considered that whatever was given was fine. In those days, too, there was no question of cash. What more do you get by asking? Whatever you get is a matter of destiny. You'll receive just as much as you're destined to, and no one can stop it. Making demands has no effect. And something will certainly be given for the sake of the nose [face]."

Prabha's younger daughter-in-law commented that a girl's parents will surely give as much as they can without being asked in order to retain their honor. Prabha agreed and began listing the items that she had presented when her two daughters were married, the older in about 1970 and the younger in 1980: utensils, clothing, and some jewelry. In the younger daughter's case, there was also a female buffalo calf, which was sent to the daughter once it had calved, some five years after the marriage.

> The boy's people didn't ask for anything, though. If they had, we'd have called off the match, for we had nothing to give. Dowry existed in the past, too. It was just the same then. It's only wealthy people who give dowry and only wealthy people who receive dowry. There's just this difference, that in those days dowry was given without demands, and it was given only by rich people. But these days, some people have begun to make demands. Say someone received a lot of things when their son got married, and they also have a girl to be married. That girl's in-laws will demand just the same dowry as arrived when the girl's brother was married. That's happened here in Dharmnagri, and now the girl's people are very worried about their daughter's marriage.

By 1985, just two of Prabha's five sons were married, and they had simply accepted what was given in their dowries. Tragically, the oldest son's first wife had five children who all died, and she herself died during an eclamptic fit in her sixth pregnancy.

> For some years after that, we didn't get my oldest son remarried. But then we went to the hills and found him a bride. There was no dowry. On the contrary, we gave the girl's brother 5,000 rupees. From the time of the wedding to now, that daughter-in-law has never visited her parents. Her brother came once to call her, but I refused to let her go. I didn't trust him. A man who's sold his sister once could do the same again. Why, when she first came here, she already had a baby girl, but her brother kept that hidden from us. We found out only when milk began flowing from her breasts. Then we fetched the baby. That's why I wouldn't let her go with her brother when he called her.

The younger daughter-in-law was married in about 1977, before this "bought bride" arrived. She rarely went to her own parents either:

> Her mother's dead and her father doesn't call her. When she wants to see him, she goes with her husband. But she doesn't stay. Rich people can call

their daughters often. Poor people can't. It was like this before as well. You see, when you call your daughter, you have to give her something when she goes back to her husband's house. It's different if she visits you without being specially invited, for if there's nothing in the house you aren't compelled to give. Otherwise, you shouldn't send your daughter back empty handed. I also couldn't visit my parents often. They didn't have much to give me and so my father didn't call me. And my husband didn't send me without an invitation.

Equally, Prabha rarely called her own married daughters, for she could not afford to give generously to them. When Prabha's younger daughter-in-law had her first son, both married daughters were indeed called. As was their right, they each selected a piece of jewelry that had originally come from the new mother's parents. But in straitened circumstances, Prabha later reclaimed and sold the jewelry she herself had presented to her daughter-in-law. The bought bride had received no jewelry from her parents' house, and her in-laws had none left to present to her.

By 1990, they were still in difficult circumstances. There was scarcely any land. Prabha's two married sons, one employed as a gardener and the other as a cycle rickshaw puller in Bijnor, both lived in separate households. Prabha and her husband relied almost exclusively on the cash incomes of her three youngest sons, all cycle rickshaw pullers in town. By now, all three were in their mid-twenties, well past the usual marriage age. Prabha was worried about how they would ever be married: "These days, the times are very bad. A girl's people only arrange their daughter's marriage if the boy's house and job are good. We're very poor and our house is also adobe. That's why no girls' people have come with any offers of marriage."

Nasiran Awaits Her Daughter-in-Law's Arrival

Nasiran's husband was a landless Sheikh in Jhakri. Ever since their marriage in the mid-1950s, they had been struggling to make ends meet, but by 1990 things were improving. Nasiran had borrowed Rs 3,000 to buy a female buffalo. The income from the milk would first be used for repaying the loan and then for household expenses. Her husband was guarding a local mango orchard for a man in Bijnor and would receive Rs 2,250 for the season's work, which entailed staying at the orchard day and night and coming home only for his meals. They were also hoping to be allocated about half an acre of the government surplus land that was being made available to landless people. They had bribed the land records officer Rs 500 a couple of years previously to put their names higher up on the waiting list. She still did not know if they would get any land or how much it would be.

They had built a kiln-brick house in 1989 and planned to have it plastered and fitted with doors after the monsoon in 1990. By now, their older son was of marriageable age: "We're just laborers. We can't do it all at once. Once the house is completed, we'll be able to get our son married. People with a son like to get the house right before they send marriage offers for a girl. That way, the girl's parents will find the house acceptable for their daughter to live in."

By spring 1991, they had made a marriage offer that had been accepted. Nasiran was eagerly awaiting the wedding and her daughter-in-law's arrival in Jhakri. Nasiran was in poor health, her unmarried daughter was still too young to be much help, and there was no other female in the house to share Nasiran's work. She would have to wait patiently for her daughter-in-law.

"Where my son is to be married, though," she commented sadly, "the girl's people are delaying the marriage. So my daughter-in-law won't be coming very soon. We do have more money and feel more at peace than before. But now that my good days have arrived, I have no strength any more. When I had teeth, I didn't have chickpeas to eat. And now there are chickpeas, I have no teeth."

Maya, Mahipal, and Their Daughter's Marriage

Mahipal, a middle-peasant Sahni in Dharmnagri, was married to Maya in 1969. At that time, Maya's father was operating both the farms he owned—one of two acres twenty-five miles from Dharmnagri, and the other of nearly five acres some twenty miles beyond. Over time, though, Maya's father found it more difficult to cope. He had no surviving sons. Indeed, Maya was her parents' only remaining child. Eventually, in the late 1980s, Maya's father persuaded Mahipal to find someone to sharecrop his Dharmnagri land, so that he could then work the larger of his father-in-law's farms.

Thus, while we were in Dharmnagri during 1990 and 1991, Mahipal was no longer living there regularly. During the year, though, he often dropped in for a chat when he was checking on his land, and Maya spent several months living in their house in Dharmnagri too. By now, their children were getting big. It was time to think about getting them married. Crucially, the four oldest children were all girls. The first had been married in about 1986. Now the second one was waiting to be married.

Maya was quite worried: "These days, the moral climate in villages is very bad. That's why we must marry the girls as soon as we can. But demands for dowry are also increasing. No matter how much there already is in the boy's house, they still ask for a lot. If the boy looks good and has land, that's good. But we don't have enough to meet people's demands."

Throughout the year, Mahipal kept updating us on his quest for a match for his daughter and his anxieties about providing her dowry. Mahipal could not afford to have his father-in-law's land transferred to his son's name yet, for that would cost him some Rs 5,000 per acre and make it impossible to get his second daughter married. As usual, the cane society was being unconscionably slow in making its payments for sugarcane sent to the Bijnor mill. Mahipal was due about Rs 5,000 and would have to wait until the next season if he failed to persuade anyone to make the payment before the mill closed in the late spring. Adding to his difficulties, wild elephants sometimes did thousands of rupees' worth of damage to the sugarcane and other crops on his father-in-law's farm. And when his sister's daughter was being married, he and his brothers had to provide the *bhāt*, comprising a couple of hundredweight of wheat, half a hundredweight of pulses, and half a hundredweight of sweetmeats. "And my first daughter's marriage must have cost over 35,000 rupees. There was a TV costing 2,250 rupees, a buffalo worth 6,000 rupees, a sewing machine and all the usual cloth, utensils, bed, and so on. There were 300 guests for two meals and heaps of sweets were eaten."

Roger listed Mahipal's estimates of what it would cost this time around: about Rs 6,000 for the engagement ceremonies; Rs 4,000 for a TV; perhaps Rs 5,000 for a buffalo; Rs 3,000 for sweets and other food for the groom's party, not counting the rice and other items that Mahipal grew himself; about Rs 4,000 for the cycle, bed, and other furniture; some Rs 4,000 for utensils and another Rs 4,000-5,000 for jewelry; and probably Rs 2,000 in cash as well. "Not far off 30,000 rupees, I suppose," Mahipal said, looking over Roger's shoulder.

So far, however, Mahipal was still trying to find a boy. If his relatives mentioned one, he would make a visit. He wanted a boy from a good family with at least two or three acres of land or some other source of income. Plenty of boys had been suggested, but each had only an acre or less of land.

"What's the use of that?" he asked. Other boys were uneducated, but his daughter had attended school to seventh class. "If the boy's educated, he could do something other than farming. Farming's very hard work," Mahipal commented. And Mahipal wanted to avoid families where the men drank heavily and shouted at their wives or beat them or where the women danced in public at weddings. "It can take three or four days checking that sort of thing with people who know the boy's family," he added.

Patricia commented that many local Muslims said they protected themselves from deceit by marrying within an extended set of relatives. Had he thought to do that? He admitted that many people exaggerated their landholding, for instance, by including other people's land that they were sharecropping or implying that land owned jointly by several brothers was owned by the boy's father alone. Mahipal would ask around for information on what the boy's immediate family actually owned.

> I heard of one Jat family that owned just two oxen. They called one Sārī [Many] and the other Bāqī [Remainder]. When guests came with a view to arranging a match with the son, the father would ask his son if the animals were back home. The son would reply, "Sārī came, but Bāqī's not yet home." They'd try to make out that they had many animals! Sometimes, too, people get a neighbor's cart wheeled up to their house to give guests the impression that they own a lot. Jats are especially notorious. But even among us Sahnis some people do that sort of thing. It's also very important to find out what the boy's people want. I shall ask straight out, "What are you asking for?" If they demand a motorcycle, I wouldn't give my girl to them. I also ask around to find how much the family gave for any of their girls who were married recently. That would indicate what they might expect. How much I give will be related to what I gave when the first girl was married. I'll have to give the same or the second girl will be angry. Perhaps a little more, because dowry is increasing all the time.

None of these calculations looked simple. Moreover, according to Maya, Mahipal was making matters more difficult than need be. Maya's father was still farming the smaller of the two farms, but he was getting too old for the work. Maya's parents would still have enough income if someone else sharecropped their land. But if Mahipal would take responsibility for both farms, she commented, all the income from both would remain within the family:

> It's something for him to consider. But he just does what he wants. He does all the calculations and doesn't consult me at all. He's even given the Dharmnagri land out for sharecropping. He works carelessly. He doesn't do things on time. He does everything late. That's why we don't get such good crops. As a result, my father gets angry. And my mother blames my father, saying that it was he alone who saw the boy [Mahipal] before the marriage. My father just says, "I saw his arms and legs, but what could I know about someone's mind?"

A Wedding Song

Fair, handsome groom, with lampblack round his eyes.

He goes crying to his grandfather's [FF] side.
"My dark-skinned bride has come!"
"What's there to fear in dark skin, brother,
Since she's brought plenty of wealth!"
Fair, handsome groom, with lampblack round his eyes.

He goes crying to his uncle's [FeB] side.
"My dark-skinned bride has come!"
"What's there to fear in dark skin, brother,
Since she's brought plenty of wealth!"
Fair, handsome groom, with lampblack round his eyes.[10]

Notes

1. The definition of "dowry" covers money demanded by the groom's family but excludes items of jewelry, clothing, and household effects. The only people who can legally complain that such demands have been made are the bride's family. They are usually too scared of the consequences for their daughter to make a formal accusation. Very few cases are registered unless the bride is killed or physically attacked in an attempt to extort more dowry from her family. Even then, few prosecutions are successful.

2. Since the late 1970s, the dowry issue has been a key one for the Indian women's movement. Deaths of young married women often used to be passed off as kitchen accidents. Suggestions that such deaths were not accidental focused attention on what were initially called dowry deaths and have subsequently become termed dowry murders. For more details, see Miller (1980); Kishwar and Vanita (1984:203ff.); Kumari (1989); Gandhi and Shah (1992:Ch. 3); Calman (1992:123ff.); Kumar (1993:115ff.).

3. Discussions of the extent to which dowry can be seen as a woman's share of the parental property can be found in Goody and Tambiah (1974); Jacobson (1976); Sharma (1980); Srinivas (1986).

4. For further on the "bought bride," see especially Chapter 14, as well as Chapters 7, 9, and 10. It is important to stress that the financial transactions entailed in buying a bride are quite different from those connected with the *mahr*, the Islamic marriage settlement ideally made by the groom on his wife. The payment for the bought bride is kept by her male kin; she herself receives none of the cash in question.

5. These themes are pursued in later chapters, especially Chapter 11. See Raheja (1988) for an elaboration of the significance of such links and the gift giving that is associated with them.

6. This wedding song is one of a genre called *bannī* ["darling bride" and by extension wedding songs], sung by women at the bride's house. It is a poignant statement of the bride's parents' fears that they might struggle to provide a dowry for her but that her in-laws may remain dissatisfied.

7. Generally the numbers of items, sums of cash, and weights of foodstuffs presented at weddings and other occasions are considered significant. It is most appropriate to give in numbers that end in one (such as eleven, twenty-one, 101, 501) or five (such as five, twenty-five, 1005). Other appropriate numbers come from *savā*, meaning "one quarter in addition" (as in one and a quarter rupees, five and a quarter, or "one and a quarter hundred" i.e. 125) and from *dhāī* meaning "two plus one half" (as in "two and a half hundred" or 250). In this book, we have retained these numbers for separate items and cash gifts. The weights of foodstuffs, however, have been converted into pounds and hundredweights, thus losing the auspicious number in translation.

8. Jats are the dominant Hindu landholding caste in the region, and Tikait was organizing a campaign to reduce the money spent on providing hospitality for the *barāt* as well as the cost of providing dowries for daughters. It is not clear how much impact he had, since items are generally presented at different stages in the arrangement of a marriage and can be given secretly.

9. Strictly speaking, a Hindu woman in this part of India cannot make a second marriage, but unions such as this were not uncommon.

10. This song is from a genre called *bannā* ["darling bridegroom"], sung by women at the groom's house. The groom's relatives (who care only for the dowry) are contrasted with the groom, handsome (i.e., fair complexioned), decked out in his finery, and eyes ringed with lampblack (used to avert the evil eye). Above all, he wants a beautiful bride, but the song taunts the bride as one who is dark skinned.

4

A Girl Seems Burdensome
to Both Her Parents

Sahnis were one of the largest castes in Dharmnagri. Locally, they had a reputation for being competent farmers who liked to grow not only wheat, rice, and sugarcane but also vegetables for market if they had enough land to do so. In Dharmnagri, about three-quarters of the Sahnis owned some land around the village. Among the better off was the extended family of Mahipal, whose mother was first married into Dharmnagri in the late 1930s. Mahipal was the younger of her two sons. After being widowed, Mahipal's mother was remarried, again in Dharmnagri. There were more children, two daughters and three other sons, of whom Devinder was the second. Like Mahipal and Maya, Devinder and his wife, Durgi, were a couple on whom we have focused since 1982. They were middle peasants, and by the late 1980s, they and their brothers had been able to build kiln-brick homes for their families. In 1982, Maya and Durgi were both preoccupied with small children. By 1990, some of these children were of an age to be married.

Weddings usually took place when people's granaries and purses were relatively full. The expenses faced by the bride's family were greatest, but outlays were also made by the groom's family. On both sides, food had to be provided for wedding guests, and items of clothing and jewelry had to be bought. In Dharmnagri and Jhakri, some weddings took place in October or November, around the rice harvest. But most were in the spring (March-May), when the wheat had been harvested and people had been receiving payments for sugarcane for several months.[1]

In spring 1991, arrangements were in hand for the marriage of Durgi and Devinder's oldest daughter, Ritu. As among other Hindu castes, the marriage arrangements had been set in motion by Devinder himself. For people with a daughter, the imperative to get her married became particularly urgent once she reached puberty. Her parents had to be constantly vigilant lest her honor be jeopardized. In arranging her marriage, then, they would hope to lift some of this burden of responsibility from their shoulders. But arranging a daughter's

Henna Drying on Ritu's Hands

wedding could be quite trying, ensuring that suitable items were bought for the dowry and that the hospitality offered to guests would bring credit to her family. Moreover, Ritu's departure was particularly poignant for Durgi and Devinder.

* * * * * *

By 1991, Devinder's elderly father was no longer much involved in the family's farming work, and he and his wife lived jointly with their youngest son and his family. Devinder's father was particularly fond of his two married daughters, and he used to visit them whenever he had the time. Indeed, he cared for them so much that for years he had always insisted on being the one to call them back to Dharmnagri, rather than Devinder or his brothers. Devinder's wife, Durgi, commented: "My father-in-law enjoys going to fetch them. Even if he has no money, he still manages to go by taking a loan. He insists on going and refuses to send anyone in his stead. One time, his sons asked, 'What, have our sisters' brothers all died that our sisters have to be fetched by their father?' But my father-in-law just ignored them."

In spring 1991, Holī—a Hindu festival when people shower one another with colored water and gaudy powder paints—took place a few days before Devinder and Durgi's oldest daughter, Ritu, was to be married. Devinder and one of his brothers had spent much of Holī drinking heavily with their father. In the evening, Devinder and his father got into a heated argument. Devinder's father stormed off to his younger daughter's home, in a village beyond Najibabad, some thirty miles away. At first, no one thought very much about it, for similar episodes had occurred many times before.

As was conventional among Hindus, the wedding ceremony was scheduled for the dead of night. But by that afternoon, Devinder's father had still not returned to Dharmnagri. The *barāt* from the groom's village would soon be arriving for the evening meal, and the priest would be coming to perform the marriage—but the bride's grandfather was nowhere to be seen. And it would not be right for the groom's party to be at the bride's house when her grandfather was not.

At about 6 P.M., Devinder's older brother Mahipal arrived at our house and explained the problem. As we surely knew, his father could be very obstinate if he was so minded. He would certainly return, however, if met with the full persuasive force of Mahipal's older cousin, the village headman, and Roger. Would Roger, in other words, drive them to Mahipal's sister's village in the jeep?

*   *   *   *   *   *

Mahipal's father sat bolt upright when Mahipal and Roger walked into his daughter's house. "I'm not going with you!" he snapped vehemently before either of them had opened his mouth. Mahipal told him that he certainly was: "You can't refuse. Just look at how much trouble you've caused Roger Sahib. He's come all this way, just to fetch you. Now pack up your things and come along right now!"

Only after more cajoling and moral pressure, more persuasion and flattery, did Mahipal's father stand up, sort out his bundle of clothes, and allow himself to be escorted to the jeep. They arrived in Dharmnagri just in time to join in the festive meal that had been prepared for the groom's party. The day had been saved. As one man commented, "It'd be absolutely disgraceful if the bride's grandfather didn't attend the wedding. Dharmnagri would get a bad reputation all around here. People in the groom's party would say, 'If the grandfather can run away, so could the bride.'"

Although the wedding took place without further hitches, people in Dharmnagri gossiped about the episode for several days. The word was that Devinder's father had said that the chairs and bed for Ritu's dowry should be wooden. Devinder had said he did not have enough money, so he had bought metal chairs and a folding metal-framed bed. Because of this disagreement Devinder's father had refused to attend the wedding. One of Devinder's sisters-in-law [eBW] was rather anxious. Metal beds were cheaper, she admitted, but a wooden bed would have been better in a dowry. "How can we tell if the girl will be troubled about it by her in-laws?"

Our research assistants, too, were perplexed by Devinder's decision. In Radha's view, metal chairs were now acceptable in a dowry: They were more expensive and fashionable than wooden ones. But the bed was another matter. People would give either an old-style bed (with a wooden frame and a base of interwoven tapes) or a bed with a wooden base. She had once been quoted Rs 4,000 for a bed with a wooden base, although Zarin thought it might be possible to get one for as little as Rs 1,500. Maybe, speculated Swaleha, Devinder's father was angry because he feared that Ritu would be taunted by her in-laws. But Zarin disagreed: Surely it was simply not customary to give metal beds in the dowry.

*   *   *   *   *   *

During the weeks of preparation for Ritu's wedding, her mother, Durgi, reminisced about her own childhood and marriage. Durgi herself was the oldest of seven children. One brother died in adulthood and there was only one other sister. Of all the children, Durgi had been her grandmother's favorite, as she was born after several sisters had died in infancy:

> My grandmother went to a faith healer after my sisters died, and she got treatment for my mother. After a long gap, I was born and remained healthy. That was why my grandmother didn't allow me to be sent to school, because of her love for me. Whenever my grandmother went to the fields, she would take me with her. And if my mother ever scolded me or beat me, I would run to my grandmother. I even used to suck on her breasts for comfort. And at night I used to sleep beside her. There was no money problem over my education. To some extent it was a question of the work in the house, and partly it was because of my grandmother. If I'd been educated, that would have been good. But education was not in my destiny. In those days, no one educated daughters.

In the early 1970s, when Durgi was approaching the age to be married, village people rarely took the level of education—either the bride's or the groom's—into account: "Rather than considering education, people looked at the girl's caste and boy's land and what his home was like. When I was to be married, my father looked to see if the boy had land as my father did, and also whether the boy was hardworking."

Durgi's father had been making enquiries about a suitable match for some time. One day he was visiting his wife's brother and chanced to meet a man from Dharmnagri who was visiting the same village. They began talking, and the Dharmnagri man said that he knew of some people with a son of marriageable age. So Durgi's father came to Dharmnagri to see Devinder. "My father liked him and immediately gave some money to bind him to marrying me. It was less than 100 rupees. In those days there wasn't as much money spent on giving and taking in weddings as there is nowadays. People then just thought, 'The house should be good, and the boy should be good.' And my in-laws didn't make any demands about the dowry."

There had previously been discussions about another possible match for Devinder, but his mother had been against it, saying that girls from that place were argumentative. Devinder's mother was happy to accept Durgi's father's offer.

> Some while later, the girl to whom he [Devinder] had almost been engaged visited Dharmnagri. She taunted him, saying he was going to be married to a very dark girl, even though she'd never seen me! He replied that it didn't matter to him if his wife was black! My mother and my aunt [MZ] were married into the same village, and when my father got home

after fixing the engagement, my aunt asked him why he was getting me married so distantly. He told her that was where my destiny was taking me. My father described the boy to my mother, saying, "He's black—but what does it matter if he's dark or fair? The man should be a working man and he should have land. And this man does farming work and he has his own land." I overheard all this only in the course of coming and going around the house. My opinion was never asked. In those days, who asked the girl or told her anything? It was a shameful matter and parents would think, "What is there for parents to ask a girl?" In any case, I was only fifteen years old and didn't fully understand what was going on.

When the marriage took place, Durgi's in-laws presented her with four *sāris* and two necklaces, three pairs of wrist ornaments, two sets of anklets, and gold earrings. "All the jewelry remained with me. My mother-in-law presented things equally to all the daughters-in-law, and she took nothing back from any of us. My husband did sell some of it when we were short of money—but my mother-in-law took nothing."

Durgi's parents gave a cycle and a watch for Devinder, as well as twenty-one metal utensils, a bed and bedding, and a low stool for Durgi to sit on. There were also five *dhotīs* for Durgi and another twenty-one for distribution to the mother-in-law, the other daughters-in-law, and other married women connected to the in-laws. Because of the distance, however, her parents decided not to give a cow or female buffalo. A year later, when the cohabitation took place, Durgi's father gave one and a half hundredweights of grain and flour, six *sāris* for Durgi herself, and clothing for all the men and women in Devinder's immediate family.

*   *   *   *   *   *

Now, about twenty years later, Durgi was concerned to get her own oldest child well settled:

Whenever a girl reaches puberty—even if that's at a young age—she seems burdensome to both her parents. They can neither send her out to work in the fields nor leave her alone at home. My own marriage took place when I was the same age as my girl is now, and we've arranged her marriage quickly like my parents did. In fact, we would have married Ritu a year back, but we had some money problems. Anyway, we didn't find a good boy at that time. We have four daughters, and the second one will have to be married in five or six years. And by the time we get her married, the two youngest will be mature. That's why we're doing the first marriage now.

Over the years, Devinder had had occasion to borrow from Durgi's family: There was still a loan of Rs 1,000 outstanding from the time when Devinder was having their home rebuilt, and that would have to be repaid sooner or later. For Ritu's marriage, too, they had turned to Durgi's father. He lent them Rs 500 when Devinder wanted to bind the boy he had chosen as his son-in-law and another Rs 500 to help with the wedding expenses. This would all be repaid when Devinder had ready cash.

In addition, on festivals or when she gives birth and when she visits her parents or when her brothers' wives have children, the out-married woman should receive clothes, foodstuffs, or jewelry—on which her parents and brothers expect to see no return. This includes the obligation to provide the *bhāt*, given when the first of the woman's children is married. If this is a girl, *bhāt* may be given again when her oldest boy is married. In the wedding season, the countryside is crisscrossed by buffalo carts loaded with women in their finery, singing lustily as they go to fetch the *bhāt* that marks the wedding of some young man or woman in their marital village. In like fashion, some weeks before Ritu's wedding, Durgi had made the lengthy journey to her own parents' village, along with some half-dozen women from her in-laws' connection and a couple of men to chaperon:

> We went to request the *bhāt*. All four of my brothers' wives gave the women with me five rupees apiece. My mother's sister is also married in the same village, and she gave all the women a rupee each and fed us a festive dish of rice topped with clarified butter and finely ground sugar. And my brothers promised me 1,300 rupees in cash and also said they'd provide one of the meals for the groom's party. My mother's sister said that they'd have given more in the *bhāt* if we hadn't asked them to provide the meal. But we couldn't have paid for both meals.

Indeed, had the timing been different, the *bhāt* might have been much larger. In recent years, Durgi's parents' circumstances had declined considerably. First, much of their land and their brick house were washed away when the Ganges flooded one year, so they had less land than before. They were still struggling to restore the farming income and replace the adobe house they had built to tide them over. Then Durgi's second brother became ill with a heart condition. Eventually, doctors talked of an operation that was beyond their purse, and despite costly medical treatments, her brother had died. And finally, just a few weeks before Durgi went to collect the *bhāt*, her mother died. Some Rs 6,000 had been spent on treatments during her illness, and Durgi's brothers had provided a meal for the whole village after the cremation.

Had it not been for all that expense, Durgi's brothers told her, they would have provided a couple of pieces of gold jewelry for Ritu. Nevertheless, they did what they could. A few days before the wedding, a hundredweight of foodstuffs—uncooked rice, clarified butter and finely ground sugar—arrived for the evening meal before the marriage ceremony. And there was also a *sārī* for Ritu to wear during the ceremony, the shawl in which she would be enveloped when she departed for her in-laws' village for the first time, and clothes for Devinder's entire household. In addition, Durgi's sister had presented two pairs of toe rings, which she wanted Ritu to wear. "But I wouldn't agree," said Durgi. "I'm not going to create new customs! In this place, the bride doesn't leave her parents' house wearing toe rings. Only the in-laws should put them on her feet."

*   *   *   *   *   *

The morning after the wedding ceremony, the men of Devinder's family entertained the guests and served them the second meal. The women, meanwhile, were thronging inside the house as final details of the dowry were checked and, periodically, women came to present another *dhotī* with cloth for a blouse, or maybe a steel tumbler or a tray. Durgi had collected all she could for the time being. In the small steel trunk packed to go with Ritu to her in-laws' village, there were seven *sārīs* for her and one for the groom's sister. In the large trunk were utensils—including five items given in the *bhāt*—and bedding. There was also a small table, two chairs, and the controversial metal bed. "We gave a cycle and watch for the groom and a TV when the engagement took place—also some 5,000 rupees in cash," Durgi told us. "We didn't give a ring for the boy, as his people had sent no earrings for our daughter. But they presented a watch and two *sārīs* to her."

Now Ritu was letting the henna on her hands dry, sitting in the midst of Durgi's female relatives who had come to attend the wedding. They were waiting for the clothing and earrings from Ritu's in-laws, which Ritu would wear when she departed for their village for the first time. Fortunately, one of Durgi's brothers was a tailor, and he was rapidly sewing the cloth into a blouse on a borrowed sewing machine. Eventually, everything was ready. Ritu was dressed in her new *sārī* and the eleven pieces of jewelry sent by her in-laws: a gold nose stud; earrings and a ring; and several silver items, including a pair of thick bracelets, a ring, a necklace, and anklets. Then she was swathed in the shawl that had come in the *bhāt*.

Meanwhile, in the courtyard, the groom was seated cross-legged on a bed. Women were making presentations to him—mainly of cash—that were placed in his lap. Then they each put a dab of turmeric and uncooked rice grains on his forehead, both symbols of fertility like the coconuts tied into the towel that was placed over his shoulder. Then came the peals of laughter as the women tried to force yet another sweet into the groom's mouth. In the midst of this, one of Devinder's cousins had the unenviable task of noting down what people were presenting—but the crush was such that he could hardly steady himself to write, and the noise made it difficult to hear the muffled voices of the women, too shy to speak up and too concealed by the ends of their *sārīs* to be recognizable.

When the women had finished, the men of the groom's party clambered into the hired bus. The trunks and furniture were loaded onto its roof. Ritu was brought outside, completely concealed under the shawl. Her relatives gathered round to embrace her in turn, Ritu and the rest of them sobbing loudly at her departure. Ritu was led out of the courtyard to the bus and guided up the steps. Rice grains and small coins rained down from every direction, and little children scrambled around under the adults' feet, gleaning as much money as they could. The engine was revved up. Final farewells were called out, and the bus lumbered along the village street, horn blaring and scattering the bystanders in its path.

*   *   *   *   *   *

A few days later, Ritu's cousin [FeBS] brought her to Dharmnagri to stay with her parents for a while. As instructed by Durgi, Ritu and her cousin had both tried to persuade Ritu's mother-in-law to keep the jewelry safely. After all, Durgi had told them, she herself was working in the fields all day, and there was no one at home to guard things properly. But Ritu's mother-in-law was insistent that a new bride should go back to her parents wearing some jewelry at least—which was perhaps surprising, since one of the many things that Ritu had to tell her parents about was the loss of her nose stud. Durgi told us about it later:

> There was no one from Dharmnagri accompanying my girl on the bus, and she pulled her shawl down right over her face. On the journey her nose stud came out—but she was too embarrassed to tell anyone. So she just searched around in the folds of her shawl, but she couldn't find it. When they arrived at her in-laws' place, she was met by my husband's cousin [who was married into the same village]. She suggested the match

in the first place. My daughter told her what had happened, and she in turn told Ritu's father-in-law. He chuckled and said, "She's a crazy little thing! Why didn't she say anything to me on the bus? We could have found it then." And my son-in-law also asked why she'd said nothing to him either. By that time, the bus had left, but my son-in-law pursued it on his cycle. He managed to catch up with it. And then he searched everywhere. He nearly gave up hope—but then he found it caught in a groove on the bus step!

After the recovery of the nose stud, the groom's sister put two pairs of toe rings on Ritu's feet. In exchange, she got first choice of the clothing from Ritu's trunk. She might have been expected to claim a *sārī*, "but she just took a cotton *dhotī*, not one of the *sārīs*," said Ritu, who also felt that her in-laws had been very generous in what they had given in the *munh dykhāī* [face-showing]. In addition, Ritu received more money when she made griddle bread for the first time in her husband's home:

> My husband's older brother asked me to make bread for the first time. He works at a sugarcane crusher and he brought his friends to eat too. They each gave me fifty-one rupees. So did everyone in the household. In all, I received about 600 rupees. My mother-in-law took the money for safe-keeping but assured me that it was still my money—whether I left it there or took it to my parents' house. "But don't spend it just now," she told me. "Wait until there's more money, and you can get something gold made from all the money from your in-laws."

*   *   *   *   *   *

Despite all these good signs, Durgi was still a bit nervous about how it would all work out. Early on, Devinder had told the boy's people he was poor, and there had been no demands about what should be in the dowry. Durgi said that Devinder had also offered to let them see Ritu if they so wished. "But they told us they hadn't seen the two older daughters-in-law nor did they want to see her. Even when the groom's older brother visited us before the wedding, he was very shy and embarrassed. He wouldn't take a look at our girl then either. The groom himself wasn't at all reserved. He was very talkative on the wedding day!"

In order to forestall problems, Durgi and Devinder had decided that the cohabitation should take place at the same time as the wedding. In Durgi's view, young men did not want their wives to stay long in their parents' home but were keen for the cohabitation to take place quickly:

> But we wouldn't have the money for the cohabitation expenses so soon. For that reason alone, I did the cohabitation customs at the same time as

the farewell customs. Otherwise, the in-laws might scold us if we delayed the cohabitation, even though we had nothing special to give. I just sent a *dhotī* for my daughter and some lentils and rice, and I told them that the cohabitation customs had been done. That means that the boy can come to collect Ritu himself whenever he wishes, and we can just give whatever we have.

Ritu reported that everyone in her new home was good. Even so, Ritu had been asked what she had brought from her parents' house and she had told them, "Nothing much at all." Then she added, with a grin, "My in-laws thought everything in the dowry was fine. But they did ask what sort of bed it was that I'd been given! It would have been better if it had been wooden!" Not surprisingly, then, Durgi was keen to continue providing as well as she could for Ritu: "When she goes to her in-laws the second time, I'll give her a nose stud and earrings. That wasn't possible at the time of the wedding. My husband doesn't understand these matters well enough to know exactly what should be given. He just bought the things that I told him to get. So nothing could be done quickly or on time. And now Ritu wants a nice *sārī* for when she goes to her husband's house the second time!"

Overall, though, Durgi felt relieved that Ritu had been satisfactorily married. So far, the in-laws seemed kindly. The boy had passed eighth class, but even with such an educated boy, there had been no demands. And he and his brothers would each inherit one and a half acres. "We've found a good, educated boy with land, and a house where people can eat and drink. That's what we wanted. And the boy's people didn't make any demands. If they had, we wouldn't have been able to marry Ritu there."

* * * * * *

Durgi's relief was somewhat tempered, however, by the loss of Ritu's help with the household work. While the children were small and Devinder still operated the land jointly with his father and brothers, Durgi never went to the fields to work, either to deal with the crops or to fetch fodder for the cattle. Her work was based in the home, cooking and cleaning for the family, caring for her children, and dealing with the cattle stalled by the house.

Now, however, Devinder and his youngest brother were together working a farm of about nine acres, the six acres they would inherit from their father and the three acres that would be inherited by another brother who had married an only daughter and was working his father-in-law's land elsewhere. Devinder's father no longer did farmwork, and

Devinder and his brother were short of labor. Over the years, Durgi had become increasingly involved in the farming; she sometimes weeded crops and helped with the harvests and was totally responsible for collecting fodder, chopping it, and dealing with the cattle.

> We tried hard to get Ritu to study, and she did complete fourth class. But she's a very slow learner. She was at school for seven years! Then we got a buffalo from my parents and that made more work. That's why Ritu stopped going to school and began doing the work in the house. Now I'm wondering how I can educate the second girl. Ritu has gone to her own house, and who will be in our house to do the work? I'm outside all day. It would be good if the girl could study a couple of classes—but I can't send her to school now. I'd like to educate my children, but what can I do? It's all a question of the work in the house.

The arrangements prior to Ritu's wedding had been possible because Durgi could delegate the work in the house to Ritu. And that had been necessary only because Durgi had no son to work in the fields in her stead. How was she going to cope now? Could she really leave her second daughter—just eight years old—in charge of all the cooking and of her two younger sisters?

*   *   *   *   *   *

Between Ritu and the eight-year-old there had been two other children. First was a girl, who was very weak because Durgi herself had been suffering from malaria during pregnancy. The child could not sit even at ten months, and she later died from measles. Next was a boy who first became ill when he was about six months old. A doctor in Bijnor said that the pulse in his scalp was very weak and that he should have a glucose drip. They had this done, but he got typhoid shortly afterward. Again they were advised to have a drip, but he died as the nurse was setting it up. According to Durgi, someone—perhaps a menstruating woman or one who had just visited a house where a baby had been born—had failed to observe the proper avoidances while he was sick and her polluting shadow had fallen on him.

Normally, pregnant women in Bijnor would not visit their parents. But because two children had died, Durgi spent a couple of months during her next pregnancy in her mother's home, getting injections and medicines to avert a further tragedy. She was pleased to be pregnant, since two children had died, and she had no son. But then, in spring 1982, she had another girl. This child's birth was met with little enthusiasm from Durgi's in-laws. There were no special celebrations apart from a naming ceremony attended only by close family members. No news of the birth was sent to Durgi's parents, and no gifts were received from them. And neither of Devinder's sisters was called to help Durgi after the delivery—or to receive gifts from Devinder and Durgi. At the time, Durgi had told us:

> If those two children were still alive, I wouldn't have had any more children. Now we have just two girls. There isn't even a single boy. He [Devinder] was angry that I'd had another girl. He took his food from his mother's hearth and didn't come into our house for three days, so how could I ask him to call his sisters? When he did come inside, I asked him to call his sisters, but my mother-in-law told us to check first that we had *dhotis* set aside. We didn't and my husband had no money, so we didn't call them. But if it had been a boy, my husband's sisters would certainly have come.

Durgi felt she must always be circumspect. Devinder had a quick temper, such that his mother had made Durgi and Devinder separate their cooking hearth from the rest: "Sometimes, if he didn't like the food he was served, he put mud or even ash into other people's food. That way no one could eat. That's why my mother-in-law made us separate. Even now that we're separate, he sometimes overturns the rice dish and throws out the vegetables."

According to Durgi, Devinder would not "go so far as to seek a woman's advice" about the farming decisions but would do just as he wished whether good or bad. And when it came to household expenses, he would decide how the money should be spent, though he would leave Durgi some money whenever he went away: "I worry when I have to spend money. If there are gifts to be bought, I first ask him. And if I spend anything without his knowledge, I don't keep it secret but tell him immediately. He alone is the earner. It's not correct to keep secrets from him."

Under such circumstances, Durgi wanted to have at least one son. So, too, did her mother-in-law. Indeed, other women in the family had already talked to her about treatments to procure a son. Devinder's younger sister had told Durgi about the three co-wives of a man who lived in a small town near to her in-laws' village. Of these women, one was particularly famed for providing treatments to help women become pregnant, to prevent or abort pregnancies, and to ensure that a pregnancy would result in a son. Devinder's second-oldest brother's wife had been treated there for infertility problems, and Devinder's older sister knew a woman in her in-laws' connection who had eight girls in succession but had a son after treatment. At this stage, Durgi told us she intended to obtain some medicines during her next pregnancy, although she feared that Devinder might not see this as a priority expenditure because he was usually short of money.

By the time of Ritu's wedding in 1991, however, Durgi had given birth to two more girls:

> I keep telling him that we have four girls and what are we not doing for them? Aren't we feeding them and giving them things to drink? What's done for boys, we're also doing for these girls, so they are now like boys for us. He drinks a lot and I keep saying he shouldn't. I tell him that however much he spends on drink he could spend on things for himself and the children, so that something will be in their stomachs. "What's the benefit of drinking?" I ask him. But he doesn't heed me. He just says, "Your brothers all have sons and your sister has a son. But you don't and you won't ever have one." He threatens to take another wife. He argues with me and beats me a lot about this, and then I cry. And if I tell anyone what he says about a second marriage, he tells me off and says he's only teasing. "Am I organizing another marriage for myself?" he asks me. He says that he talks like that in anger.

And now, at the time of Ritu's wedding, Durgi was pregnant once more:

> I want a boy because the girls will all go to their own houses. There has to be someone to help us two in our old age. Now I'm three or four months pregnant. A short while back I got the ANM to buy medicines in town to obtain a son. They cost thirty-one rupees. She told me I was late taking them. I took them in the third month, but they should be taken in the second month. When my sister came for the wedding and heard about this, she was cross with me. She asked, "Why didn't you say anything to me? There's someone in a village near my in-laws' place whose medicines are absolutely guaranteed. He doesn't take any money until your wishes have been fulfilled and then you give him whatever you want." Now, we'll soon know what will happen. But even if I have a boy this time, I won't be able to say anything about not having any more children. If one boy is born, the people in the house can also say, "What is one boy? There can also be sadness and happiness, wasting and illness. Call a second boy after the first!"

Once again, however, Durgi's wishes remained unfulfilled. She had another daughter, who lived only to six months: "I myself would like one son. And I don't want many children. But it isn't a question of what I want. Until I have a son, I won't stop having children."

Notes

1. Marriages do sometimes take place during the monsoon (July-August). In addition, Muslims will not hold weddings in the Islamic months of Ramzān (since people should be fasting between sunrise and sunset) or Muharram (the first month of the Islamic calendar, during which the Karbela massacre is commemorated). These shift back by ten days each solar year, so there may be periods during the conventional marriage seasons when Muslims cannot hold marriages.

5

Leaving Her Father's House

Our jeep was often drafted into service for weddings in Dharmnagri and Jhakri. Roger would go to the bride's village with the barāt to participate in the wedding festivities and bring the newly married couple back to the groom's home. As with Ritu's wedding, the bride's departure from her parents' home was always a protracted affair with the men restlessly pacing while the women said long and tearful farewells. Eventually, the bride would be bundled into the waiting jeep with the groom and several members of the barāt. To Roger's discomfort, many a journey home would be in virtual silence, punctuated only by the bride's stifled sobbing.

For the bride's parents, the dowry was not the only source of anxiety. Many people in Dharmnagri and Jhakri were explicit that sons had always been preferred over daughters, and not just because the provision of a dowry had become more difficult in recent years: When the daughter married, she became "someone else's," thus "emptying" her parents' house in more than just a material sense. The new bride's arrival at the groom's home, however, would be a source of excitement and happiness. There would be no tears and no laments sung.[1] The house would fill, not empty. The new bride would bring the prospect of children, of an additional worker, and of care and support in old age, aside from the material provisions her parents would make.

Yet if the significance of marriage differed for the two sets of relatives involved, there were points in common. Settling children in marriage was an important parental obligation. It should not and could not be left to the children themselves. Indeed, in rural Bijnor, it was inappropriate for the bride and groom either to be asked their opinion or to speak up during the marriage negotiations. Parents with adolescent children would be roundly criticized if they failed to execute their duties in a timely and careful fashion. But doing so often seemed a heavy responsibility. There would be urgency but also fear that excessive haste could result in mistakes, especially during the delicate negotiations when arranging a marriage with virtual strangers.

For the bride's parents, it was not merely a matter of judging if their daughter's in-laws would make demands about the dowry, whether before or after the marriage, or of making fine calculations about how much they could afford to provide. They would also be concerned about their daughter's happiness in her marital home. Would she be treated well? What reliable information could they glean about the groom's family? Would they be hoodwinked about the groom's personal qualities or his mother's character? How had other young women married into the same household fared? Might they be deceived about the groom's education and occupation or about his family's standing and wealth? In what sort of house—and household—would their daughter be living? In short, how best could a girl's parents ensure her future well-being and comfort?

From the other side, too, fears of deceit played their part. If they visited the bride's home and viewed her, what would they be able to judge about her? Could they discern her character satisfactorily? Would they miscalculate and face years of contending with a lazy worker or a woman with a sharp tongue who failed to keep silent when she should or who spread dissent within the family? And how could they ensure that the girl they had seen was the one who would arrive as the bride on the wedding day?

Many Muslims argued that arranging marriages among quite closely connected people protected them from the worst hazards. Indeed, our assistant Radha claimed that precisely this reasoning lay behind recent decisions in some urban Hindu families known to her to arrange marriages between people more closely related than would have been acceptable only a few years ago. Yet nothing could be guaranteed. Even when great care was taken, even when marriages were arranged between relatives, tensions and problems could all too easily arise.

A Wedding Song

Leaving her father's house,
Our darling has become someone else's.

Grandfather [FF] is crying, grandmother [FM] is crying,
All her girlfriends are crying.
And, clutching her finger, her little brother is crying,
"Where are you going, my mother's daughter?"

Leaving her father's house,
Our darling has become someone else's.

Uncle [FeB] is crying, aunt [FeBW] is crying,
All her girlfriends are crying.
And, clutching her finger, her little brother is crying,
"Where are you going, my mother's daughter?"

Leaving her father's house,
Our darling has become someone else's.[2]

The Arrangement of Qudsia's Marriage

Qudsia, a Sheikh woman in Jhakri, remarked that even her own mother had played little part in arranging her marriage to Qadir in the late 1970s:

> My father made all the decisions about my marriage. My mother's opinion carried no weight. The cock gives the call to prayer. Who's ever heard the hen's call to prayer? My father saw that he himself and the boy had land, so he arranged my marriage here in Jhakri. There was no go-between. Maybe two or three other offers of marriage came for me, but I don't know where they came from or why my father refused them. He didn't talk about it inside the house. The offers were brought by men, not women, and my father talked to them outside. He refused those he didn't want to accept. Parents don't ask the girls' opinion. But they also don't ask the boy either. The marriage just takes place wherever the parents wish. Even if the girl is pushed into a deep well, she can't say anything. And the boy doesn't speak either. At the time of the *nikāh* [Muslim marriage ceremony], the boy is asked if a blind, one-eyed and lame girl is acceptable to him. And he says, "Yes." He's asked that because he must keep whatever sort of wife he receives.

A Bride for Rakesh

Subash was a middle-peasant Sahni in his mid-forties. He had seven children, and the oldest—a girl—had been married in spring 1987. By 1990, Rakesh, Subash's second child, was about twenty, and Subash wanted to get him married. A couple of months after our arrival, Subash told Roger that a party of men had come from a girl's family to view Rakesh just a couple of days previously:

> We fed fifty people. And we spent another 150 rupees on gifts. At first, the girl's father took fright when he saw our house. He began saying, "I'm just a poor man" and "How can I afford to arrange my girl's marriage here?" But I told him we didn't want anything except that we'd like to see the girl ourselves. Those people liked my boy, and they gave eleven rupees to bind the match. We'll just send men from the family when we go to see the girl. It's not right to send women these days. If we took two men and two women, the men would sit outside with the men of the girl's family, and the women would be taken inside. And if our women said they didn't like the girl, the men and women of the house could lock them inside and threaten to molest them. There'd be such compulsion and force that we'd have to agree to the marriage even if we didn't like the girl. People with girls are very cunning these days. I'm

rather anxious about all this. That's why you must come with us in your jeep. And Patricia must come too. They wouldn't dare to molest a white woman.

Thus we became involved—not wholly willingly—in Rakesh's marriage arrangements. It would, of course, be interesting to accompany Subash and hear how he arrived at his decision about the girl. What sort of criteria would he use to gauge if she would be suitable? How would he decide what gifts to take for her? But what if Subash began placing great reliance on our opinions? That would be quite another matter. Did we really understand these things well enough for our judgment to be added to the discussions? What if we got it all wrong?

A few days later, the girl's father came to set the date for seeing his daughter. He wanted things settled, for Subash had told him of other offers coming for Rakesh, including one from a man who was promising to give a generous dowry with his only daughter. Subash had reassured the first girl's father, for he had refused to consider the second man's offer: "I told that other man I didn't need anything. Anyway, I told him that nothing could be done now, as the matter had already been settled elsewhere. I told him there were plenty of other boys available."

Then Subash showed us the watch costing Rs 350 that he would present to the girl—provided that she met everyone's approval. "She'll wear it on the wedding day. That way we'll know the right girl has been sent," he explained. He bought fruit and sweets to present to the girl's family. And there was also a *sārī* (costing Rs 250) and cloth for a blouse (costing Rs 21). He asked our assistant Radha to check it over. Was the quality acceptable for giving to the girl? Radha fingered it carefully and then spied the price label. "It says 150 rupees here. That is the correct price for a *sārī* such as this," she commented. "You shouldn't have paid so much."

"What do men know about these things?" Subash lamented. "But nothing can be done now. And I'd intended to buy some cloth for a petticoat, but all the shops were closed because of these Hindu-Muslim troubles," he added.

Roger and Patricia climbed into the jeep with Subash, one of his younger sons, his brother and his brother's little daughter, and his wife's sister's husband, who was the go-between. When we arrived at the girl's home, Roger and the men went to the men's sitting room near the courtyard entrance; Patricia was taken to one of the family rooms. It was not quite the "poor man's house" we had expected. The girl's father's comments had clearly been posturings connected with the dowry negotiations. Shortly, tea and snacks were served to the men. The girl came in, shrouded in a new red *sārī* and with her head lowered, carrying a tray of sweets, which she placed on a low table. Then, to indicate her respect for the guests, she bent down and touched the feet of the men in Subash's party. As was proper, she then went straight inside the house without saying a word.

Subash was almost overwhelmed with nerves. He took Roger aside and asked if he thought the girl was suitable. Roger had no idea what to say. Was his opinion about a lifetime match to rest on this brief sighting? He would happily have evaded answering, but Subash persisted.

"If you think she's suitable, then she is suitable," Roger said diplomatically.

Subash seemed satisfied. The gifts were fetched from the jeep, but Subash had forgotten new Rs 50 notes for presentation. For a moment he was flustered. Under his breath, he asked if Roger could oblige. Then the gifts were placed on trays, the *sārī* in a box to which Subash added Rs 5, and Rs 101 was given separately to a man acting for the girl's father.

Meanwhile, inside the house, Rakesh's bride-to-be was serving tea and snacks to Patricia and Subash's little niece. The child was utterly daunted by the occasion. She had to be cajoled into eating anything and would only whisper inaudibly when someone talked to her. After Patricia and the girl had eaten, the future bride touched their feet. Then she fled into an inner room, having uttered not a word. Her mother and aunts began asking Patricia what Rakesh looked like. Was he like his younger brother, for it was important that the bride and groom matched one another. Patricia reported that Rakesh was quite dark, like their girl, and they nodded in satisfaction.

Next came the photograph that Subash wanted Roger to take so that all his family could see what Rakesh's bride was like. It would also ensure that the correct girl was sent to Dharmnagri on the wedding day. The bride was extracted from the inner room. She stood with her head bowed, nervously fiddling with a blue kerchief. As soon as she could, she rushed inside once more.

Then there was a meal, followed by presentations to Subash's party, Rs 50 for Subash, Rs 20 for Roger, Rs 10 for the others, and some cloth lengths placed in Rakesh's brother's lap. It was almost time to leave, but Subash was in a fluster again. How many sisters did the bride have, and how much should he be giving them? He asked Patricia's advice. After a brief debate with the go-between, Subash settled on Rs 11 for his future daughter-in-law and Rs 5 each for her two younger sisters. Patricia went inside to present the money.

As we set off for Dharmnagri, everyone commented on how successful the mission had been. The only thing Subash had forgotten to ask was the girl's age. His brother reckoned she looked about sixteen or seventeen. That was a correct age for a bride. Admittedly, she was dark complexioned—but so too was Rakesh. And Rakesh and the girl were both the oldest children in their families, so the bride would know how to handle her husband's younger siblings. Patricia asked if it mattered that the girl was uneducated, since Rakesh had studied to eighth class. "Not at all," said Subash adamantly. "I don't need an educated daughter-in-law. What, am I going to send her out for employment? No! I just need a strong girl who's capable of doing farming work. Isn't that so?" The others nodded in agreement. The gifts they had received were all appropriate, too, and the girl's family seemed very straightforward. And the girl's father was so well mannered, for he kept honoring his guests by insisting that they sat at the head of the bed. Yes, the matter had been settled well.

Subash was building a new room for Rakesh and his bride, so he could not afford to hold the wedding in November 1990, as the bride's people wished. The wedding eventually took place after we had left Dharmnagri. And the cohabitation was to take place in November 1991, shortly before we returned for a further brief visit. On arrival, Patricia headed straight for Subash's house. Subash was sitting by the hearth with his wife, who was stirring a pot of water containing water chestnuts. As she fished them out, Subash peeled them, scalding his fingers as he did so. He motioned Patricia to sit down, and he began passing her water chestnuts. Patricia looked around as she ate. There was no sign of the new bride. Had she already gone back to her parents after the cohabitation? Subash and his wife looked awkwardly at one another. "What's happened?" Patricia asked.

"Well, the bride came," explained Subash. "It all seemed fine at the beginning. But then my wife refused to let the bride stay. She sent the girl back to her parents."

"But why? What was wrong?"

"You ask my wife," snorted Subash. "It was her wish, not mine."

"That girl wasn't right for our Rakesh. True, she's dark like he is. But what about her features? Our Rakesh has a fine nose, but her features are heavy. Her features wouldn't look good on his children."

"But what do features matter if the girl's character is good?" intervened Subash.

"That was another problem. It wasn't so bad until she started to speak. But didn't you hear her? She sounded just like a Chamar [Harijan] the moment she opened her mouth. We're Sahnis. We can't have a bride like that in the house!" retorted his wife.

"So you see," said Subash to Patricia, "my wife insisted that Rakesh's bride be sent back to her parents. The girl's honor has been broken."

So Subash would have to find another bride for Rakesh. This might not prove too easy. News of this incident had spread throughout the Sahni networks in Bijnor. No one wanted to marry their daughter to Rakesh. Maybe, some people suggested, Rakesh would have to be married to a girl from outside the district.

Fatima Reflects on Marriage Between Close Kin

Fatima was married to Farooq in Jhakri in the early 1970s. At the time, her father's older brother arranged all the marriages in their extended household in Qaziwala:

> With us, when we're arranging a girl's marriage, we consider whether there's land in the other family. We may also consider if the boy's educated. But village people think mainly about the land. My uncle didn't think about whether he was marrying the girls close by or distantly. The important thing is to find a good boy. But in fact, nearly all of us girls were married close by, apart from one of my cousins [FBD]. Two aunts [FZ] and my oldest sister were all married within Qaziwala itself. And my second sister and I were married in nearby villages. I don't think that marriage within the village is good. But if a girl's married too distantly, there are great problems in times of happiness as well as times of sadness, problems of coming and going and making sure people hear the news. Being married in a nearby village is the best.

Certainly, Fatima and her second sister had been able to keep in touch much more easily than if they had been married more distantly. They often met when they visited relatives in Qaziwala. And Fatima, as younger sister, even visited her sister in the village where she was married. By 1990, Fatima's oldest surviving child, a daughter, was of an age to be married. But it had all been settled some years previously, for Fatima's second sister had asked for the girl for her own son:

> A girl's father's sister or her mother's sister can ask for her in that way. It was a childhood engagement. My own engagement wasn't like that, though. But in neither case was the girl's opinion asked. We people don't ask the girl what she thinks. If a marriage were done according to the girl's wishes, the parents' nose is cut [they are dishonored], because people say the girl's arranging her own marriage. The parents decide. And if the girl faces any difficulties later in her in-laws' house, her parents will tell her she must tolerate everything.

The match would be a good one for Fatima's daughter. The boy's family owned land and her aunt would become her mother-in-law. Moreover, the boy himself was studying. He had already read the Qur'ān Sharīf completely and was studying in ninth class.

> It's important for us Muslims to make every effort to get our children to learn about matters of religion. My daughter also went to the *madrasā* for a while, but we aren't sending her now. She used to go with another girl from Jhakri, but every day they used to say some boy or other wouldn't let them walk along the road or was taunting them. That's why we stopped her education. Being uneducated is better than that sort of education. So she went to the *madrasā* for only three or four years. Since then she's been at home learning how to keep house. She's very capable now.

The only difficulty was that Fatima's nephew was smaller than her daughter even though the girl was younger. And it would not look good for a tall girl to be married to a small boy. "There's this problem with thinking about a match too soon. When someone's engagement is settled in childhood, no other offers of marriage come because everyone knows the matter's settled. Anyway, if I break the engagement, my sister would think very badly of me. So we'll have to wait till he grows bigger before we can have the wedding."

Then Fatima would have to sort out the dowry. This would probably be difficult, however. Farooq's father was one of the wealthiest Sheikh farmers in Jhakri, but he still controlled all the land and was not generous with the gifts he made to his grandchildren. Fatima feared that Farooq would have to meet the dowry expenses alone, using income from some land they had bought by saving the small sums of money her father presented when he visited Jhakri.

> If Allah gives a girl, he ought also to give plenty of money. We are praying that disappointment won't lodge in our hearts because we couldn't give generously to our girl. In our family, there are no demands, although in some families relatives are making demands, and some unrelated people don't ask for anything. But there's nothing better than relatives if they're prepared to arrange marriages with one another. You know exactly how much land there is and what the people are like. You can be sure of the future in store for your daughter or of the character of the bride coming into your own home.

Patricia mentioned that many people in Dharmnagri had been commenting on the deceptions that could arise because Hindus did not marry close relatives. What did Fatima think? "There's deception among us Muslims, too. There's a woman in Qaziwala who told me about her daughter's husband's sister, who was married far away to unrelated people. The boy's people showed the girl's people a boy. But after the marriage it turned out that the groom was another boy who had a plastic leg. The girl went just once to that house. Then her parents didn't send her again. That happened two years ago. That's why marrying among relatives is correct."

And that was why Fatima was thinking of asking formally for her brother's daughter as a bride for her son:

> One day I was visiting Qaziwala, and my brother's daughter was crying. My brother said I should get the girl engaged to one of my sons. I didn't say anything at the time because I was worried about my daughter's marriage. But I've kept my brother's words in my mind. I've told him and his wife that they know my house is a poor one, but they should marry their girl to my second son if they consider him a good boy. But the matter has gone no further because I'm anxious to settle my daughter's marriage first.

Urmila's Widowed Mother Is Deceived

Urmila's father had arranged the marriages of Urmila's three older sisters before he died in the early 1970s. There were still six other children to be married; Urmila was the oldest of them and next in line. Urmila was perhaps fourteen or fifteen at the time. Within a year, her family considered her ready for marriage.

> There's another Sahni woman from my father's village who was already married here in Dharmnagri. That woman's brother told my mother there was a suitable boy in Dharmnagri. My mother said that since she was a widow and since her sons were all small, there was no one to go to Dharmnagri to see the boy. She asked that man to bring the boy to her, which he did. That man told my mother that the boy's house owned eight acres and that the house was also very good. My mother was very happy with that. On the spot, she gave five rupees to bind the boy. My mother never visited Dharmnagri to check whether there was land or what the house was like.

At this point, Urmila's mother-in-law intervened. There had been land, she insisted, but it had subsequently been compulsorily purchased when the Madhya Ganga Barrage across the river Ganges nearby was being constructed. Urmila was furious at this:

Just how much land was there? There were just a couple of acres that were owned. And then there were eight acres that weren't owned but were being sharecropped! My poor mother hadn't looked anywhere else for a boy for me. When she visited Dharmnagri after the marriage, she came to know the situation, and she was very upset. She fought with that man who'd been the go-between, saying he'd deceived her and she'd sent her girl into a family where the house was no good and there was no land all because of him. She hasn't spoken to him since.

By the time of Urmila's marriage in 1974, there was no adult worker in her mother's house. The land had to be sharecropped, so there was less income. But there were no demands about the dowry. Thus, Urmila's dowry was very modest compared with those of her older sisters. She received no jewelry at all from her mother's house. There were just kitchen utensils and *dhotīs* for distribution among Urmila's in-laws. At the time of the wedding, Urmila's in-laws gave her nine pieces of silver jewelry weighing over two pounds. Only after the cohabitation did it become clear that the land owned by her in-laws would be taken for the barrage construction. Her father-in-law should have received compensation for it, but the land records officer refused to hand it over unless he was given Rs 500.

But my father-in-law had no money, so he took back my jewelry and pawned it. My father-in-law said we could easily get it back if my husband did laboring work for a month. He could earn that much and use it to reclaim the jewelry. But my husband wouldn't do that, so the time ran out for reclaiming it. We'll have to begin organizing our older daughter's marriage in four or five years from now, when she's fifteen or sixteen. For one thing, the moral climate in villages is very bad. What's more, village people don't leave you alone. They taunt you and torture you, saying, "Your girl's become so big! She's still seated at home and her marriage hasn't taken place yet!" When we have to begin buying things for our own children's marriages, my husband will understand the value of flour and lentils.

Javed's Bride Comes to Jhakri

Javed was one of Khurshid Ahmed's first cousins. He was about twelve years old when we first knew him in 1982, and was still studying at the Begawala *madrasā*. Like Khurshid Ahmed, Javed had been intrigued rather than frightened by us, and—with a second cousin from the same compound—he used to spend quite a bit of time at our house playing with our three-year-old daughter. By 1990, Javed was a grown

man. In the May before our arrival he was married to the daughter of
one of his father's cousins [Javed's FMBSD], from a village about
twenty-five miles beyond Bijnor. The cohabitation kept on being
delayed, however, and relationships between the two families were in
danger of being seriously soured.

According to Javed, his in-laws had originally intended to have the
marriage and the cohabitation take place at the same time, but the
bride's younger sister had been injured by a couple of oxen shortly
before the wedding. Her treatment had cost some Rs 8,000-9,000, a
totally unscheduled expenditure; thus Javed's in-laws could not
immediately afford the expenses of the cohabitation. Then Javed's wife
was bitten by a snake. Apparently, she had seen a snake slithering
underneath the tubewell engine as it sat in the courtyard. Later, when
she and her father went to fetch the engine and lifted up the cover, the
snake bit her finger. She was treated by a snake-bite specialist and was
soon recovering. But again, the cohabitation was delayed. Then, at the
end of October 1990, serious communal tensions in Bijnor town erupted
in rioting and looting, and the cohabitation date was again postponed.

In early 1991, when the cohabitation had still not taken place, Javed's
married sister in Qaziwala told us how the matter was becoming
protracted:

> The bride's people settled one date, but the fighting in Bijnor last autumn
> made everyone nervous, and my father postponed the arrangement. Then
> my father told them that ours is a large family, and he was planning to
> take fifteen men with him when he went to collect the bride and bring her
> to Jhakri for the cohabitation. The bride's father said that was too many,
> and he refused to let the cohabitation take place at the rearranged time.
> Then the bride's mother began saying that the jewelry we'd given the
> bride was artificial. You know, the ring the girl's people gave our Javed
> was adulterated, though they claimed it wasn't. Then my parents said
> they'd take all the jewelry back to the jeweler and ask for their money
> back. Then the girl's mother could get jewelry she liked made for her
> daughter.

A few days later, we talked to Javed's aunt [FZ] who was also
married in Qaziwala. Her husband had relatives in Javed's in-laws'
village and they were hearing reports about Javed's father through
those connections. "Javed's in-laws are bad-mouthing my brother," she
said. "They're saying he's constantly causing them trouble over the date
of the cohabitation. They say they were ready to send the girl the day
my brother went there recently. But my brother told them he hadn't
come to collect the bride then, he just wanted to settle the date for the

cohabitation. That made Javed's in-laws even more annoyed." Javed's uncle [FZH] joined in: "I don't want to listen to either side. If someone would just tell me when the girl is to be sent to Jhakri, I'll go to her parents' house and collect her myself! Both sides are alike. Now that they've both become heated, the matter can't be settled easily. That's why it's all escalating."

And Fatima's aunt [FBW] in Qaziwala, a woman originally from the same village as Javed's bride, had also been hearing about the dispute from her own relatives: "It's all the fault of Javed's father. He's repeatedly caused those people worries. Several times, they've gone to trouble and expense over the preparations for sending their girl, getting in food for the men from Jhakri coming to collect her. And several times, he's postponed the date."

In mid-January, Javed's father sent the village barber to the bride's village to say that he wanted to go the next day in the hope of straightening things out and maybe bringing the bride back to Jhakri. The barber returned with a message that the next day was not suitable.[3] Roger asked Javed's father what the difficulty was. "I don't know. The wedding was on May thirtieth. And the date for the cohabitation was set for November twenty-fourth. But then there were the troubles. For a month no one could go anywhere. It would have been dangerous to go all that distance with a tractor and trolley. I explained that to them, so I can't understand why they're still creating all these difficulties. They aren't crooks. They're my cousin-brothers. I don't know what the problem is."

The next day, despite the barber's message, Roger drove to Javed's in-laws' village with Javed's father, Javed's uncle [FZH] from Qaziwala, and a couple of young men married to Javed's paternal cousins, who were visiting Jhakri at the time. When they arrived, the hostility was palpable. Some women challenged Javed's father and asked why he had come when he had been expressly told not to. The bride's father was fetched from the fields, and he promptly began shouting at Javed's father. "Why didn't you come on November twenty-fourth as arranged?" he demanded. "There wasn't any trouble then, just rumors. You should have come."

"But a bride must come to her in-laws' place dressed in finery and wearing her wedding jewelry. It was too dangerous at that time. We might have been looted," responded Javed's father.

"And you didn't even get the dates for the wedding right," protested the bride's father.

"No, it was clear to us. We wanted to have it on May first because my nephew was also getting married that month. If thirty men had attended that wedding, thirty would have had to come on Javed's wedding too. That's why we wanted to set the date earlier, for your benefit. But then you set the date for May thirtieth."

"You shouldn't have sent the barber. You should have come yourself to settle the date," exclaimed the bride's father. "And anyway, after you failed to come on November twenty-fourth, how could we manage to arrange the cohabitation things for December thirtieth as you suggested?"

"But surely you had all the grain ready for November twenty-fourth," interjected Javed's father.

"Yes, but people don't keep grain set aside indefinitely. We couldn't have got everything ready again so quickly."

One old man commented that there were faults on both sides—which neither side would accept. Some other family elders tried to calm things down. There was some coming and going with men from the two sides going up onto the roof or into quiet corners for private conferences. Eventually, it seemed to be smoothed over. On the date settled for the cohabitation, Roger drove to the bride's village again with Javed's father and a party of men from Jhakri. The ill feeling appeared to have dissipated, and they were entertained to a sumptuous meal by the bride's family. Indeed, the occasion would have been uneventful except that the bride—who had never been in a motor vehicle before—was violently carsick three times on the way to Jhakri.

Adesh on Childhood Weddings

Ashok was one of two Rajput brothers in Dharmnagri who owned one of the largest farms in the village. They owned several farm animals and a tractor and had a large home with two stories at the front and a sizable courtyard behind. When we arrived in 1990, Ashok's wife, Adesh, began telling us about the marriages of her second and third daughters some three years earlier. The two girls had been married into one house, to a pair of brothers. Adesh reeled off the details of the dowries they had given—jewelry, clothing, household effects, and so forth with everything in pairs so that the two dowries would be identical. By the sounds of it, the marriages had been quite grand. By contrast, Adesh's own marriage in about 1952 had been a rather low-key affair.

"My father died when I was very young," she explained. "I can hardly remember him at all. All the responsibility for the work in the house and on the farm and for arranging the children's marriages rested with my mother. My mother was very capable and wouldn't accept her in-laws' offers of help. She did all the farm management herself and employed laborers to do the farmwork. With us, marriages used to be arranged *sate.*"

"*Sate*? What do you mean by that?" Patricia asked.

"It's sometimes also called *adlī-badlī* [exchange] or *sājhe-ki-shādī* [marriages together]," our assistant Radha commented. "People used to do that when there were shortages of girls, so that they could ensure the boys could be married." Adesh continued the explanation:

> That's right. If someone had a son to marry but they had no daughter, they'd ask among their relatives to find someone else with a girl who needed to be married and then find another family with a boy and a girl needing to be married. In my case it happened this way. My aunt [FZ] wanted to get her son married. My aunt came to my mother and said I should be married here, and then her own son could be married. His bride was my husband's cousin. I was just seven years old at the time. The cohabitation didn't take place for another seven years. Even then I used to come for just a short time to my in-laws' place. In other cases, a boy and his sister might be married to a girl and her brother. That's exactly what happened with my older sister and one of my brothers. My sister was of an age to be married, but my brother was still small. The party of men collecting my sister from her first visit to her in-laws' place was also the party of men for my brother's wedding. The marriage ceremony took place with all the circling round the fire and so on—and then the bride and groom went to play outside. My brother was five at the time and his bride was just three! The party of men who went with the groom didn't take the bride away with them, of course. The cohabitation took place eight or nine years later.

Zubeida Complains About Her Marriage

Zubeida's father died leaving three little girls for her mother to look after; Zubeida was the smallest. Soon afterward, Zubeida's mother was married again (as often happens when a woman is widowed young) to a younger unmarried brother of her first husband. In due course, the second of Zubeida's sisters was married to Zakir, a landless Teli from Jhakri. Zubeida's sister had one daughter but died in childbirth at the end of her second pregnancy. At this time, Zubeida herself was still a child. After four years, Zakir had still not remarried, and Zubeida's mother arranged the match between Zakir and Zubeida.

> In fact, my marriage had been decided years before, when I was a tiny child. I was to be married to my father's sister's son. My aunt had asked for me for her son when I was just four or five years old. But then my sister died. My mother began saying she wouldn't give me to my aunt, but she'd marry me to her son-in-law instead so that I could look after her

granddaughter. That's why I was married here when I was about thirteen years old. I wasn't even mature. My mother didn't heed a word my stepfather said. She just insisted that no other woman would look after her little granddaughter properly. Eventually my stepfather gave in. And that's how my mother ruined my life for the sake of a son-in-law and a granddaughter.

There had been no other offers of marriage for Zubeida because people believed that her marriage had long been settled in her aunt's house. But then, in about 1975, she was married to Zakir. She was furious about the whole business.

My parents didn't ask me anything about this. I'd have refused if they had asked me. I knew what I was coming to, but my parents' honor would have been destroyed if I'd said anything. My stepfather was against the match. At the time of the *nikāh*, he tried to insist on a large *mahr*. He wanted it to be 5,000 rupees in addition to the jewelry, because I was still so young. But my husband refused until some four days had passed. Then he agreed. I still have the jewelry, but he made me forgo the *mahr* after I came to Jhakri. My cousin is much better than this man here. My cousin was young and a good earner. But this man is old compared with me, and he beats me a lot. If I'd gone to my aunt's house, I'd be living a pleasant life. If I'd moved my tongue, it would have been better, but my parents' honor stopped me. Enough, I'm just managing to endure my life here. Now I must simply live out my time. But if I'd refused the marriage at the time of the marriage ceremony, I'd have escaped this calamity. A boy should be good, he should earn and feed his family, and he shouldn't beat his wife. All a woman needs is to obtain two pieces of bread and two pieces of clothing in peace.

A Wedding Song

The darling bride's huge eyes are brimming with tears.
Just as she's leaving, the girl says this:
"Father, don't get me married,
My life will be afflicted by calamities."
"Child, you'll be left alone in this house,
Your mother will taunt you, she'll make you cry."

The darling bride's huge eyes are brimming with tears.
Just as she's leaving, the girl says this:
"Uncle [FyB], don't get me married,
My life will be afflicted by calamities."
"Child, you'll be left alone in this house,
Your aunt [FyBW] will taunt you, she'll make you cry."[4]

Notes

1. For examples of songs sung by women at the groom's home, see the one at the end of Chapter 3 and the one at the beginning of Chapter 9.

2. Both songs in this chapter are from the *bannī* genre, sung at the bride's house when the bride is departing for her in-laws' house after the wedding ceremonies have been completed. This one focuses on the sadness of her relatives at her departure.

3. Village barbers often conveyed messages in this way, and they frequently acted as go-betweens in wedding arrangements. Since their work took them to many villages, people generally regarded them as a good source of gossip and of information about potential matches.

4. This *bannī* (see note 2) voices the bride's fears and her relatives' insistence that she must go to her husband's home.

6

Who Would There Be
to Sit with Our Boy?

One of the largest and most impressive compounds in Dharmnagri had been built by three Dhimar brothers who farmed some twenty acres. By 1990, their father was perhaps in his nineties. He had become very frail, and he died while we were there. In his younger days, he had been a prosperous farmer. The land remained in his name until his death, but his sons had already been farming it separately in three equal portions for several years. When we first stayed in Dharmnagri, the old father, his three sons, and their wives and children all lived in kiln-brick houses built around a courtyard, at a time when most people in Dharmnagri were still living in single-storied and single-roomed thatched adobe houses. Inside the spacious courtyard, several milch animals would be stalled. Outside, the pillared veranda to the front of the complex, with yet more tethered cattle and equipment such as plows and the fodder chopper, stood in marked contrast to the houses round about. By 1990, the marriages of six of the old man's grandsons and a growing generation of great grandchildren had impelled several of the couples to relocate to new homes on the outskirts of Dharmnagri, built on sites where their cattle byres had previously stood.

The old man's eldest son had been married to Anjali in the late 1940s. In about 1971, Anjali's second son, Krishnu, was married to Kamla, the oldest daughter of a man who operated a farm in a village beyond the market town of Mandawar, about six miles to the northwest of Bijnor. But the match had not been readily agreed to by Krishnu's relatives, for Kamla had no brothers. Given the levels of child mortality in rural Bijnor, it was not particularly uncommon for a couple to have no surviving sons. From all angles, though, this would be a problem. The parents themselves would face old age with an empty house and no one to work the land or care for them. Their daughter would worry about who would visit her in her husband's home or collect her when she was due to spend some time at her parents' home. She would fear that she might cease to receive her entitlements from her parents' property or that she would not be given protection if necessary in the years to come.[1] And the son-in-law would have no one to fête him when he visited his wife's natal village: His father-in-law's seniority would preclude the informal and relaxed chatting that would be appropriate only with a younger man. Moreover, he might find himself pressured to become an "in-living son-in-law" [ghar jamāī], a somewhat derogatory term for a man living in his wife's village. This usually happened only when a woman had no brothers capable of farming her father's land and caring for her parents. The in-living son-in-law would expect to be accused of taking land from his wife's cousins, and he would have no ready allies. Few men would happily consent to such an arrangement.[2]

* * * * * *

After several years of marriage and a host of medical treatments, Kamla eventually gave birth to her first child in 1977. From the start, she had had menstrual problems, including light periods only every eight or nine months. She was plagued by "heat" because the menstrual blood accumulated in her body, and she was unable to eat any "heating" foods in case the effects went to her head and she became insane.[3] For some years, her mother-in-law, Anjali, took her for treatments at various places. By the time Kamla had been married for five or six years and still shown no signs of pregnancy, her in-laws began saying that as she did not menstruate, how could she have any children? And the healer who was being consulted at the time said that her menstrual problems must be cleared up before there was any question of fertility treatment.

By this stage, Kamla's parents were anxious in case her failure to have children would make her position in her in-laws' house insecure. Kamla herself spoke to her mother about getting medicines to help her conceive. She went back to their house, and from there they sought and paid for her treatments. They began taking her to local healers, who also refused to begin fertility treatment until her menstrual problems were solved. Subsequently, at various times, she was treated in Nizampur, Najibabad, and Sahanpur, and she had tablets from the ANM in Dharmnagri and from a private female doctor in Bijnor. "But I got no benefit from any of these treatments. That was why I stopped taking the medicines. Even now my periods are not regular. But this much was good: Eventually I gave birth without any other treatment!"

By the beginning of 1983, she had three small children, the oldest a boy of five, the second a girl of not quite three years, and now another baby boy. Her in-laws were delighted that she now had two sons. On the day of the birth, they had marked their happiness by breaking a large lump of unrefined sugar over Kamla's daughter's buttocks because she had "brought a brother" in her wake. And the other women of the compound sang birth songs to celebrate the birth every day before the

A Father Sits with His Daughter

baby's naming ceremony. Kamla's own response, though, was moderated by the feeling that her earlier problems had been reversed:

> I was neither happy nor sad to be pregnant the third time. It was not something under my control. But I didn't want to get pregnant again so soon because the girl was too young. It would have been better if the third child had been born later. The spaces between my children are too short. I don't want to be sterilized. I'd like to have as many children as my mother-in-law! No, really, we might like to have one or two more children, so I don't want to have the operation. That's why I want to get medicines. We both think that if there's to be another child, it should only be born when this baby boy is five or six years old.

Kamla's menstrual problems, however, had put her into a quandary about how to achieve this goal. A well-known local remedy to prevent conception was to eat carrot seeds, which were believed to make a woman so "cold" that her husband's seed could not germinate inside her. Kamla believed these would be useless for her, since the carrot seeds must be taken a few days after a menstrual period. "My periods haven't begun again after this baby. When they do, I'll go to Bijnor with my husband and get some pills to make the gap long. He also agrees with that. His mother has no say in this. It's for the two of us to decide. My mother-in-law will find out about the pills once I start taking them. But I won't say anything to her beforehand."

But now, Kamla's third baby was still tiny, and she was looking forward to a visit with her parents. She had not visited them since she was about five months pregnant. "But I'll have to wait until someone comes to fetch me. They haven't been able to call me for some time, not since I was heavily pregnant. Now, if someone comes to collect me, I'll go with them. It's such a long time since I've been, and I very much want to go. I don't go there alone. And since I have no brothers, there's only my father who can fetch me."

* * * * * *

Kamla's father farmed about eight acres of land, more than enough for his family's needs. But he had to run the farm single-handed, for he had no living sons. Kamla explained:

> There was a brother and a sister older than me. But my sister died from typhoid when she was about two and a half. And when my brother was being born, my mother was given an injection to increase the pains, but it wasn't done right. My mother says that the doctor gave it when she was having only light pains. Because of that, the baby died inside her. After I

was born, my mother had other babies, but there were two other stillbirths, both girls. In that fashion, her babies died during her pains. My mother had all her children with a lot of trouble. She would have pains for three or four days. And previously, doctors weren't easily found in villages. So now just we three girls remain.

As the oldest daughter, Kamla would be the first of the sisters to be married. So, when she reached puberty, her father began making enquiries about suitable matches. Kamla's father often used to go to Mandawar in connection with his farmwork. One time, in the course of conversation, he asked if one of his friends knew of any possible matches for Kamla. "He told his friend that his girl was ready for marriage and if the friend knew of any boy, he should tell him. That man has relatives in Dharmnagri, and he told my father about the boy. At that time, my in-laws were very influential because my grandfather-in-law was still alive and all the land was in his name. Previously, it was thought very impressive if twenty acres were in the name of one man."

Kamla's father liked the sound of such a match, and he visited Dharmnagri to see the house and the boy he had been told about. He greatly approved of Krishnu. The boy had studied at school, had passed the eighth class examinations, and now was farming with his father. Then and there, Kamla's father said he wished his daughter to be married to Krishnu. The match seemed ideal, but only to Kamla's father. "My father-in-law and his two brothers refused to go ahead with the proposed marriage," Kamla explained. "They said that since I don't have any brothers, they wouldn't arrange this boy's marriage with me. They said, 'Who would there be to sit with our boy when he visits his in-laws? Who would there be for him to talk to? He would just be left alone.' At this, my father became very saddened and he returned home, weeping with hopelessness."

Even so, Kamla's father persisted. According to Kamla, he made several return trips to Dharmnagri to try to persuade Krishnu's relatives to agree to the match. But it was all to no avail. They would hear nothing of it. One time, Kamla's father went to Dharmnagri with several other men, including the man who had first suggested the match. They tried to pressure Krishnu's father and uncles: "They spent a lot of time exhorting them to accept the match. They told his family that my people are very honest and simple, that my father also has plenty of land, and that I was also very good. They also said the boy could visit his in-laws a couple of times after the marriage. If the boy's family found that his visits went well, they could continue sending him. And if not, they could keep their daughter-in-law in their house and not send her to visit her parents."

These efforts at persuasion met with no more success than Kamla's father's. He himself made several more visits to Dharmnagri and was repeatedly refused. It was only when Krishnu himself spoke up—something quite daring for a boy of sixteen to do—that his relatives agreed to proceed. "He was beginning to feel bad about the way I was being rejected simply because I had no brothers. No one was saying anything else against me. So he told his parents that if he was to be married, he would be married into that very house or he wouldn't marry at all. And then my in-laws became willing to accept the match."

* * * * * *

Of course, it had not been for Kamla to decide how far from her parents she would be married, but she did not like living in such a distant place. "If your in-laws' village is close, then news of sadness and happiness can be received quickly, and other essential work can be done at any time. Also, I could come and go alone."

But the journey to her parents' home took a long time and entailed taking a cycle rickshaw three miles into Bijnor, going by bus for the six miles along the metaled road to Mandawar, and changing there for a bus to her home village, a further three miles beyond. Either her father would come to collect her or her husband would take her and the children and leave them in her parents' house. As she commented after the birth of her third child in 1983,

> I haven't gone there by myself and I don't want to. How can I go alone with small children? Going alone with small children causes a lot of trouble. Anyway, my parents' village is quite far away and I have to change buses twice. Generally, my in-laws don't prevent me if I want to visit my parents. But in any case, my mother doesn't call me for visits often because the children always become sick when they go. And they're too small for me to leave behind in Dharmnagri. The youngest is still drinking my milk. That's why my mother fears for my children and doesn't call me often.

Normally, then, she would just go for the Tījo festival during the monsoon.[4] Once, though, her mother-in-law had said she should not go even then, as the signs were bad: One of Kamla's relatives had died on each of the previous two occasions she had gone for Tījo. Sometimes Kamla managed another visit to her parents in the course of a year. But although Krishnu would give his permission, he would not let her stay away very long, usually no more than "ten-fifteen" days. "I would like to visit my parents more often. I get peace in their house. But who would make his food for him? And there are animals too. Who would also do the work for them? Nor do my parents stop me from returning to Dharmnagri. My mother says, 'What's the point of making them angry, since Kamla has to live in that house?'"

Parents would generally feel embarrassed to visit their married daughters in their in-laws' village. Normally, a married woman would expect to be visited by her brother, who would keep their parents in touch with her situation. If Kamla had had a brother, she would have expected the same. But she had no one to visit her apart from her parents. Unlike most married women in Dharmnagri, she had been visited a few times by her mother. Her father even stayed overnight sometimes, carefully giving her a small sum of money after his visit to ensure that he was not accused of taking hospitality from his married daughter. But he could not leave his farmwork for longer.

*   *   *   *   *   *

If Kamla regretted that she could not meet her parents often, she had no complaints about their generosity. Indeed, their substantial contributions to the well-being of Kamla's household over the years had been the hallmark of their relationship with her and Krishnu. There were the predictable gifts of clothing and foodstuffs for her immediate household when she visited her parents. When her older son was born, her parents sent clothes for the whole compound, as well as clothing for Kamla, Krishnu, and the baby and small items of jewelry for the baby. "The things that cost 500 rupees in those days," Kamla commented in 1991, "would not be available for 1,000 rupees now." After returning from a couple of weeks in her parents' house over the Tijo festival in 1985, Kamla listed what had been given to her: "Three *dhotīs* for me, about half a hundredweight each of rice, pulses, and flour, and clothes for all my children. My mother has no son. That's why she gives me so much."

The giving had begun with Kamla's engagement and marriage in the early 1970s. When Kamla and her sisters became "big," her father would first make all the arrangements for the dowry, each time accumulating things "till the world was overflowing," according to the expectations of the day. Only then did he go in search of a boy. Her in-laws did not make any demands in relation to the dowry, but even so, her father made a "good marriage" for her. There were nine *dhotīs* for her and several others for distribution among the women in Krishnu's compound, a bed and stool, a table and chair, a watch and cycle for Krishnu, and some fifty thick metal kitchen utensils. She was also given more than two pounds of silver made into various pieces of jewelry.

When I was married, my grandfather-in-law and his three sons were all living jointly. The things [jewelry] that had been presented to Jumni [Krishnu's older brother's wife] were all still with her. She refused to give them up so that they could be presented to me. At that, my husband's two aunts [FBW] said that new jewelry shouldn't be made—they would present me with their own. They told my mother-in-law she would have to present things from her own side when their sons were married.

So Kamla had arrived in her in-laws' house in her wedding finery and wearing jewelry presented by each of the three women, as well as the jewelry that her parents had had made for her.

My mother-in-law saw that my parents had given me plenty of things. So she immediately returned everything that had been presented by my husband's aunts. She did that because she herself would have to get things made for the weddings of her sisters-in-laws' sons, and the sisters-in-law would say that she had given them things made of adulterated metal and they wouldn't like them. So she gave their things back straightaway. When their sons were married, she didn't have to present anything. The only item that remained with me was the collarbone that my mother-in-law gave me herself.[5]

The cohabitation, six months after the wedding, was again an occasion for her parents' generosity. In addition to clothing for Kamla and Krishnu and all the members of Krishnu's compound, Kamla's father sent one hundredweight of foodstuffs and Rs 10,000 in cash, a not inconsiderable sum in the early 1970s. The foodstuffs went into the common compound granary, and the money initially went to Krishnu's father. But then Krishnu decided to go into business—hiring fruit orchards by the season—rather than work the family land with his father. Krishnu asked for the money to get established. Prior to that, Krishnu had never been in business. At first he took heavy losses.

But he didn't lose courage. Bit by bit, he sold off some of the jewelry my parents had given, and he put that money into the business. I agreed to that, since I reckoned that it would be for the benefit of my own household. Now I have just a few items of my dowry jewelry and those I'm keeping in my parents' house so that no more will be sold. Then, when he was short of money again, he asked his father for more money. His father told him he shouldn't stay in business—but he didn't listen. He couldn't see how he could pay his debts otherwise.

Up to that point, Kamla had been living with Krishnu in a joint household with her parents-in-law, Krishnu's older brother and his wife and children, and Krishnu's unmarried siblings. But then, shortly before the birth of her third child, Krishnu and his father had an argument. Krishnu was making no contribution to his father's farming work, yet he was asking for more money to cover his business losses and was eating grain from the family fields. "My mother-in-law never criticizes me or fights with me. But my father-in-law is a very angry man. One day he told my husband and his older brother that since they do no fieldwork, their households should become separate. They would get grain only if they worked."

And so Krishnu's father gave him one and a half acres of land and told him that whatever he decided to do was no longer of any concern to his parents. There was no argument between Kamla and her mother-in-law, Anjali. Indeed, the two women still often helped one another with their work. But Krishnu could not rely on his parents to feed his family if his business ran into difficulties. Kamla's father, however, continued to provide basic security for the household as a backdrop to Krishnu's activities in Dharmnagri. For many years, for instance, Kamla received three to four hundredweight of grain twice a year after the rice and wheat harvests. That accounted for almost all the rice they ate and about a third of the wheat. "Since we constantly receive so much from my parents, I don't have to ask for anything. Nor has anyone among my in-laws ever told me to bring anything back with me after I visit them. I have no brothers, so whatever my parents have will be received by the three sisters."

By 1991, Krishnu's orchard business as well as his farming in Dharmnagri were both flourishing, and Kamla was content with her financial position. Moreover, she and Krishnu were in accord on their household finances:

> His income and mine are not separate. Both our concerns are one. Whatever comes into the house is spent on the house only. When the sugarcane money comes, I myself ask how much has to be repaid to whom, and he tells me everything. And if I have to buy something, I first tell him about it. Then he tells me to buy it, for I am not one who spends money wastefully. I buy only essential things. And he knows that too. There's nothing hidden from him. What is to be done happens after we've both agreed to it.

*   *   *   *   *   *

Kamla's father, however, was beginning to find running his farm a strain. Throughout the 1980s, he repeatedly tried to persuade Kamla and Krishnu to move to his village, where they could take possession of a portion of his land and cultivate it for him. Kamla's parents were keen for this to happen, because they would obtain respite from the heavy burden of work and a guarantee that they would be cared for in their old age. And Kamla felt that such an arrangement would be beneficial for her, for she could expect support and kindnesses from her mother.

Krishnu, though, was adamant that he did not want to leave Dharmnagri. Certainly he was treated as a guest whenever he visited Kamla's parents, and he was well fed and made comfortable. As a son-in-law, however, he had to be quiet in his behavior and complain about nothing in front of his parents-in-law. Living there on a regular basis would mean suffering the indignities of being an in-living son-in-law. But Krishnu had further reasons for not wishing to move there:

> He also doesn't want to go because there's a lot of fighting. People make false reports to the police and people end up spending a lot of money on bribes to the police. That's why he thinks that peace is better than fights. And in addition, my father has taken in my mother's brother's widow. She lives in a separate house and refuses to speak to my mother. That woman alone helps to plow and plant my father's land. She's eaten carrot seeds so that she doesn't have any more children. People would talk if a widow had children, though everyone knows that my father is having sex with her. My mother is silent because she doesn't have any sons. If she were to say anything, my father could throw her out of the house.

By 1991, Kamla's father was no longer sending grain to his two married daughters. Instead, he had given one acre of land to each of his sons-in-law, and he told them to cultivate the land and take the crop. "Since he had to give us grain anyway and he can't cultivate all the land by himself, he reckoned he should just give the land. When my third sister is married next winter, he'll meet the costs of her wedding. Then he'll register more of his land in the names of all three sons-in-law. He and my mother will have power of attorney."

Moreover, there was a solid brick house available for whichever of the sisters wanted to shift there permanently. Kamla's father continued to say that Kamla should go there to live, and she was considering doing so if neither of her other sisters decided to. She and Krishnu could keep an eye on things both there and in Dharmnagri. Such a peripatetic existence, however, would not be without its drawbacks, especially for a family with school-aged children.

* * * * * *

After the initial anxieties about whether she could have children at all, Kamla was rather less than pleased to have had five children by

1991. Kamla's menstrual irregularity, however, had not made it easy for her to determine when she should begin using contraception.

After the birth of her third child in December 1982, she did not obtain contraceptives before she became pregnant again. Her fourth child, a girl, was born less than two years later in late 1984. At that stage Kamla began to consider being sterilized. "I don't have periods, so how could I take pills to lengthen the gap between pregnancies? I talked to my mother-in-law about being sterilized and she said I should do as I wish. But if she didn't agree, I'd just do what I wanted. My husband also wants me to stop having children. But I've also spoken to my mother and my married sister. They both say I shouldn't have the operation, since I have no brothers."

The weight of their opposition was augmented because the family's continuity rested so much on Kamla's ability to bear children. Kamla's youngest sister was still unmarried, and her second sister (who was married to Krishnu's father's sister's son in Mandawar) had gynecological problems: "When she has her periods, she has great pain. Her breasts become badly engorged—very large and painful. She's also had a lot of treatment. She's even been taken to the lady doctor in Bijnor, but there's been no benefit. Nor has she had any children."

In any case, when Kamla consulted a doctor about the operation, she was told that she could not have it done for some time, since she was suffering from "gas" and "heat." And Krishnu did not want to be sterilized. "Then someone told me about a Bengali doctor in Mandawar. I went there when the girl [born in 1984] was about one and a half. I had an injection [of hormonal contraceptive] that would last for three years. Now I'll have a new injection every three years. That injection cost forty rupees then, now they cost sixty to seventy rupees."[6] That first injection, however, had worsened her symptoms of "gas" and "heat." Her food was not properly digested and she constantly felt nauseous. The doctor gave her "cold" medicines and recommended that she eat "cold" foods. "But the injection was hot. Because of the cold medicines, the injection soon became ineffectual. So I became pregnant again. But this last time, when my son [born in late 1988] was a year old and I wasn't taking any cold medicines, I had another injection. And now there's no question of getting pregnant."

She commented somewhat ruefully that her last two children had come without being wanted. Now she wanted absolutely no more: "Two or three children are good. If there are more children, no one is prepared to marry their own daughter into a house. They'd say they wouldn't give their daughter to a house with many children because she'd die just cooking bread the whole time!"

* * * * * *

Nonetheless, Kamla remained hopeful. They had no serious money problems, so there was plenty of food for them all. Nor were there any worries about finding enough money to educate the children. Kamla felt she herself had missed out, however, and bitterly regretted her loss:

> There was a school to fifth class when I was a child, but I didn't attend it. My mother now tells me that she sent me to school many times, but I didn't enjoy studying and didn't like being in school. That's why I'm not educated. But being uneducated has caused me lots of sadness. I get so much pleasure from religious books that I get my children to read them to me. Books contain such good matters. If I could read them myself, it would be even more interesting. Then, when I have free time, I could pick up a book of my own and sit down to read. Only if I were educated though. Human beings learn a lot from books. They become very aware. An educated person can never do bad work because they think before they act. Nor do they jabber disrespectfully. They learn how to make sensible conversation. Education is useful in every activity. If my husband had wished, he could have taught me to read, but he just didn't have the time. Both his older sisters were completely uneducated, but both their husbands had studied to fourteenth class and taught them to read and write. Now my husband's sisters can read any book at all properly.

Thus, she was very keen that her children do well at school and not have their education disrupted or curtailed. There was now a school as far as tenth class in her parents' village, but Kamla's three oldest children were already settled in school in Dharmnagri, and she was planning that they continue there. Her oldest son was in the junior high school (up to eighth class). The next two were together in one class in the primary school: Kamla had sent her daughter rather older than usual and her son rather younger to ensure that the girl would always have someone to chaperon her. Kamla's enthusiasm for her children's schooling was mirrored in the children themselves: "They themselves get such pleasure from studying that I don't have to tell them to go to school. They go to school at their own insistence. And since our children want to study, we shall get them married only when they have completed their education, at a good age."

The considerations for girls and boys were somewhat different, however. The girls could study only near home, in Dharmnagri. But Kamla did not intend to take them out of school after fifth class as many others did: "They can carry on studying in Dharmnagri as long as they like. We don't intend to marry them at an early age. Nor shall we take them out of school and sit them at home until they are to be married."

Boys, however, could be sent to Bijnor to study once they outgrew the Dharmnagri school. Her oldest boy was keen to study for as long as he could:

> The two of us told him we'd educate him as far as Inter [twelfth class]. But he said there's no education before Inter, and he would study well beyond that. He said he can get regular employment once he's studied. At present he's studying, and he also helps with some of the farming if need be. That's why we don't stop him studying. These past two years he's been marketing the *parwal* [a monsoon vegetable crop] for us. He goes to Bijnor by himself and brings back the full amount of money. Sometimes he brings back as much as 2,000 rupees.

But decisions about this boy's future would not rest with him alone, or even with his parents: "We don't want to marry the children too young. But it's possible that we shall be forced to get our oldest son married quickly. You see, my parents want his marriage to take place while they're still alive. My father wants to go on a wedding party to a bride's house. He wants to bring a new bride into his home. He couldn't do that because he had three daughters. But now he wants to do it for his grandson."

Notes

1. A woman's reliance on her natal kin is explored in Chapters 10-13.

2. See Jeffery, Jeffery, and Lyon (1989:36-38) for more on the in-living son-in-law.

3. Chapter 1, note 9. Menstrual blood was considered both polluting and "heating." Excessive "heat" could also make a pregnant woman miscarry. Excessive "coolness" was associated with infertility.

4. Tĩjo—also known as Tĩj—is a Hindu festival marked by women fasting for the day; worshipping the goddess Parvati; and asking for a good husband, prosperity, and children. Married women would return to their parents' home if at all possible and enjoy themselves singing on swings especially constructed for the occasion.

5. The "collarbone" is a heavy ornament for the neck, an incomplete ring of solid silver worn hanging down over a woman's collarbones with the opening at the back of the neck.

6. The use of injectable hormonal contraceptives is very controversial (see Ravindran 1993). There are issues connected with the long-term effects, and a woman experiencing side effects must simply wait for them to wear off. In addition, injections are often given under nonsterile conditions, bringing the danger of blood-transmitted infections, including AIDS. Still, many women find the injection attractive, in some measure because they can get it secretly. See Vishwanath (1994) for more on the social marketing of contraceptives in India.

7

No One of Your Own Will Be There

People in Dharmnagri and Jhakri often raised topics of conversation that we had been diffident about initiating because they seemed too close to the voyeuristic. Wife beating was one such, sex was another. On numerous occasions, Patricia was asked how often Roger beat her and on what pretext. "No one here escapes a beating," was the common refrain if she asked further about it. Men, too, would bring up the subject with Roger, asserting that it was a necessary and legitimate part of men's means of controlling their wives. Again, especially in 1982, women were fascinated by our sleeping arrangements and often heartily criticized us because our young daughters slept in a separate room. "What?" Patricia was continually asked, "Do you prefer your husband to your daughters?" And then someone would almost certainly ask Patricia how often Roger caused her "trouble" [taklīf, pareshānī] by demanding sex. Yet despite this and the openly sexual references contained in many women's songs, discussing sex much further with the women proved immensely difficult. They generally insisted that we were shameless if we tried to do so. On occasion, enquiring about the gaps between a woman's children or asking women where they had given birth—in their husband's home or elsewhere—would bring forth a diatribe of abuse and accusations that we would soon be asking about what happened at night. Many young men, by contrast, openly asserted that sex—like wife beating—was a key part of their repertoire to control their wives. But it was hard to go beyond this. Was it all just bravado? How did they regard their wives? We found it difficult to fathom.

Women in Dharmnagri and Jhakri had generally been married by their mid-teens. Most had established homes and relationships with men who were strangers when they married. Their adult lives would be spent in their husband's village; they would be expected to work for his household and to bear and look after his children. Very few women remained unmarried. Marriage, then, had a centrality in women's lives for compelling reasons. And women's marital situations were a common focus of conversation among women themselves. Women often talked about "ādmī-ka-rāj" [husband's rule] or referred to the husband as the "ghar-ka-mālik" [master of the house].

Husbands who beat their wives to excess would become the focus of gossip and criticism. Yet women also considered that men were entitled to use physical means to chastise wives who had failed in their work or who had been too assertive. Apparently, to varying degrees, most men did so.

A husband's rule, however, was not sustained simply by overt violence and coercive sexual relations. The bulk of household finances and decisionmaking would normally rest with the husband. Most men made decisions about the sale or purchase of livestock or the planting of crops without any input from their wives. Generally, too, a village husband would himself select and purchase the cloth for his wife's clothing without consulting her. Few women had sources of independent income sufficient to enable them to make more than very limited purchases.[1] Among Muslims, the mahr *specified in the marriage contract might have provided a measure of financial and marital security that was unavailable to Hindu women. In reality it did not. None of the women in Jhakri had received their* mahr.[2] *Indeed, it was shameless for a woman to insist on being given it. Many had been expected to "forgive" their husband and relinquish their claims, sometimes under considerable pressure. Several women in Jhakri did not know what* mahr *had been settled on them. Others reported trivial sums—some as little as Rs 25—that could provide no meaningful economic security. Even in the event of divorce, Muslim women in rural Bijnor could not be certain that the* mahr *would be given.*

But in any case, few women sought economic independence. Ideally, a husband and wife should be interdependent. The husband should be continually mindful of the needs of his wife and children, and his wife should have no call for income of her own. Women who held the family purse rarely controlled it. Rather, it was held in trust and they felt diffident about buying things for themselves. Within the constraints laid down by their incomes, most men in Dharmnagri and Jhakri did indeed provide for their families as best they could. And although most men belittled the work their wives did, many also cared for their wives. Indeed, the prospect that a newly married son might "put his wife on his head" made many a mother feel threatened by her daughter-in-law's arrival.[3]

A Wedding Song

Don't cry so much, my darling!
You must go to your husband's house.
That place will be someone else's.
No one of your own will be there.
Tears will stream from your eyes,
You'll have to mop them with the end of your *sārī*.
Neither your aunt [FeBW] nor uncle [FeB] will be there.
No one of your own will be there.

Don't cry so much, my darling!
You must go to your husband's house.[4]

The Innocence of Gulshan's Mother-in-Law

Gulshan was from the same Sheikh extended family as Khurshid Ahmed. She was married within Jhakri to a young man in a neighboring courtyard in spring 1982. A few months after this, Patricia went to visit her in her in-laws' home with our assistant Swaleha. Gulshan was smashing some unrefined sugar on the stone used to grind spices. She asked her mother-in-law how much water should be added, and her mother-in-law added the water and said she would fetch a dung cake so that they could cook the syrup on the hearth. Gulshan began kneading the dough and told us that we would now have to stay so that we could eat the sweetened bread she was preparing.

"Is this the first thing you've cooked in your in-laws' house? Is that why they've asked you to cook something sweet?" Patricia asked.

Gulshan explained, "No. I cooked something sweet the very first time that I came here. It's just that I don't like sitting idle. But yes, there is this custom in some houses that the bride first cooks something sweet for her in-laws. What, are you wanting to write down all the details of the work that I do here?"

Swaleha explained that we wanted to record the maternity histories of all the married women in Jhakri. "Fine!" said Gulshan. "Then you should write down that I've been married for three months and that I have six children!" And she went to call her mother-in-law.

Gulshan's mother-in-law reckoned she had been married about twenty years, but Gulshan said it must have been longer than that, since she herself was fully nineteen years old and her husband was older. "And was he your first child?" Swaleha asked. Gulshan's mother-in-law nodded. "And how long after your marriage was he born?" Gulshan's mother-in-law replied that it was some six or seven years after her marriage:

I was very small when I was married. I wasn't mature. My husband was, though. I was afraid of him and used to run away from him. I used to sleep beside my mother-in-law or my husband's sister. After I'd been married for four years or so, some women began telling my mother-in-law that I kept running away from my husband. They told her to put the two of us in a separate house and prevent me from sleeping beside her any more. When I was made to sleep in a separate room, I didn't understand why they were putting a bed there. When we all used to sleep in one place, my husband used to pinch me in order to call me. I complained to my father-in-law about it and he said he'd beat my husband! I didn't have a clue! These days, even little girls are very knowing.

"My mother-in-law is very *sīdhī* [innocent]!" laughed Gulshan. And at that very moment, Gulshan caught sight of her father-in-law coming into the courtyard. She hastily covered her face with her shawl.

"But why are you doing that?" Swaleha asked her. "Hasn't he been able to see your face since you were a little child?"

"Yes, of course. I didn't want to keep *purdah* from him. I said so when I arrived here. But all the women of the family said they wouldn't do the *munh dykhāī* [face-showing]. They said I must keep *purdah* from him."

Khurshida Mixes the New Wheat

Khurshida was a live spark, always joking and teasing us and the other women in her compound with mischievous twinkles in her eyes. One day in spring 1991, however, we found her crying her eyes out. When we asked what had happened, she denied that anything was wrong. Firdausi—her sister-in-law [HyBW] and Khurshid Ahmed's wife—explained what had happened:

Our father-in-law got a stone of new wheat seed from the Co-operative Society to test for them. He planted the seeds in a special plot. Now the grain's been harvested. While it was being cut, it was collected separately from all the rest. My father-in-law wouldn't let it get mixed with even so much as a single stalk of wheat from another field. Before the new wheat was threshed, he had the ground swept to clear away the grain from the other fields. You see, he was going to weigh that grain separately to see how much he had managed to grow and what it was like. It was put into separate sacks as well.

The farming was being done jointly by Maqsood and his two sons, Khalil and Khurshid Ahmed, though the two younger men operated two households for consumption purposes. Their wives, Khurshida and Firdausi, organized the storing, milling, and cooking of the grain separately. But it was dark by the time the grain sacks were brought back to the house, and Khurshida had forgotten that some of the sacks were to be kept apart from the main crop. She opened the sacks and divided all the wheat crop into two portions. When Khalil found out what had happened, he began shouting and swearing at Khurshida. Firdausi continued the tale:

This morning he was still furious. He went off to the fields with his goad and now he's beating his oxen. He's taking his anger out on them. Khurshida has just come back from taking his food out to the fields for him, and even now he's angry. "You've finished off in five minutes several days of our hard work!" he shouted at her. Khurshida's even more afraid of our father-in-law's anger. She's afraid he'll swear at her as well. But I think, let him swear at her! Khurshida should remain silent. If he doesn't swear at Khurshida, he'll probably slander her parents! But he can't beat us. If he ever gets angry with me, I just stay silent.

Trying to cheer Khurshida, Firdausi told of how she had once annoyed their father-in-law, but she had not had "enough spirit" to answer back when he shouted at her. Their father-in-law kept taunting her by repeating, "You don't have enough spirit to answer! You don't have enough spirit to answer!" After a while, when she had still said nothing, he went away, muttering the same words. Firdausi told Khurshida it was useless to cry so much. In any case, Firdausi said, her own husband had admitted they could buy more seed and that nothing could be done now that this year's grain had been mixed. But Khurshida was inconsolable. "I've never before done anything as wrong as this," she moaned.

That evening, according to Firdausi, Khurshida took her children and hid in another house in the compound. Firdausi was alone when their father-in-law arrived home. He swore roundly for a while, but Firdausi said nothing in response. He went out to the animal byre and shouted some more. But after that, he said nothing:

> It was Khurshida's fault, for she knew about the seeds. Our husbands brought the sacks to the house, and she should have asked them. But her husband is also to blame. He should have told her which sacks were which. Some wheat was put on one side. Khurshida thought it was the special wheat, and she left it alone. Then she ended up mixing the seeds. The fault was on both sides. But I told Khurshida not to cry. I told her to remain silent. One silence can defeat a hundred angry words.

Politics, Both Electoral and Domestic

Shortly before the general election in May 1991, Radha and Patricia went to visit Kamla. All three older women in the compound—Kamla's mother-in-law and both aunts-in-law [HFyBW]—were working in the fields. We were soon joined by Hiran and Gita, the wives of two of Krishnu's paternal cousins. They were all about thirty years old, and they were relaxed and lively without their mothers-in-law hovering in the background. We began discussing the political situation. Which party, we asked, would the people in their compound be voting for? A babble of voices erupted:

"There's still lots of time to decide!"

"Nobody's thought about it yet."

"We'll have to vote how our husbands tell us to."

"And they'll do that on election day itself!"

"But doesn't your opinion carry any weight with the men?" Patricia asked.

"There's a great difference between towns and villages," said Hiran. "In the town, men listen to what women say. In villages, only the men's opinions carry weight."

"A village woman can give her vote only to the person her husband tells her to vote for," explained Kamla.

"If a woman says she'll vote for someone else," Gita interjected, "her husband will say, 'What, do you know some man from that party? Then go off and live with him!'"

"It's like this in a village," Kamla continued. "Even if a man does wrong, the women in the village can't stop him. Whatever a man wants to do, that's allowed."

There was more to it than that, as Hiran explained:

But it isn't just the men! Village women can't put on makeup. If they do, it's not so much a question of what the men think—the women gossip among themselves, saying, "Look at her, see how much she's decorating herself." That's why you have to live like the other people around you. If any woman with a daughter-in-law in the house becomes a grandmother and wears nice clothes and puts on makeup, it's considered bad. The other women say, "Her daughter-in-law has come, and there are also grandchildren. But she's still thinking herself in the prime of her youth!" And about the woman whose children have reached puberty, women will say, "Look, her sons and daughters have become mature and just see how she's wearing plenty of makeup!" That's why you have to live simply in the village. If a woman so much as talks to her husband's younger brother, other women immediately start saying she's living in his house. In the city, there's nothing like that. In town, women generally wear makeup all the time whether they're old or young. In a village, too, there's more work. And because of that village women don't have time for such things.

Sudesh's Daughter Is Remarried

Sudesh was a Sahni woman in her forties who lived in a small adobe house behind the dispensary, where we lived. The family was poor and it had been a struggle to provide enough for the daughters' dowries. Shortly after we returned to Bijnor in 1990, Sudesh told us about the troubles she had been having over her daughter's marriage. Sudesh's son-in-law used to beat her daughter frequently. If she visited a neighbor's house, he would accuse her of having sexual relations with the men of the house, and he would insist that she was "spoilt":

> And when she was pregnant, he even sat on her chest and began throttling her. At that point I brought her back here to Dharmnagri. I didn't send her back to her in-laws for seven months. Then again, her husband began beating her, and again I didn't send her back for seven months. My son-in-law isn't in his right mind, nor is his father. Do you know, the father-in-law wants to keep my daughter in his own house? He tried to do so several times. But she wouldn't agree. The next time my daughter was beaten, she ran away. At that very time, my husband's cousin was going to Bijnor and she met my daughter on the way. My daughter explained everything, and my husband's cousin brought her back here. Since then, I've never sent my daughter back to her in-laws.

Often, such matters end at that point, but not in this case. Sudesh was fearful because her daughter's in-laws had tried to pay Rs 500 to some men to surround Sudesh's family and keep them captive until they let their daughter return to her husband. The men had apparently refused on the grounds that there were too many people with guns in Dharmnagri. Then the aggrieved in-laws came to complain to the big landowner in Dharmnagri, alleging that Sudesh had deceitfully called her daughter home and was wrongfully refusing to send her back to them. The landowner summoned Sudesh and her daughter and talked to each of them separately.

> He told my girl's in-laws that they'd caused a daughter of his village a lot of grief. He wouldn't let them take her away. Then my daughter's mother-in-law came and so did my son-in-law's sister. They tried flattering us to persuade us to send my girl back. But I absolutely refused. I said I wouldn't send her back ever again. My daughter's mother-in-law took away all the baby's clothes and all my daughter's clothes too, except for the *dhotī* she was wearing. When my daughter came home, we paid 1,000 rupees to have a police report made. Now we're safe from those people and they can't do anything to harm us. We didn't get a single item back from my daughter's dowry. If we'd asked for anything, those people would have demanded that we return everything they'd given her. So we said nothing. And then, a year after that, we got my daughter married again. The wife of my oldest son-in-law's cousin [his MBSW] drowned, and there were no children. Now my daughter's with him. He cares for her very well. And he's very fond of her little daughter too.

Some Sheikh Women Discuss Marital Violence

Our research assistant Swaleha was unmarried. Over the years, several offers of marriage had come for her, but she had simply refused. Her parents and brother had eventually accepted that she could earn her own keep. This so perplexed women in Jhakri that Swaleha was repeatedly asked when she would be married. One time in late spring 1982, Swaleha was adamant: "Men think of their wives as slaves. I don't want to make a slave of myself."

Patricia held her breath. Surely research was not supposed to be quite so combative? There was a brief, stunned silence followed by a torrent of comments. The consensus was that marriage was no great thing—even that marriage was a calamity. Swaleha was right, they said, but she had been able to avoid marriage because she was educated. Would they have chosen to marry if they were educated enough to find employment? Without education and income, they answered, village women had no such choice.

"Men don't just think of their wives as slaves, they beat them too," added Nusrat, who had been married just a few weeks earlier to a young man in nearby Begawala.

"All the men here beat their wives," intervened her cousin Hanifa, whose marriage within Jhakri had been in the same week as Nusrat's.

"With hunks of wood," added Nusrat.

"Has your husband beaten you, then?" asked Patricia.

"Nusrat's had that experience. That's why she's telling you," said her aunt Khushnuda, a woman in her forties.

"Yes," agreed Nusrat. "And one day my husband's uncle took some wood off the cart and began beating his wife!"

Patricia asked if other people tried to restrain a man who was beating his wife.

"Who is there left to reason with him, since the old men also beat their wives!" interjected another aunt, Jamila.

"But my husband has never beaten me!" exclaimed Khushnuda. "He sometimes swears at me though." Hanifa queried her aunt. She had seen her uncle hitting her.

"But I was under the influence of evil spirits and I don't know exactly what happened," Khushnuda explained. "And there was another time, when my oldest girl was little and I hit her. When my husband heard what I was doing, he picked up a piece of sugarcane and flung it at me. But it got caught in the thatch and it didn't hit me. Since that time, he's never hit me. Men are not all the same."

"But if a man doesn't beat his wife, other women start taunting him," added Nusrat. "They'll say that he's let his wife sit on his head. And about the wife, they'll say that she's seated herself high up, on her husband's head!"

Khushnuda went on. "There's a man in our compound who beats his wife. No one tries to stop him, for if they do, he beats her more. If women try to protect her, he tells them they're simply ensuring that the beating is even more severe. If no one tries to save her, he just hits her two or three times. Then he goes and sits down silently." Nodding in the direction of her two nieces, Nusrat and Hanifa, she commented, "He beat his wife one time when these two were little, and they both said they'd never get married if their husbands were going to beat them!"

"But my father never beats my mother," insisted Hanifa. "If he even swears at her, she begins to cry. And then we children start crying too. And we refuse to eat our food."

Seema's Punishment

One day in 1982 when Patricia was visiting Maya with our assistant Radha, we could hear a woman sobbing and moaning loudly in the abutting house. It was Seema, a woman from another Sahni middle-peasant family. She had been married for only a couple of years. Apparently, her husband, Siddarth, often beat her. Maya, however, was simply carrying on with her work, scouring the dishes at the handpump. "I don't know what it's about. It's just some trouble between husband and wife. I get beaten sometimes, too. All men here are the same. They all beat their wives. He beats me over any little matter, like if I hit the children, then he in turn beats me."

Maya's younger sister-in-law [HyBW] said that she too got beaten, perhaps three or four times a year. For instance, if she failed to cook any vegetables, her husband would overturn the dish of cooked rice and begin to beat her. As we were talking this over, Seema's own sister-in-law came into the courtyard. She reported that this episode had begun because Seema had been swearing at Siddarth and was calling him *tū* [the least respectful form of "you"] and not *tum*. Siddarth had become so angry that he had repeatedly beaten Seema across the shoulders with a large wooden spoon.

I didn't try to stop him because Seema and I aren't speaking at present. Our parents-in-law tried to stop him, but he wouldn't listen. He just carried on beating her all the more. She'll spend the rest of the day crying. Then she'll become silent of her own accord. I wouldn't try to quiet her. If I tried to, she'd start fighting with me as well. It's a daily matter. Anyway, who'll rescue her from her husband? If she keeps saying upside-down things to him, he's bound to beat her. And what can we do about that?

Tahira Praises Her Husband

In 1991, we met a Sheikh woman in Qaziwala who had first been
married to Taslim in Jhakri. She had been very young when she was
married, and she had gone to Jhakri just a few times. But after a while,
she refused to return because Taslim beat her a lot. She remained in her
parents' home for three or four years before being married to a man in
Qaziwala. Meanwhile, in about 1980, Taslim himself remarried. Taslim
had a bad stammer and his father had sold off practically all their land,
so in combination with his failed first marriage, Taslim could not find a
second wife locally.

Taslim's second wife, Tahira, was born in eastern Uttar Pradesh, and
had been married to her older sister's brother-in-law [her ZHyB]. Tahira
had had a daughter who died, and Tahira's husband had accused her
sister of killing his daughter: "That man was no good. He told lots of
lies and caused me a lot of trouble over that child's death. That man
wasn't honorable. He threw me out. But I put my thumbprint on the
divorce papers."

Taslim's sister had been married nearby, and she suggested that
Tahira be married to Taslim. Thus, Tahira was brought to Jhakri by
Taslim's sister's husband, and she and Taslim were married.

> No one has ever been to visit me from my parents' place. Nor have I ever
> gone to see them. In effect Jhakri is now both my mother's place and my
> in-laws' place.[5] When my husband beats me, I feel very homesick and I
> think about my brothers and sisters. But my husband never complains
> that I brought no dowry or other things with me. He doesn't smoke and
> he never goes to see films. Just occasionally he complains that he never
> gets to spend any money on himself. He gives everything he earns as a
> laborer to me, but we can't meet all our expenses even then.

Because of family illnesses, everything Taslim earned was spent.
They were still living in an adobe house and were finding it hard to save
even the money that would be needed to replace the thatch. But at least
Taslim was a man prepared to spend money when his wife and children
were ill:

> Even if he's angry, he still pays attention to me when I'm sick. At the
> beginning of this winter, I had a septic lump in my belly. It was so painful
> that I couldn't stand up straight but had to walk bent over. He took me to
> a doctor who said it was either a septic lump or cancer and that I needed
> an operation. I was also examined by one of the Qaziwala *dāīs* who said
> there was nothing wrong with my womb, it was just something in my
> belly. Then I was seen by another doctor in Bijnor, who said he'd give me

treatment. He said he couldn't tell if I'd recover. I'd need two months of treatment before he'd know. For one week, he gave me three injections daily, and there were also pills and a syrup. It was costing 100 rupees each day. Then after a week, the medicines were costing 60 to 70 rupees a day. It went on like that for two months. Then the lump burst. I'm still taking medicines. I've been having treatment for three months. We're very troubled by this treatment. There have also been all the problems with my older girl born here in Jhakri. She started having fits when she was about one and a half. We had a lot of treatment for her, but she didn't improve. Then I took her to a *maulvī*. I gave him 300 rupees, but the girl still didn't get better. Then I showed her to another doctor and to another *maulvī*, and that cost another 400 rupees. After that, I visited my husband's sister, who arranged for another *maulvī* to see the girl. That *maulvī* gave her an amulet to wear. That's about three years ago, and she hasn't had a fit since then. She keeps on getting fevers, but she gets better without medicines. And the second girl is always getting ill, and we're constantly having to get medicines for her.

How Swati's Efforts Were Perceived

In 1985, Patricia and Radha talked to several women in Dharmnagri and Jhakri about how their work had changed over the years. Among these was Swati, a Jat woman in Dharmnagri who was in her early forties at the time. She had been married to Brijpal in about 1954 and the cohabitation had taken place a couple of years later. When she first began living regularly in her in-laws' house, she and Brijpal were in a joint household with his older brother and his wife and children. Together, the brothers operated a farm of some twelve acres. At that time, she did no work outside the house, and her duties basically consisted of cooking, cleaning dishes, and keeping the house in order.

My husband and his brother used to do the work in the fields with the help of two or three farm servants. One of the servants used to bring the fodder back home, and another used to chop it by machine. And in those days, the dung cakes were made for me by a Bhangan [Harijan woman]. She used to come to the house, lift up all the dung, and deal with it. In the monsoon, she tipped it into the midden. At other times she made dung cakes. But in those days, there was more wood fuel available, so we didn't need as many dung cakes as we do now. We used them only for simmering the milk and in our *huqqās* [tobacco pipe smoked through water]. So one dung-cake stack would be enough. Now we need at least two or three stacks because we use just a couple of sticks as kindling in the hearth and all the cooking is done with dung cakes. What's more, these days the Bhangans and Chamars [Harijans] have been empowered and they won't make dung cakes for other people. So now I do all the dungwork myself, throwing it in the midden or making dung cakes. Once my daughters got big enough, I made them do the cooking and other housework, like spreading dung paste on the floor and whitewashing the walls, and then I did all the animal work myself.

We asked further about the work for the animals. Who did the milking and who brought the fodder for them?

The fodder is organized by the men. My husband used to have a servant to help. My son helps now. Animals used to be grazed more, and we had a servant who did that work for us. But now there's less fodder available in the scrubland, so we don't put the animals out to graze. Milk animals were never sent out, though, as they wouldn't get good stuff to eat, and then where would their milk have come from? That's why they're given good food at home, so that they can give more milk. We have some ten animals. I've done all the milking since the very beginning. It takes about fifteen or twenty minutes to milk a cow, but only about ten for a buffalo. Cows' udders are harder and my hands always ache after I've milked a cow. These days, I sell some milk to a man from Bijnor who comes twice daily to collect it. He pays us every week, and whoever is in the house takes the money. I also set milk to warm to make clarified butter for household use. When the cold weather comes, I'm going to sell the milk from one buffalo and make clarified butter from the milk of the other one. There's more advantage from selling clarified butter than milk. It sells for twenty-four rupees a pound.

Did she ever do any work in the fields?

I never went to the fields in the old days. I still don't, though there's just this difference, that I do go at harvest times. I collect any grain that's been left on the ground, and I check that the laborers are doing the work properly. They won't unless you keep an eye on them. The work processing the crops—winnowing and drying the grain for storage—is much greater nowadays, as there are more crops than there used to be. And so I also have to make a larger grain store. The grain mill was already in Dharmnagri when I was married, so I've never had to mill the wheat at home regularly. Once, though, there was no electricity for several days and I had to make the flour. It was so exhausting that I was ill for six months afterward! Then, we still grow a little cotton on our own land. It's not enough for the whole household to use, so I just card it at home and use it for making the bed quilts and mattresses. And I also spin the old cotton into coarse thread and then make it into a thick cloth covering to go between the mattress and the interwoven strings on a bed. I can earn twenty-five to thirty rupees for each one I make. And these days I do sewing work at home. I sew for myself and the children. I also sew things for other people in the village if I have time. I charge three or four rupees for making a cotton shirt, and four rupees for synthetic material. I take ten rupees for making a man's shirt and cotton trousers. The sewing machine wasn't part of my dowry. I bought it secondhand after the children were born because my husband said I'd be able to make money from sewing clothes. I could make quite a lot of money if I had more spare time from the housework. Once my son is married, I'll be able to spend more time on the sewing. I keep all the money—but it all gets spent on household items. My husband even asks me for money for his cigarettes and matches! And even with all that work, men still don't understand that women do any work. On the contrary, they say, "You just remain inside the house in the shade. What do you know about the sun's glare in the fields? It's men alone who do fieldwork in the water and in the sun. What work do women have? Just cooking some bread and scouring the dishes!"

And then she dragged her millstone into the center of the floor and began grinding some mustard seeds. Her buffalo had given birth a week earlier, she explained, but it had not bled completely afterward. The mustard would be cooked together with unrefined sugar—both considered "heating" in their effects—and then fed to the buffalo so that it would be properly cleansed.[6]

Ghazala and the Household Purse

Ghazala had no income of her own apart from presents from her parents. Even some of those remained with her mother-in-law, since Ghazala was still living in a joint household with her. And when we asked Ghazala about her *mahr*, she was sceptical about its value to her: "I don't know what it was. I'll have to ask him [her husband]. Then I'll be able to tell you. I just can't remember. But he didn't make me forgo it, nor did I ever ask him for it. Anyway, what would happen if I did so? The money would still be his alone. And what expenses do I have that I should claim the money?"

Her husband, Ghulam, was the second son of one of the wealthiest Sheikh farmers in Jhakri. Ghulam and Ghazala had been married for about twelve years and were still living in a joint household with Ghulam's parents, along with Ghulam's two younger married brothers and their wives and children and Ghulam's two remaining unmarried siblings. All Ghazala's living expenses were met by Ghulam and his mother. Ghazala felt she had little need for cash:

Whatever I need, he [Ghulam] either fetches or gives me the money to buy it. I don't have any income of my own. But he's rented some land separately from the rest of the family, and our personal expenses are met from our income from that. His younger brother's wife sells milk from their buffalo to meet little expenses. But our mother-in-law provides most things, since we're still living jointly with her. If we or the children are sick, my mother-in-law immediately gives money for treatment. And what other expenses do we have? We don't wash our faces in soap! We don't use creams or talcum powder!

Ghazala had never attended school and could not do the household accounts, so she would keep no more than ten or twenty rupees with her. Basically, money matters were all handled by Ghulam, who had a masters degree in commerce and was the most educated man in Jhakri. If she needed new clothes for herself or the children, she would simply tell him:

We usually get new clothes made once a year, for the Eid festival—though we had new things made when my brother was married recently. At that time, too, I spent 150 rupees on cloth for my new sister-in-law [BW]. I had to borrow the money. When my husband came back home in the evening, I told him I'd bought the cloth and needed to repay the money. Straightaway he gave me the money. He told me the cloth I'd bought was very good and there was no need to ask him in advance. I should just buy good things.

A Wedding Song

I won't leave in the heat of the day, put the palanquin away!
The first summons came from my father-in-law,
But I won't go with an old man!
I won't leave in the heat of the day, put the palanquin away!

The second summons came from my husband's older brother,
But I won't go with an elder!
I won't leave in the heat of the day, put the palanquin away!

The third summons came from my husband's sister's husband,
But I won't go with an outsider!
I won't leave in the heat of the day, put the palanquin away!

The fourth summons came from my husband's younger brother,
But I won't go with a child!
I won't leave in the heat of the day, put the palanquin away!

The fifth summons came from the king [husband],
And I'll go just now!
I'll even go without my shoes on! Bring the palanquin right here!
I won't leave in the heat of the day, put the palanquin away![7]

Notes

1. Bijnor rural women's economic dependence is discussed further in Jeffery, Jeffery, and Lyon (1989), chapter 3.

2. This was also the case in the other villages where we have worked, both in Bijnor and in Hazrat Nizamuddin in Delhi. For the latter, see Jeffery (1979:57-59).

3. See Chapter 9 for more on relationships between women.

4. Both songs in this chapter are *bannī* sung at the bride's home shortly before her departure. The first one focuses on the bride's unhappiness at leaving her parents' home.

5. Tahira, like other women cut off from their natal kin, often used this form of expression as an ironic comment on her isolation.

6. As with women who give birth, the blood that cattle lose when calving is considered polluting. The blood must flow properly to ensure that the animal is not harmed. For more on the postpartum period for women, see Jeffery, Jeffery, and Lyon (1989), chapter 7.

7. This *bannī* is in an ironic tenor: When the bridegroom summons the bride, she is in such haste that she has no time to put her shoes on. But such unseemliness would be very unlikely in a real bride.

8

I've Become Shameless Because of the Children

Dilshad was the only surviving son of a rich-peasant Sheikh in Jhakri. Two brothers had died in infancy; several sisters had survived. Of Dilshad's two elder sisters, the older died in childbirth in the mid-1960s. The second, Gulistan, was married to her sister's widower. Dilshad's three younger sisters were all married after Dilshad. Dilshad's land would remain intact, but the entitlements of his four sisters might strain his resources. Indeed, this was a central issue in the troubled relationship of Dilshad and his wife, Dilruba. If Dilshad felt he was giving his sisters their due, Dilruba felt she was fighting a rearguard action against in-laws intent on depriving her children of their inheritance. That Dilruba voiced her resentments did not aid her cause, however. Indeed, her married life was peppered with acrimonious squabbling and marital violence—and Dilshad divorced her in spring 1991.

In November 1990, the first major assault was made on the Babri mosque in Ayodhya.[1] Unlike several neighboring districts, Bijnor had no history of communal troubles, yet tensions between Muslims and Hindus erupted in Bijnor and its rural hinterland.[2] The Ayodhya affair had been brewing for some years, part of a complex choreography of events that had come to a head in the mid-1980s, when the claim of a divorced Muslim woman, Shah Bano, for maintenance from her ex-husband was upheld in the Delhi Supreme Court.[3] This event marked the beginning of a campaign by those Muslims who saw maintenance as un-Islamic and the judgment by Hindu judges as Islam under threat. Their campaign culminated in the Muslim Women (Protection of Rights on Divorce) Act 1986, which explicitly prevented divorced Muslim women from appealing for maintenance under the Criminal Procedure Code. Many liberal Muslims and feminists opposed this legislation, essentially because it deprived Muslim women of a right that women of all other religious communities in India still possessed. Organizations associated with the Hindu Right opposed the legislation on different grounds, arguing that the government was appeasing Muslims in order to maintain their electoral support. In 1990-1991, this line was still being strenuously and articulately argued by many Hindus in Bijnor. And the view that Muslims had been allowed to evade the law of the land was regarded as justification for the lawbreaking of those who marched on Ayodhya.

For people in Jhakri, the Ayodhya affair had a drastic impact on the tone of life in the area for many months. By contrast, though, the Shah Bano controversy had affected neither the terms under which married Muslim women lived nor their experiences of marital breakdown. As with Hindu women in Bijnor, marital breakdown usually meant simply a return to the parents' home without any formal divorce, attempts by relatives on both sides to mend the rift, and remarriage elsewhere if these failed. Dilruba's case was unusual partly because she was formally divorced—but also because of how she returned to Jhakri.

* * * * * *

One day in mid-1982, Patricia and our assistant Swaleha were chatting with several Sheikh women and girls in a courtyard in Jhakri. Zahida asked Swaleha when she would be married.

"What would I do if I'd been married?" asked Swaleha.

"Marriage is essential. Everyone gets married," Zahida insisted.

"But I have an aunt who's a teacher and says that she's bringing in her own salary. Why should I marry and make myself into a slave? I've another aunt who owns land. She has enough money to live on too."

"What will you do, Swaleha?"

"I'll get a job."

Zahida's married sister, Mehsar, was visiting just then. "But even so," Mehsar said, "you should get married."

"But I don't want slavery!"

"Is it because you don't like the idea of your husband hitting and beating you?" asked Mehsar.

"In my family, no one thinks it's good to hit other people. If anyone even speaks loudly to another, people ask why and think badly of him."

"All the women in Jhakri get beaten quite a lot," asserted Mehsar.

"Does your husband beat you, then, Mehsar?" asked Patricia.

Mehsar's younger brother was standing nearby, listening. "It's not that she hasn't been beaten," he said. "She's been beaten once or twice. Jhakri men take a lot of pleasure in beating their wives."

About five years previously, when she was about seventeen, Mehsar had been married to a man from a rich-peasant household on the far side of Jhakri from her parents' home. At her husband's house, one of her near neighbors was Dilruba. According to Mehsar, there was often trouble between Dilruba and her husband, Dilshad:

Marital Discord in Jhakri

Dilruba gets beaten a lot. She's very sharp. Once her husband beat her, and she ran inside their room and shut the door. She began shouting at him from inside. He told her to open the door but she refused, and she just carried on wagging her tongue at him. She was threatening to strangle his son. He even tried to break the door down with an axe because she wouldn't keep quiet. Then his mother began to restrain him. His mother asked him what was the benefit of breaking down the door, and he said that he wanted to beat his wife. To that, his mother asked who'd repair the door and what would happen if his wife were to die at his hands. Only then did he become silent. Men beat their wives over little matters.

Even then, Dilruba and Dilshad's marriage was known throughout Jhakri to be a stormy one. And little had changed when we returned in 1990. The marriage was still tempestuous, still the focus for gossip. Many years ago, according to Khurshid Ahmed, his brother, Khalil, had almost been married to Dilruba. The matter had been discussed and nearly settled. But Khalil's mother had been from the same village as Dilruba, and her relatives warned them off the match: "It was very fortunate that we heard she had a reputation for being hot tempered before my brother was married to her. Our lives would have been wretched with her living here. Dilshad's also very sharp tongued. The two of them are fighting all the time. Thanks to Allah, we escaped from that!"

*   *   *   *   *   *

On the face of it, though, the match between Dilruba and Dilshad had been a good one. Dilruba was the older of two surviving siblings. She was married in 1973, when she was about sixteen years old. Dilruba's father owned about five acres of land. Dilshad was the only son of a rich peasant, in line to inherit all the eight acres owned by his father. Many women would have considered themselves fortunate to have been married into such a house.

Indeed, such was the work on the land that Dilshad and his father could not manage to cultivate the farm on their own. For some years before Dilshad's marriage, while he was still a young boy, Dilshad and his father had come to rely heavily on the efforts of Dilshad's oldest sister's husband. This man was from a village on the outskirts of Bijnor, where he owned some three acres. Since moving to Jhakri to help his in-laws with the farmwork, his land had been sharecropped for him by relatives. When his wife died in childbirth, leaving a small daughter, he remained in Jhakri. He subsequently married Gulistan, Dilshad's second sister, saying that his daughter would blossom only with her mother's sister as a stepmother.

When Dilshad married Dilruba, three other younger sisters were still unmarried. They would lend a hand around the house and even in the fields when the workload demanded. Indeed, they also used to do a lot of the jobs that many other young married women would have had to do single-handed. About five years after Dilshad's marriage, the oldest of these sisters was married into Qaziwala, and the next one followed her into the same household some three years later. By this time, Dilruba had had four children, one of whom had died. With small children constantly around her, Dilruba said, she could get no peace to do her work. What was more, Dilshad's mother had poor eyesight and was incapable of doing a lot of tasks. But for several years after their marriages, even after Dilruba had separated her cooking hearth from Dilshad's parents, Dilshad's two sisters married in Qaziwala continued to spend a lot of time in Jhakri, helping Dilruba and their mother. Dilruba explained: "They're married to two brothers and they're both still joint with their mother-in-law. That's why they can come so often. If they were separate from her, they wouldn't be able to stay for such long periods. What happens is this. When one goes back to Qaziwala, I call the other one here. They do all the work when they come. Whatever happens, one of them stays here. We always send them back to Qaziwala with cloth and foodstuffs."

Consequently, for much of the time, Dilruba's work consisted of just cooking, cleaning, and childcare. She rarely had to collect the cattle dung and make dung cakes, for instance, because Dilshad's sisters usually did it all. Generally, they would also take food out to the fields for the men and collect fodder for the stalled animals. Sometimes, too, they might do Dilruba's work when she was visiting her parents. When Dilruba was pregnant, they would certainly be around for a lengthy period before the delivery. After each of her first five deliveries, Dilruba had several weeks when she just had to care for the new baby and wash its clothes. In that respect, she was one of the most favorably placed women in Jhakri.

Dilruba, however, had gained a reputation among her in-laws and their neighbors for ingratitude and laziness. Once when we were talking to Dilruba about her work, a neighbor caustically intervened: "You're asking Dilruba all about her work. But I'll tell you about it properly. Her greatest work is to fight five times a day. She has no other work. She just argues with her mother-in-law and her husband's sisters all the time. There's no one here who gets so much rest. She gets all her work done for her by Dilshad's sisters. And then she fights with them!" And when we asked Dilruba why she had separated her cooking hearth from Dilshad's parents, one of Dilshad's sisters butted in to comment: "She became separate after fighting with my parents. She separated because she sometimes had to do the cooking while she was living jointly!"

Then, a few minutes later, when we were asking about the gifts Dilruba had presented to Dilshad's sisters after she gave birth, Dilruba's account was again cut short by Dilshad's sister. Dilruba was explaining that three of Dilshad's sisters were still unmarried when she had her first child and that she had given them each suit lengths of cloth. "And she even took those back after an argument," muttered Dilshad's sister.

Nevertheless, because Dilshad's two sisters were in a household with their mother-in-law and two other daughters-in-law, the labor of one or the other of them could be spared fairly easily, if somewhat grudgingly. As the younger of the two sisters explained:

No, my husband doesn't send me to Jhakri. This time, I came to Jhakri only after a great deal of pressure was put on him to let me come. I'd been back in Qaziwala for just three months. He didn't want to send me at all. And now—don't tell anyone—I haven't had a period for one and a half months. That has never happened to me before. Usually I have a period after twenty-five days. I have a feeling that I'm pregnant. Now I can come often to Jhakri, but once I have a child, I won't be able to come so easily.

*   *   *   *   *   *

Indeed, both sisters gradually became more and more tied to Qaziwala by their own children. By the mid-1980s, they were making only infrequent visits to Jhakri. Dilshad's youngest sister was married into nearby Burhanuddinpur in 1988. When we returned in 1990, Dilruba had given birth for the ninth time just a couple of weeks before. She had been doing all the housework and the dungwork from the time the baby was three days old, a marked change from her earlier experiences.

By this stage, Dilshad's parents had both become very frail. His father could no longer work the land, and his mother was now totally blind. Even with the help of his two oldest sons, Dilshad was finding it hard to cope. Dilshad's second sister, Gulistan, was still in Jhakri, though. Her husband had taken over some of Dilshad's land on a sharecropping basis, and he was also employed as a laborer on the land that remained with Dilshad. On occasion, too, Dilshad had to employ other men in Jhakri. Dilruba herself had perforce taken on more and more of the animal work. But she refused to cook for her parents-in-law.

For the cooking, they relied on their daughters, sometimes the ones married in Qaziwala and Burhanuddinpur but generally on Gulistan who lived next door in Jhakri itself.

It was with Gulistan that Dilruba had had the most acrimonious relationship for many years. The two women had next to nothing to do with one another. Gulistan, for instance, never helped Dilruba after childbirth, although she lived in an adjoining house and the husband's sister is one of the most appropriate helpers for a woman who has just delivered. Contacts between the two women were often acerbic. One time, Gulistan said she would mix the broken straw and mud together if Dilruba would make her a new cooking hearth with it. As quick as a flash, Dilruba retorted, "I'll get my daughter married if you provide the dowry!"

Over the years, Dilruba had repeatedly voiced her suspicions about Gulistan. She was convinced that Gulistan was living in Jhakri in the hope that she and her husband would gain control over Dilshad's land, land that Dilruba felt entitled to regard as her own security for the future: "Gulistan lives in Jhakri all the time, and his [Dilshad's] parents love her best of all. She wants to get everything from his parents."

Dilruba widely proclaimed this allegation. It was equally widely discounted. Qudsia, for instance, could see no sense in this view of Dilshad's sister: "Gulistan isn't living in Jhakri to get the land. And her parents didn't call her here. What sort of a man would Gulistan's husband be to try to insist that his wife gets a share of the inheritance? Gulistan has a brother, Dilshad. He's not going to give his land to anyone else!"

But Dilruba felt that Gulistan and her sisters had already been benefiting constantly. For instance, Gulistan was living in a solid kiln-brick house when we first began visiting Jhakri in 1982, but Dilruba's house was still a thatched single room of sun-baked bricks in 1990. Dilruba was angry:

> One of his [Dilshad's] sisters was just married a short while back. There are four sisters and he's an only son. There's only one earner but there are plenty of expenses. That's why we haven't been able to build a kiln-brick house. And you know how a man has to provide *bhāt* when his sister's child gets married? Well, there was the daughter of his sister who died— the girl whose father married Gulistan and lives here in Jhakri. A few years ago, we had to spend quite a lot on the *bhāt* for that girl's marriage. Then there are plenty of expenses on the children. Three of our sons still have to be circumcised. We'll do the two older ones together, but the baby will remain to be done. Their circumcisions will cost a lot because we'll have to give a feast. That's why we can't do everything all at once.

One of the crucial points for Dilruba was that she had no control over the resources coming into the household, and no control over how they were spent.

> When the harvest comes in, my parents-in-law divide the grain into two portions. They give me half. They keep the other half for themselves so that they can give grain to their daughters. All the money from the sugarcane is under their control. I don't buy anything myself. My husband gets clothes made for me when he wants to. I still have the utensils and jewelry that my parents gave in my dowry. I don't have any of the jewelry that my in-laws presented to me, though. My father-in-law pawned it, but he failed to keep up the payments; so it all remained at the moneylender's house. The only things I got to wear were the clothes my in-laws had made for me. My parents-in-law keep all the money in their hands. If I need money for any reason and I say anything angrily about it, my in-laws accuse me of speaking out of turn and swearing at them.

* * * * * *

There had been many occasions when Dilruba felt she had not obtained the necessary cash for herself and her children. She had her children in rapid succession—in all but one instance, about two years apart. With each pregnancy, she had to wean her previous child. She felt this was too soon to be weaning her toddlers, but she could not afford to buy powdered milk for them. "Each new child arrived before the previous one had become big. That's why all my children are small and weak," she said. During one of her pregnancies, Dilruba had severe headaches and pains in her body, but she had no treatment. "I don't have any money. It's my husband who has the money. And I didn't say anything to him." After another pregnancy, Dilruba had trouble breast-feeding the baby, since one breast had become septic. The baby became seriously emaciated and she herself had no treatment. In 1985, when Dilruba had just four living children, she was saying she wanted no more: "When I became pregnant last time I wasn't at all happy. But what could I do? To have an abortion is a sin. It's also dangerous. I don't want more children. Bringing up the children falls on me, not my husband. Now my own health is not improving. The more children, the more my health sinks."

Dilshad's perspective on the subject could hardly have been more different. "I'll take as many children as God gives. There can never be too many. I'm on my own here, and there's lots of room. We don't have enough people in the family to do the work. We have lots of land and not enough workers. When the boys grow up, they'll work alongside me. When I'm old, they'll save me from being the only worker like I am now."

By 1990, though, Dilruba had six sons and a daughter. Two other girls had died. She felt that her concerns over their well-being and her own health were not taken seriously by her in-laws: "The go-between in my marriage lives here in Jhakri. And now he too says nothing to back me up. My husband and his family have put him against me. And some of the women say, 'What do you need? Don't you have a couple of pieces of griddle bread to eat?' But in addition to food, other things are needed. You need clothes. If you're ill, you need medicines. There are plenty of other expenses. Who says we don't need anything?'"

*   *   *   *   *   *

Over the years, Dilruba had circumvented these obstacles through her visits to her parents and brother. They lived about four miles from Jhakri. Dilruba used to visit them every ten days or so, sometimes returning the same day, sometimes staying for several days. That in itself had generated a lot of tension with Dilshad:

> She goes there 50-60 times a year. She goes to her parents too often. Her father calls her, and she sometimes goes alone with the smaller children. I should finish this marriage and make another one much farther away. Then my wife wouldn't be able to go so often. It would be too far for her to go alone, and I wouldn't give her the fare anyway. This woman sometimes goes without even asking my permission. I've tried beating her, but it does no good. She just goes anyway, and I get into trouble with her father. He might refuse to let her come back to Jhakri, and then I'd look very bad. I'd never hear the end of it.

For Dilshad, the issue was not simply that Dilruba willfully continued to visit her parents but that she complained about her situation in Jhakri to them:

> If your wife's father is nearby and you fight with your wife, he hears about it straightaway. Even if you just swore at her, they could come immediately and there'd be trouble. If you're married far away that doesn't happen. That's why people arrange marriages more distantly now. There are fewer marriages between relatives too. Those are the marriages that go bad because the wife's relatives interfere. For instance, my son was once in my wife's village and he spread malicious stories about what I'd done. Then someone from my village was informed, and he came and told me I'd done wrong. Things like that wouldn't happen if I were married somewhere else, no matter what I did to my wife.

By the mid-1980s, Dilshad was already aware of the antagonistic relationship between him and Dilruba's family. No longer was he the honored guest when he visited; no longer did he receive the customary gifts of clothing and cash from her parents. "Last time she went, I didn't receive a single paisā. The relationship has become cold now. I don't get much from them anymore."

* * * * * *

Given this stormy history, no one was unduly surprised when in Ramzān 1991, Dilshad and Dilruba fought yet again. But this time, it was much more serious. Dilshad had uttered the divorce formula three times and sent Dilruba back to her parents' home.[4] He was apparently saying that he would never call her back.

But just a few days later, Dilruba returned to Jhakri. What on earth had brought her back? Surely her parents had not refused to keep her at their house? Did they resent having to meet her expenses there?

My parents always give me grain after the harvests and also the things that parents give at festivals like Eid. My brother has a separate hearth, so he and my parents each give me things. For the past two years, though, I've been leaving the things at my mother's house so that I could buy my own necessities there. If I brought everything to Jhakri, it would all be consumed in the house. He [Dilshad] never gives me money. If I ever need anything, I can't ask for any money. Last Eid, for instance, I received five pounds of sugar, twenty-five pounds of unrefined sugar, eleven pounds of rice, and five pounds of flour. I just brought the sugar and left everything else at my mother's house. When he [Dilshad] divorced me and put me out of the house, I went to my mother's home. I sold some unrefined sugar and rice so that I could buy what I needed. Now I'm returning after six days, and my mother and my brother each gave me twenty-five pounds of wheat. I've left it all in my mother's house. What could I do with it if I brought it here?

So why had she come? Had Dilshad summoned her even though he had divorced her? "No, I came back without being called. Now Gulistan is saying that if I were of good breeding I wouldn't have come. She says I've returned shamelessly. Gulistan wants to see me pushed out completely. She wants me to leave. Then everything will be under her control. The parents prefer the daughter. They don't care about laying waste to their son's house."

But Dilshad had sent her away without any of the children, and she had been worried about their welfare: "I've become shameless because of the children. I couldn't live without my children. I came back only because of them. I shouldn't have come. But the baby's still drinking my milk, and the girl's still so young. Could she have managed all the housework and looked after the small children? I've got six sons and a daughter. I don't want their lives to be ruined."

When Dilruba returned to Jhakri, she found that Dilshad had used up all the sugar she had brought from her parents' house. She had kept it aside to make sweet tea for the small children. While she was away, her children told her, Dilshad had made a sweet rice dish for himself. Now she was having to sweeten the children's tea with unrefined sugar, which was very "heating": "My second son is frying with fever, and all I have to give him is tea with unrefined sugar in it. It'll cause him damage. He'll certainly come out in boils because of all the heat. I have to care for all the children. My husband doesn't even understand that he should be getting medicines for them."

She was also scathing about Dilshad's knowledge of Islam. As a child, Dilruba had read the Qur'ān Sharīf at the mosque in her father's village under the guidance of a Hāfiz Qur'ān [a man who could recite the Qur'ān Sharīf by memory] and a couple of religious books in Urdu, which Dilruba said she could no longer remember. She knew how to pray, she said, though generally managed to do so only a couple of times a day. "How can a woman with children find the time to cleanse herself properly for praying?" she asked. But Dilshad did not even know how to pray. Nor did he know that he should no longer be having sexual relations with her: "I've plenty of children. But they don't receive proper consideration. Nor do I. So what would I do with any more? I bought contraceptive pills when I was at my mother's house. By the way, I don't know how I should be taking them. I'm taking the red ones now. Am I doing it right?"

We explained that she should start taking the white ones right after her menstrual period and the red ones at the end of the month. Then Dilruba continued: "You know, my husband is bad. He's uneducated. That's why he doesn't know that there should be no sexual relations after divorce. He has no knowledge of what's prohibited and what's permitted. This man will not stop. That's why I bought the pills. They cost three rupees. But I didn't know how to take them. If there were any injection to stop me having children, I'd have it right now."

If this were not a clear enough indication that Dilruba's presence in Jhakri was fraught with problems, Dilshad's return from the fields while we were talking touched off a conversation peppered with bickering and tension. Formally, Dilshad should have given Dilruba the *mahr* specified in the marriage contract when they were married. At the very least, Dilshad should have given it when he divorced her and sent her away. We asked—sotto voce—how much her *mahr* had been. She said it had been the *mahr Fatimi*—the settlement that the Prophet Mohammed had required for his daughter Fatima's marriage. But Dilshad pricked up his ears:

"No it wasn't! It was 500 rupees," he snapped.

"Well, are you going to give it?" she retorted. And then she turned to us again. "It's written into the marriage certificate that it's the *shar'ia mahr* [marriage settlement sanctioned by Islam]. But he hasn't given it yet, nor have I asked him for it."

They let the matter drop. But a few minutes later we were talking about her hopes for the children. Over the years, the children's schooling had been another contentious issue. Dilruba was keen to see them all educated, but Dilshad did not want to bother: "He just says they'll still get married even if they aren't educated. My oldest boy studied to second class. When he came to the third, he asked his father for the money for fees. He [Dilshad] wouldn't give him anything. That's why the boy stopped studying. Just look at my husband sitting there. You should ask him if I want to get these children educated. But he doesn't."

She inclined her head in Dilshad's direction, joining her hands in supplication to him, and asked him to send the children to school. He looked blankly at her and ignored her plea. She continued:

But you see, it's not a matter of a connection between marriage and education. It's a question of education coming in useful for the children. They'd be able to fast and pray properly. It would also be useful in their lives. They'll have to get the sugarcane receipts and the water-tax bills read for them by someone else. If they'd studied they could do their own work themselves. If there were ever any money in my hands, I'd never stop my children studying. I'd certainly get them educated. You know, I wanted to send my daughter and two of the middle boys to my parents' house so that they could go to school there. But my husband wouldn't even agree to that. All the children in the next compound go to the *madrasā* in Begawala but no one at this side of the village does. The *maulvī* in the Jhakri mosque is blind, so no children are studying here with him. I've forgotten nearly everything I learned to read, so what was the use of that? If I were more educated, at least it would be useful for teaching my children.

The more distant prospects seemed no brighter for Dilruba's children or for her ability to influence events: "Where do I have any control over the children's marriages? Whatever he sets his heart on, he'll do. Since none of these boys will be educated, how would anyone give us their educated daughter? I can't say anything in this regard. Whatever he wishes will happen."

Her parents and brother could continue to ease her position by presenting her with grain and other foodstuffs. But the scale of their giving was modest and quite insufficient to enable her to pay school fees for her children. Her parents were unable to do more, and her brother now had children too: "I tried to scare my husband, saying that I'd insist on getting my rights to maintenance from him. To that, he said the children would all stay with him, and then how could I demand anything from him? What can I do myself? And my parents are not powerful enough to do much. They can't do anything with the courts and lawyers. That would take a lot of money."

When Dilruba's parents were arranging her marriage, she said, they were looking for a boy who was hardworking and who did farming. In Dilshad's case, they saw eight acres of land, and they believed he could feed their daughter properly:

> But my fate was to be broken here. That's why my marriage took place here. My parents didn't know that there was all this in my destiny. Of course, my opinion wasn't asked about the marriage. If I'd known what was in my fate, I'd have refused to marry here. But there's no knowledge of the future. My parents didn't know my destiny. Otherwise, perhaps they wouldn't have married me here. Perhaps they'd have given me some education. But, then, my destiny was here. Even if I were educated, all this would still have come about. Swaleha is right not to have married.

Notes

1. For more details on the Ayodhya issue, see Ramaseshan (1990); Engineer (1991); Gopal (1991); Sarkar (1991); and Basu et al. (1993). The mosque at Ayodhya was destroyed in December 1992.

2. See R. Jeffery and P. Jeffery (1994); and Basu (1994).

3. For more details on the Shah Bano case, see Engineer (1987); Das (1995); Kumar (1993); Mody (1987); Hasan (1989; 1994); Parashar (1992); and Pathak and Rajan (1989).

4. Some Islamic legal theorists argue that a couple are permanently divorced if a man says *talāq* ["I divorce you"] three times without rescinding it.

9

The Daughter-in-Law's Era

In July 1982, Jumni, the older sister-in-law [HeBW] of Kamla in Dharm-nagri, gave birth to a son. Celebrations were held, including the "taking out-side" a few days after the birth, when Jumni would be briefly brought out of her house for the first time after the delivery by a younger brother of her husband, Jagram. And Jagram's younger brother and other relatives (particularly his sister) would each receive honoraria. Jagram's married sister had been called back from her in-laws' village to participate. We always enjoyed her visits to Dharmnagri. She was lively with a quirky sense of humor. And this occasion was no exception. Before the "taking outside," some of Jagram's female relatives were to make a circuit of Dharmnagri, stopping briefly to pray at each of the three satī shrines on the village outskirts.[1] Patricia went along with them. Any piety attached to the prayers was thoroughly undermined by the antics of Jagram's sister. At one shrine, she took on the persona of an aged woman with a quavering voice, beseeching the other women by turns to give her a blind bride for her son. Everyone dissolved in giggles, including the Brahman woman performing the prayers. But there was more to come. With evident planning, Jagram's sister had brought a segment of sugarcane about a foot long. She positioned it horizontally at the top of her thighs and with a lascivious leer began making prancing lunges at the other women present. By this stage, we were all laughing helplessly.

Women in Dharmnagri and Jhakri had often been explicit about the contrasting situations of a daughter and a daughter-in-law, and this episode resoundingly brought the point home. While Jagram's wife was still inside her home, Jagram's sister—on leave from her husband's village—played a high-profile (and sexually suggestive) part in the proceedings. Back in her husband's home, however, Jagram's sister would have to revert to the demure behavior expected of a young married woman. Although the relationship between a mother and daughter could not be one of equality, people would presume it to be loving and warm and would regard the mother's home as a place where a young woman could shed many of the restraints required of her in her husband's village. By contrast, people's stereotypes of a woman's relationships with women in her in-laws' home—her mother-in-law, the wives of her husband's brothers, her husband's sisters—hinted at power and control, competition and disunity. This was where people expected to see women's agency in conflict.[2] *Yet women's experiences were far more complex than these images might suggest.*

The relationship between a woman and her mother-in-law would be central in both their lives—but the differing positions and interests of the two women were liable to generate tensions and difficulties. The son's wife would bring hopes of care and comfort in old age, and the mother-in-law would feel entitled to obedience and respect for her seniority. Sometimes older women were sorely disappointed in their daughters-in-law and accused them of insubordination. Some women attempted to control their daughters-in-law, but others avoided open conflict. And the older woman's desire for respite after a lifetime's work was often coupled with allegations about the younger woman's laziness. For many older women, their situations seemed to parallel the specter of the "daughter-in-law's era" portrayed in the song that follows. From the other side, though, younger women often complained about the power wielded by the mother-in-law, about how much work she insisted they do, about her ever-watchful and critical eye. Some young women might refuse to take orders from their mothers-in-law, but it would not be easy to do so without being punished. The daughter-in-law in the song, so aggressively scorning her mother-in-law's skills, would be hard to imagine unless the older woman was a widow. Just as women talked about the "husband's rule," so did they talk about the "mother-in-law's rule" [sās-ka-rāj]. Among women, indeed, the word "susrī" [derived from "sās," meaning mother-in-law] was used as a term of abuse.

Moreover, tensions between brothers—over work or jointly held resources, over the school fees or wedding expenses of nieces and nephews—could play themselves out in their wives' refusals to help one another or in their mutual taunting. And the grudges of sisters-in-law who felt that their in-laws' jewelry had not been equitably distributed or that one among them was especially favored by their mother-in-law might precipitate antagonisms that threatened the integrity of the household itself. The husband's sisters could add further strains through their insistence on treating visits to their parents as holidays from the rigors of their own in-laws' place or because of their claims on the jewelry belonging to their brothers' wives. Sometimes, the husband himself was his wife's best defense against other women, maybe deciding to separate their cooking hearth from the others in order to protect her from excessive work or constant criticism or to take control over their expenditures and their work.

Yet if the potential for division was endemic to household organization, kin also represented one's best prospects for help and security. And there were, of course, households where women shared their duties amiably and supported one another through illness and childbirth, where the mother-in-law gratefully acknowledged the "shade" provided by a devoted daughter-in-law, and where the younger woman had nothing but praise for her kindly mother-in-law.

A Wedding Song

Gone, gone is your rule, O mother-in-law,
The daughter-in-law's era has arrived!

Mother-in-law, poor thing, scours the pots,
Daughter-in-law goes to see:
"Filthy-dirty are your pots, O mother-in-law!"
Gone, gone is your rule, O mother-in-law,
The daughter-in-law's era has arrived!

Mother-in-law, poor thing, mills the grain,
Daughter-in-law goes to see:
"Coarse-thick is your flour, O mother-in-law!"
Gone, gone is your rule, O mother-in-law,
The daughter-in-law's era has arrived!

Mother-in-law, poor thing, makes bread,
Daughter-in-law goes to see:
"Tough-uncooked is your bread, O mother-in-law!"
Gone, gone is your rule, O mother-in-law,
The daughter-in-law's era has arrived!

Mother-in-law, poor thing, is going to her natal village,
Daughter-in-law goes to see:
"Bow down and press my ankles, O mother-in-law!"
Gone, gone is your rule, O mother-in-law,
The daughter-in-law's era has arrived![3]

Deepa's Views on Mothers-in-Law

Deepa was married into a poor-peasant Sahni household in the mid-1930s. Her husband died before she had any children, and she was then married to his younger brother in about 1941. When her first son was born a few years later, her mother-in-law caused her a great deal of trouble:

On the third day after the birth, my mother-in-law gave me just enough wheat and pulses for a meal. She told me to mill the wheat and make some bread. So I did that. In the evening, she did the same. It continued like that until the fifth day. All this time, my husband was eating food cooked by his mother. On the fifth day, they did the *jasthawn* [naming and cleansing ceremony] and then I was given all sorts of food. In those days people used to cook wheat and barley bread. In the evening, they gave me root artichoke and lady finger. They're both unsuitable for a new mother as they cause flatulence. But I just had to eat whatever was being cooked.

Not only was there little care over the new mother's diet but Deepa's mother-in-law hit the baby's head with a stick, and he was quite badly hurt. Deepa called all the people in the locality to see what her mother-in-law had done. She told them that if the child died, she would report the matter to the police. Deepa's neighbors began shouting at the mother-in-law, calling her all manner of names:

> From that time, I separated my cooking hearth from my mother-in-law. She had troubled my older sister-in-law [HeBW] in the same way. That was why my brother-in-law had made his hearth separate from his mother. My mother-in-law was very bad, and she used to fight with everyone. No matter how much work I did, she'd follow me around and make a fight out of nothing. She'd refuse to feed me. She made me sleep in the open in the courtyard, not in the house. My husband did what his parents told him. He didn't listen to me at all. He'd even beat me if his mother told him to.

As a result of the trouble her mother-in-law caused her, Deepa used to spend six months or even a year at a time in her parents' village. "But these days, a mother-in-law can't say anything to her daughter-in-law. If she did, the daughter-in-law would just walk out of the house. And the husband will take his wife's side and talk only about his own parents' wrongdoings."

By 1985, Deepa had two daughters-in-law of her own. The younger one, who had been married just three years previously, was sitting there listening. Deepa said there was no question of their cooking at separate hearths. Deepa now had no unmarried children; no more daughters-in-law would be arriving, and no daughters remained to be married. There was just Deepa and her husband. In any case, this daughter-in-law's children were small. Deepa looked after them to free her daughter-in-law for working around the house, caring for the cattle, and sometimes going to the fields to work or collect fodder. Deepa looked over at her daughter-in-law, chuckling: "And for as long as you remain joint with me, you won't be able to go to your parents' home just when you like! You won't be able to do what you want to! Your husband will have to obey us! If ever you don't heed what I say, I'll make your hearth separate from mine and I'll begin to cook for myself!"

Afsana's Troubles with Her In-Laws

Afsana was from a rich-peasant Sheikh household in Jhakri. In 1981, she was married into a village some distance away to the west of the river Ganges. Her husband had been reared by his aunt [FyBW] because she had no children of her own, and this woman was originally from Jhakri, from a house on the same side of the village as Afsana's parents' home. But now, despite these close connections, Afsana was troubled about her situation. Just a year after her marriage, while visiting her parents, Afsana asked our assistant Swaleha to write a letter for her to send secretly to her father-in-law:

> He's in the position of my father. But I'm very worried because he's saying bad things about me to other people and giving me a bad name. If I've done anything wrong, why does he talk to other people? He should come home and tell me. Why does he listen to those people who tell him bad things about me? My honor is just the same as his daughters'. Those people who are saying bad things about me also have daughters of their own. The same could happen to them as has happened to me. I'll ask my father-in-law to tell my husband that he sits among the women too much. He pays heed to what they say. He should learn to sit among the men. And if he wants to divorce me, my husband should come to Jhakri and do the divorce properly.

After finishing the letter, Afsana explained that there would be a letter coming for her after the forthcoming Eid festival: "I wanted to have a letter ready to send in reply. How else could I do that? I couldn't have asked the men in my family. Now I'll return the letter to my in-laws with the letter you've just written for me, Swaleha. Now I won't be afraid of anyone. I've heard so many things. But I'll say everything now. I'll answer everything they've said about me. And I won't go back there in a hurry."

Afsana's brother's wife was also sitting there. She had been in a similar plight since her marriage some fifteen years earlier. Because she seemed incapable of bearing children, she was taunted by Afsana's mother and the wives of Afsana's other brothers. She joined in: "I, too, returned to my in-laws after staying a long time with my parents. I wouldn't return until they promised not to trouble me anymore. My parents live in Bijnor itself, which is not a great distance. I could easily answer anything that happened here or anything that my in-laws said about me. In the end, they got tired of troubling me and they stopped saying bad things about me to other people."

Afsana remained in Jhakri for some nine months after our conversation. Then her husband's uncle [FyB] came and collected her. But Afsana's mother was quite anxious: "Afsana's husband is under his mother's [the woman who reared him, his FyBW] control. He listens to her and not to our Afsana. My husband himself will go in a while to see how things are."

Prabha's Complaints

"My younger daughter-in-law remained joint with me for just three years," Prabha told us. "Then my oldest son got married again and the two daughters-in-law used to squabble about their work. Neither of them likes to work, so I myself made them become separate. When their children are born, though, or if there is anyone ill, I'm the one who helps. I sometimes call my daughter from her in-laws' place. People of the house do the helping. Who would come from outside to help?"

In 1985, Prabha was nearly sixty. In comparison with the old days, she asserted, young women these days had a much easier life than she had in her youth:

> These days, there's no need to handmill the wheat. All they have to do is make the bread from the flour. And water can easily be obtained from the handpump. You can practically do it still sitting down by the hearth! But young women nowadays have the wrong attitude to their elders. When I was young, I didn't say anything or answer back even when someone beat me and left me hungry. Enough, I just stayed silent. But today's daughters-in-law, that's enough! Say one thing to them and hear two! Who wants to waste their honor and standing? It's better to remain silent. Who can beat them? You can't even tap them with a single knuckle!

Prabha's younger daughter-in-law was sitting on a cot nearby. Prabha looked over at her and continued: "Now that they're separated from me, they do whatever they want. These daughters-in-law don't take so much as advice from me. This one here was two months pregnant but she didn't tell me a single thing. Then she lied to me when I saw her taking some medicine. She said it was because she had a fever. But she'd asked her husband to bring some medicine. She ate it and then her period began."

Prabha's daughter-in-law, silent thus far, retorted: "When my husband decides something, why should I ask anyone else? I should do what the person I live with says I should do."

Prabha, though, remembered this daughter-in-law's second pregnancy in 1980, when bleeding had prevented her from doing anything active for several months. Prabha had obtained treatments for her, but they had no effect. When the baby was born at seven months, the placenta was retained. It was delivered some days later, after the dispensary compounder suggested they put a hot-water bottle against her belly. The daughter-in-law said she narrowly escaped death: Just as the placenta was being delivered, she became cold and was revived with great difficulty. Prabha was responsible for nursing her back to health but was annoyed to receive no gratitude: "The only person who knows how much effort I made is myself. Yet I don't get any acknowledgment for it. I did everything, including cleaning up the blood-soaked clothes. I haven't seen her face but I've certainly seen her arse!"

Providing Shade for the Mother-in-Law

While recording maternity histories from women in Dharmnagri and Jhakri during our first research in Bijnor, we came across a woman nicknamed Gungi [Mute]. She seemed to follow what we said, but she replied only in sign language that her neighbors interpreted for us.

She had been married into a poor-peasant Sheikh household in Jhakri in the mid-1960s. Before her marriage, her prospective in-laws visited her parents' house in nearby Burhanuddinpur, and she served them tea and biscuits. The occasion did not demand that she talk to anyone. On the contrary, it would have been extremely inappropriate for her to have done so. Thus, no one in Jhakri realized that she was deaf-mute until after the marriage. Her mother-in-law was furious at the deceit and wanted to send Gungi back to her parents. But Gungi's husband resisted, saying that she was now his wife and he would not let her be sent back to have her future destroyed.

As we later learned, things did not always run smoothly. Gungi's sister-in-law [HeBW]—some ten years older than Gungi—told us how the two of them had been tormented by their mother-in-law:

> Daughters-in-law used to be afraid of their mothers-in-law. We used to tremble with fear. In the old days, a son would follow his mother and do what she told him. He would heed her words. My husband still doesn't listen to me. He does just what he wants even if it's harmful. Gungi and I used to do exactly what our mother-in-law said because she would beat us both, especially Gungi. But I was stronger than our mother-in-law and used to catch her by the arms to stop her beating Gungi. My youngest child was just three days old when our mother-in-law died and I had to bathe her for burial. These days, it's the mother-in-law who fears the daughter-in-law. The daughter-in-law doesn't listen to a word the

mother-in-law says. And now a man speaks up for his wife. These days, a mother is not thought of like she used to be. And the wife has become like a queen.

If Gungi's sister-in-law was dissatisfied with her sons' wives, however, Gungi was better placed in her husband's house than she had ever been. In 1989, her oldest son had been married to Gungi's niece [ZD], who seemed determined to provide the "shade" for her aunt that was the unfulfilled dream of so many mothers-in-law: "I still call her aunt, not mother, and I'm still living jointly with her. I'm doing all the work at present, since my aunt has just had another baby girl. My aunt is almost fully occupied with her tiny baby, though she sometimes helps me a bit with lifting the dung from the tethered cattle. I'm not going to separate from my mother-in-law. For one thing, she's my aunt. For another, I'm the only daughter-in-law at present. And her other children are still very small."

Adesh's Frustrations

Adesh was married into a rich-peasant Rajput household in Dharmnagri when she was seven, and the cohabitation took place about seven years later, in the late 1950s. Her first child—a girl—was born about five years later, and the second was a boy born in 1967. At this stage, Adesh told us, she had wanted to stop having children: "Two children are enough. So I asked my husband to see the big landowner about it. You see, my husband relies on the landowner for getting things like gun permits, so I thought that we should get the sterilization organized through him."

When the landowner discovered that Adesh had just two children, he advised against the operation, saying that they should wait until Adesh had a second son. After that, Adesh had another girl, followed by a second son. The landowner then said that they should arrange the operation, but when Adesh discovered that the intention was for her to be sterilized, she refused:

> I said that I wouldn't have the operation. I told my husband he should be sterilized himself. After all, I told him, I have heavy work to do. If he has heavy work, he can get it done by a farm servant, but I can't. So, carrying on like that, three more girls were born. Then our second son fell into the well and drowned, so there was no question of the operation then. The landowner said nothing more about it. When the youngest girl was about five, I became pregnant again. Before that, I'd thought that perhaps I wouldn't have any more children. Then I thought that maybe this one would be a boy, so I decided not to take any medicines to abort the baby.

In 1982, however, she gave birth to another girl: "When we had one girl and one boy, we shouldn't have heeded the landowner's words. It would have been good if we'd agreed to the operation then, for these girls wouldn't have been born. There was only one son in our destiny, but in searching for a second one, four more girls were born. We own over twenty acres and have just one son. And we've opened a grain mill too. Sometimes we have to get someone to sharecrop some of our land. One man can't watch over so much land alone."

In some ways, though, the heavy burden of work to be covered by her husband, Ashok, and their son was the least of Adesh's anxieties: "I have only this one son and he just does what he wants. When he was younger, he refused to continue his schooling, but he wouldn't help with the farmwork either. My husband gets very angry. I'm always afraid our son will leave home. That's why we're scared to say too much to him. If we had a second son, we wouldn't have to tolerate his obstinacy so much."

With her daughters growing up and getting married, Adesh had pinned her hopes on her daughter-in-law to furnish the care that her son was failing to provide. When Adesh's son was just crawling, Adesh had taken him to her father's sister's house for a visit. While there, she met a man who insisted on settling a match between his infant daughter and Adesh's son. When Adesh's son was about ten years old, the man sent some money to make the arrangement binding. At the time, Adesh felt that her son was still small and that they might be able to marry him elsewhere. If they took the money, they would be tied. But her father-in-law insisted. He said he had accepted *lakshmī* [wealth and good fortune] from the girl's house, and it could not be returned. By 1990, though, Adesh's hopes had been dashed:

They were married ten years later [in 1986]. The wedding and cohabitation were at the same time, but nothing special came with the bride. Those people aren't poor, but they don't have the intention to give generously. Even those who have things don't give generously. The bride studied to eighth class, but I haven't received a single letter from her while she's been visiting her parents. That's why I'm angry. I haven't sent her a letter either. My daughter-in-law doesn't want to work when she's here. She sometimes cooks bread and pulses if she wants to. Otherwise, she spends the whole day sitting down. And I don't tell my daughter-in-law to do anything, because I'm angry with her. She asks why she should do any work, since I still have unmarried daughters in the house. But I have no mother-in-law. I'm alone here. And now my daughter-in-law is saying she wants to separate her cooking hearth. People in the village would gossip if that happened. They'd say that I have just one daughter-in-law and that I can't even tolerate that one. That's why I stay silent.

Sisters-in-Law and Sisters

In 1986, after Khalil and his widowed father, Maqsood, had a bitter argument about how to run the farm, Khalil's wife, Khurshida, would cook food only for Khalil and her children. Maqsood and Khurshid Ahmed (Maqsood's son by his second marriage) were worried about how to feed themselves. Khurshid Ahmed was still at school, and he had little time to help even with the farmwork. Khurshid Ahmed had recently been married to Khalil's cousin [MBD] Firdausi, but she had not yet come to live in Jhakri. Khurshida began taunting Khurshid Ahmed, saying he should bring his wife to Jhakri if he was so worried about getting food. But it would have been shameless for a young man to collect his own wife, at least so soon after the marriage, and Khalil refused to collect her on Khurshid Ahmed's behalf.

Maqsood had been married three times, but all three wives had died. In desperation, Maqsood announced that he would have to get married again. Khurshid Ahmed told us how he had been unhappy with this plan: "So I gave my father 1,200 rupees and told him to go to Bihar by train and buy some woman. I also gave him some ready-made clothes for the new bride. Then I asked a neighbor to go too, and I explained to him that they should spend some money on the way. There are a hundred stations, and they could buy food and drink. That accounted for maybe 200 rupees. So when they arrived in Bihar, they didn't have enough money left. People over there ask 4,000-5,000 rupees for a woman."

Consequently, when Maqsood returned to Jhakri, he brought back the ready-made clothes but no new wife. Khurshid Ahmed said he told his father that the two of them were not being fed but that he himself was already married. He would go to collect his wife, and she could use the clothes. Maqsood told him to talk to his father-in-law about it:

So I went to see my father-in-law and explained that Khurshida was refusing to cook for me and my father. I said we were having great difficulties over our food. My father-in-law said I could collect my wife whenever I wanted. "We don't intend to keep her here indefinitely," he said. "Are we expecting to pickle her?" So I went back the next day and brought her with me to Jhakri. Khurshida was angry. She and Khalil wanted us to remain worried, so she hadn't wanted my wife to come. Khurshida asked, "Whenever did a new bride arrive like that?" You see, there was no party of men to collect her. I brought her by myself. I told Khurshida, "Did I chase her all the way here? I'm married and I've brought my wife to live with me."

Khalil then began asking for the land to be divided. Khurshid Ahmed suggested that they make three plots, one for Maqsood and one for each of the two brothers. Khalil protested, saying that he would be unable to feed his children. But Maqsood agreed to the division, since Khalil had first asked for it. So Khurshid Ahmed left school and began farming. Grudgingly, Khalil accepted the situation, but he began taunting Khurshid Ahmed and telling their relatives that his brother had been at school so long he would not know how to farm properly. And Khurshida complained about an outstanding loan for Rs 10,000 that had been taken out when Khurshid Ahmed was married.

Khurshid Ahmed managed to get some ploughing done for him by tractor. Then he bought two oxen to make a ploughing team and a female buffalo to provide milk, and he paid off the loan in full. Clearly, he was coping very well with the farming. Khalil was so impressed that he suggested that the land should again be held jointly, since his expenses were greater. But Khurshid Ahmed insisted that even if the three men did the farmwork together, the crop itself should be divided when it was brought home. Thus it was that the two sisters-in-law [HBW], Khurshida and Firdausi, had cooked at separate hearths from the start.

After a woman gives birth, she can usually expect help from other women in her husband's family. In Khurshida's case, though, Khalil's mother and stepmothers had all died and there were no sisters. As a result, ever since her marriage in 1975, Khurshida had always obtained help from Khalil's cousins, often unmarried paternal cousins living in the same compound. On a couple of occasions, Firdausi was called to help even before she had been formally engaged to Khurshid Ahmed.

When Firdausi's own turn came, however, she refused to ask Khurshida for help. Instead, after Firdausi had a son in spring 1991, she asked her parents to send her unmarried sister. They were happy to do so. As Firdausi's sister herself commented to us, Khurshid Ahmed did not "trouble" her and so her parents were willing to send her to Jhakri. And Firdausi was grateful that her sister had been able to help: "I had lots of peace while my sister was here. I've had to work only since she went home. Now I'm having to do it all. I lifted a full basket of dung and watered the buffalo. Since then I've had pains in my belly."

But was it not possible to get some help from Khurshida if she was feeling unwell, Patricia asked. "Yes, my sister-in-law certainly could do the work for me. But after doing it, she'd taunt me with, 'Co-wife [a term of abuse], I've done this work of yours and that work of yours!' I'm not prepared to listen to that sort of thing."

Santosh's Critics

Sunil was a poor peasant, who was widely known for having a way with sick animals and children. One day in 1982, Kirpal—a landless man in his late twenties—went in search of Sunil when his little daughter was ill. Sunil was not at home, but his nineteen-year-old wife, Santosh, was. What happened next was never entirely clear to us, but a furor erupted that was to take hold of Dharmnagri for several days.

Kirpal began telling people that Santosh had grasped his wrist the day he was trying to find Sunil. He insisted that Santosh had asked him why he was not wearing the bracelet that (he claimed) Santosh had given him some time previously. Meanwhile, Santosh had told Sunil that it was Kirpal who had grasped her by the wrist. As if this would not have been bad enough, Kirpal was a Chamar [Harijan] and Sunil and Santosh were Dhimar [a middle-ranking caste]. Sunil told us that he himself had given Kirpal the bracelet because Kirpal and another man had helped lift Sunil's thatch roof onto his house the previous spring. As far as Sunil was concerned, Kirpal had made a pass at his wife. In Kirpal's section of the village, the consensus was that the incident was Santosh's fault.

Sunil claimed that his five brothers and three paternal cousins were ready to fight, for no one in Dharmnagri had been able to lift so much as a finger at their family before this. To add to their anger, they asserted that they never touched Kirpal's wife, who regularly collected fodder from their land. Sunil tried to restrain his relatives, saying that Kirpal had always been a womanizer. Nevertheless, fearing either attack by Sunil and his brothers or being reported to the police, Kirpal vanished from the scene for several days. His mother and married sister even went to Sunil to beg forgiveness. Sunil refused to hear them out.

Within days, rumors were rife in Sunil's part of the village, not all of them taking Santosh's side. Some people were saying that Kirpal had grasped Santosh's breast, others that he had grabbed her groin. Yet others claimed that Kirpal had indeed grasped Santosh's wrist—but that Santosh had then followed Kirpal to his house, where he had done it again.

One elderly woman considered Sunil and Santosh shameless. She told us with overt disgust that she had once caught them embracing with their lips touching. She said she had told them they were acting like donkeys who did not understand that such things are not done in public. Another woman remarked that she was unsure what had happened, but there were certainly several suspicious things about Santosh:

Santosh's father wanted the marriage done quickly. That's always a bad sign. It usually means there's something wrong with the girl's character and her parents want her married before anyone outside the family finds out. And then Santosh didn't even hit that Chamar with her sandal. And why didn't Santosh call out to her mother-in-law and sisters-in-law when it happened? They were all close by, but she had to go searching for her husband instead. And then again, Santosh doesn't behave properly when she walks around her in-laws' village.

She stood up to demonstrate. First she showed Patricia how a demure young woman should walk, with her head bowed and fully covered with the end of her *dhotī* and with her chest properly concealed. Then she showed how Santosh walked around with her back erect, her head upright, and her *dhotī* falling round her shoulders and leaving her breasts covered only with her shirt. In similar vein, Sunil's sister, Mamta, had no sympathy for Santosh. She criticized Santosh for reporting the incident to Sunil rather than to the women of the family. And she regarded Sunil himself as stupid:

> He shouldn't have made the matter public. And he should have forgiven that Chamar's mother and sister when they came to him. In spreading the story he was dishonoring himself. Even the postmaster's wife has been asking me what went on. She wouldn't have known anything about it if Sunil had kept quiet. He handled the whole thing badly. Anyway, Santosh walks around the place improperly. A young women in her in-laws' village should cover her head, face, and chest with the end of her *dhotī*. But Santosh doesn't know what's proper. What can we do if people don't heed the advice we give?

Once more, to underline the point, Patricia was given a demonstration. Mamta stood up with her feet apart. She arranged the end of her *dhotī* on her head so that her face was uncovered and the fabric went down her back behind her shoulders. Mamta looked straight ahead and drew herself up. And then she began taking huge strides along our veranda, swinging her shoulders and arms as she went.

When Santosh became pregnant soon after this, people were no less scathing. Santosh had insisted on visiting her parents when they were sick, despite Sunil's mother's objections. She was furious when Santosh returned to Dharmnagri ill herself. And then there was the question of the special foods that Santosh was asking Sunil to provide for her. Mamta was disdainful: "How could Santosh ask for things like that when she's pregnant? She thinks she's so important that she doesn't think about her elders. She asked Sunil for things right in front of them. Santosh has no sense of shame. Why, my brothers' wives have even begun saying that Santosh is bringing a Chamar baby into our court-yard. Sunil and Santosh? They're both stupid! And Sunil has let Santosh sit on his head."

Ghazala Tries to Avoid Being Taunted

One day in 1985, Ghazala arrived at the Dharmnagri dispensary with her husband, Ghulam, a Sheikh man in his mid-twenties. Ghazala was clutching a vial of fluid for an injection. Ghulam wandered a discrete distance away, looking embarrassed. Ghazala explained in low tones: "My period was some three or four months overdue, so I got him [Ghulam] to fetch some medicines from the compounder here. I took them and the baby fell [aborted]. Then I became very weak, so we went to the big doctor in Bijnor. She prescribed a glucose drip and a course of injections. I've come here to ask the compounder to give an injection."

Some weeks later Patricia and our assistant Swaleha were chatting to Ghazala's older sister-in-law, Fatima, who was telling us how exhausted she felt by her pregnancies (six by that time) and that she now wanted no more than the four children still alive: "The more we don't want children, the more God sends them. So now I'm going to give God this prayer, 'Please send me lots more children.'"

At that moment, Ghazala arrived. She had prepared some mud, and the two of them could now busy themselves making Fatima's new grain store. Ghazala announced that she had a headache. Like a flash, Fatima retorted, "There are medicines for sore heads, too!" Ghazala looked downcast and muttered to us that Fatima had found out about her abortion: "Even after an abortion, I have worries about it. People shouldn't get their sons married until they have their own separate income. If he [Ghulam] had work, I'd just tell him what I need, whether medicines or other things, and no one else would be involved."

By the time we returned in 1990, Ghazala had three children. She wanted no more and she insisted that Patricia give her information about contraceptive pills. Another Jhakri woman teased her, saying, "Why are you talking like that when Ghulam wants ten children!" Ghazala denied that he did, but she let the subject drop because of the other women present. A few weeks later, when she was alone with us, she brought up the issue again.

> I took pills for a while, but I began having trouble with my eyes. I even told him [Ghulam] he'd have to stop this baby-making work! Then we started using condoms. I haven't told anyone. No one else knows but us

two. The other women make up a lot of stories. That's why I'm saying nothing. After my oldest son, I had an abortion [in 1985]. Everyone began taunting me. My health got bad and my husband took me to my parents' home so that I'd get peace and wouldn't have to listen to what they were saying. My mother-in-law was angry. She didn't even come to my parents' home to ask how I was. That's why I'm not saying anything to anyone. For one thing, my health isn't good and the children are often ill. And what would we do with more children? He [Ghulam] also doesn't want any more. Some women are asking me why I've had such a long space after my last pregnancy. I just say, "I don't know. God knows."

A Wedding Song

Darling, we've found a bridegroom for you,
After a long, long search.
Darling, grandfather [FF] is going,
Always bidding you farewell.
Darling, grandmother [FM] is weeping,
Always hoping for your happiness.
Darling, we've found a bridegroom for you,
After a long, long search.

Darling, we've found a bridegroom for you,
After a long, long search.
Darling, uncle [FeB] is going,
Always bidding you farewell.
Darling, aunt [FeBW] is weeping,
Always hoping for your happiness.
Darling, we've found a bridegroom for you,
After a long, long search.[4]

Notes

1. Although these were called *satī* shrines, people in Dharmnagri denied that they marked places where widows had been immolated on their husbands' funeral pyres. Rather the shrines were said to commemorate dutiful and devoted wives. For more details on this episode, see Jeffery, Jeffery, and Lyon (1989:143-144).

2. For further discussion of this point see Jeffery, Jeffery, and Lyon (1989:28ff.); and Sharma (1978b).

3. This is sung at the groom's house. The mother-in-law is told that her rule is over and that she is incompetent in all her work, using the most demeaning form of "your" (*terā* and *terī*, rather than *tumhārā* and *tumhārī*). The final verse also hinges on an inversion of people's expectations. It is a mark of respect and submission for a subordinate to bend over before a senior person and touch their feet. Among women in Bijnor, the daughter-in-law would be expected to

do so before departure to her parent's home and on her return. A slightly different version of this song is given in Wadley (1994:237).

4. This is a *banni* sung at the bride's house; it contrasts the men's preoccupation with seeing the bride off with the women's primary concern—her future happiness.

10

Love and Peace in My Mother's House

Om Prakash must have been about fourteen when his father died. His mother never remarried, and (as often happens in such situations), her six sons were denied the full fruits of their father's land. Thus, when Omvati was married to Om Prakash in the early 1970s, his financial situation was less secure than it might otherwise have been. For several years, they coped moderately well. But there was no margin for the disruptions that illness might cause.

The government's health care system could not meet the demand, and free medicines were a rarity. Generally, people in rural Bijnor would expect to pay for medical consultations and drugs. For the relatively wealthy, this might pose no great problem. For the poor, it could create a crisis, perhaps precipitating the pawning or sale of assets or loans at such high interest rates that they could not be repaid. "Distress sales" often left families unable to replace valuable possessions after the immediate crisis was over. Generally, people would prefer to sell a woman's jewelry before selling productive resources such as land or livestock. On occasion, this put women under considerable pressure to part with jewelry that (formally) was their own security.[1]

Moreover, an adult's incapacity would normally have a serious effect on household well-being. A man's ability to earn from laboring or to farm his own land adequately would be seriously compromised. Equally, a woman's work with livestock and other aspects of farming activities, let alone her home-based work, would be sorely missed if she could not fulfill her duties. The need for women to do their work regularly often made it difficult to grant them much leave before or after childbirth, and many women we knew continued working at other times when they were quite incapacitated by ailments such as malaria and intestinal infections.[2] When serious problems arose, people might have no choice but to place themselves at the mercy of their relatives.

The crises experienced by Omvati link the previous chapter with the one that follows, in which we highlight the continuing reliance of married women on their natal kin. As the mother-in-law's favorite, Omvati's sisters-in-law claimed, Omvati had abused her position. By the time disasters struck, she had

171

Feeding an Invalid Breadwinner

truly antagonized them all and no help was forthcoming. Without her parents and brothers, Omvati's dreadful situation would undoubtedly have been even worse.

*   *   *   *   *   *

Omvati's parents lived in Harganpur, a large village near Nagina and some twenty-five miles from Dharmnagri. Although her father owned no land, he had a modestly successful tea stall—much frequented by travelers and locals alike—on the main road near the village. Her parents also had several milk animals. Omvati was the second of six children. Once her older brother had been married, her parents began looking for a suitable match for Omvati: "I was first engaged to a boy in Bhurapur, near Nagina. That's where my father's sister lives. My father heeded his sister's words because she's his sister. She insisted that if he didn't accept the match she was suggesting, all kinship between them would come to an end."

At first, Omvati's mother had been against the match. She was sad that her husband was planning to send Omvati to such an inaccessible village. It was not that it was very far from Harganpur but the two villages were linked by an unmetaled road that went through a riverbed that flooded during the monsoon. How would the poor girl be able to visit for Tījo and other festivals that always took place in the rainy season?[3] But Omvati's father listened to his sister and handed over Rs 5 to the boy to bind him to the marriage.

A short while afterward, Omvati was chopping fodder by machine along with a friend:

> It was the day of the bazaar—my village is not small and there are two bazaars each week. While we were cutting fodder, an oldish man came up. He began talking to me and asking where my father was. I said he wasn't at home. Then the man asked where my brother was and I said he'd gone to Moradabad. Then the man asked if I cut grass and brought it from the fields, and I replied that I can do all types of work. I didn't know that this man was from Bhurapur. The next day, someone came from the boy's family and began refusing the marriage with me. You see, that man who talked to me had gone to the boy's people and told them I was very fat and black.

Aside from the slur, Omvati's mother was delighted, as Omvati's aunt had compelled them to accept the match in the first instance. A potter woman who had moved from Harganpur to Bhurapur and who still visited Omvati's home quite often, heard what had happened:

That potter woman promptly went to the boy's people and upbraided them for breaking the engagement. She told them they'd never find a girl like me or a house like my father's anywhere else. When they heard that, the Bhurapur people came to my father's home. They flattered and cajoled, and they begged my father to marry me to their boy. They said they'd been mistaken, and such a thing would never happen again. But my mother told them straight, "I'm not going to marry my girl into your house even if it means she remains a virgin for the rest of her life."

The matter was soon resolved, though. There was a mendicant from Harganpur and among the villages where he went begging was Dharmnagri. He told Omvati's parents that they should marry her to Om Prakash instead of the boy from Bhurapur. Omvati was not asked about this marriage, but "I did know about it. When something's being discussed in the house you get to know. It was just that I didn't come forward to listen. But I increased my needless coming and going so that I could overhear the discussions!"

The mendicant told Omvati's father that there were two households, that of Om Prakash's widowed mother, and that of his uncle [FeB].[4] Both households had boys in them, he said, and there were "ten to twelve" acres of land. Omvati's father and older brother went to Dharmnagri to see Om Prakash. There and then, they gave Rs 5 to bind him.

* * * * * *

With hindsight, Omvati's parents might have done well not to arrange her marriage simply on the mendicant's say-so. As Omvati acidly commented, the claims he had made about Om Prakash's family were exaggerated and held out a promise of security that had eluded her ever since.

Omvati's father-in-law had died in the mid-1960s. He had lived long enough to arrange only the marriages of his oldest son and his only daughter. The remaining five sons—among them Om Prakash—were still small, the youngest a toddler, when their father died. Om Prakash's uncle had helped to rear the orphaned children, but he had also contrived to put in his own name some of the land to which they were entitled. Of the twenty-seven acres inherited jointly by Om Prakash's father and uncle, the uncle and his three sons took about eighteen, leaving only nine for Om Prakash and his five brothers.

Om Prakash's uncle had managed to build a spacious house: a men's sitting area at the front and a large courtyard behind with separate houses for the women and children. Despite the unhappy family relationships, the uncle's home was always the place where visitors were entertained, as when Omvati's father and brother went to propose the match with Om Prakash. To the side and behind the uncle's extensive complex lay the thatched adobe single-roomed houses occupied by Om Prakash and his brothers. According to Omvati, though, none of that was pointed out to her father. Nor was her father told that Om Prakash was being employed by his uncle to look after the animals and that he was being paid just Rs 35 per month. Apparently, Omvati's father believed that he was marrying her into a moderately prosperous farming family. His main concern was for Om Prakash's widowed mother. So he set the marriage date for a year later to enable her to make the wedding preparations for her son gradually.

Om Prakash was the third of the six brothers. The oldest brother had set up a separate household many years before, and he contributed nothing to Om Prakash's wedding expenses. The second brother, Rohtash, was married some years after Om Prakash.[5] Thus, in 1971, Om Prakash paid for his own marriage without any help from his older brothers. He could do this only by taking a loan, for his regular income was insufficient.

Once married, Om Prakash began farming on the nine acres he shared with his brothers. And during the first ten years after he and Omvati were married, the land provided enough—just—for the family members to live on. As Omvati put it in 1982,

> We don't have shortages of food during the year. Sometimes the grain from our own fields isn't enough, so we have to buy some from the bazaar. That's what we're doing these days. We're buying from the bazaar and eating it straightaway. Last time I was pregnant, I very much wanted to eat special food. But where does anyone obtain special food in this house? Sometimes my husband bought things, but they all got divided among the children, so I didn't get anything. Who wouldn't want special food during pregnancy? Everyone does. If a woman is ever to get special food, she should certainly get it during pregnancy. That way the baby is healthy and the woman stays healthy too.

Omvati and Om Prakash were by no means comfortably off, then, but Omvati was quietly confident and making plans for her family. She had hopes of replacing their thatched adobe house with a more substantial and spacious one built from kiln-baked bricks. Moreover, she felt she had enough children, and had tried to abort her fifth pregnancy in 1982:

> When I knew I was pregnant, I wasn't at all happy. I didn't want another child. I even took some medicines to make the baby fall. My husband got

pills for me from a doctor in Bijnor. But I had no benefit from them, as three months were already completed. Only we two knew about this. Later, when his mother found out, she was very angry. I don't want more children, but I can't have the operation. I'd consider getting it done today but for the work. After the operation, I wouldn't be able to do the work that has to be done in this house. After the operation, I wouldn't get as much rest as I ought to. When my periods begin again, I'll get some pills from Bijnor to delay another pregnancy. My mother-in-law wouldn't stop me doing that.

*   *   *   *   *   *

Over the succeeding years, however, Omvati's confidence was sapped as her family was struck by a series of calamities and her situation became more and more precarious. First, their oldest child contracted polio and became paralyzed in one leg. Then the youngest child, the girl born in 1982, had malaria and died during a fit of convulsions. After this, Om Prakash became sick with a chest complaint, probably pulmonary tuberculosis (TB). The cost of his treatment—several thousand rupees for various doctors' fees and medicines—had serious consequences for the family, especially as Om Prakash was unable to work for some months. In 1985, Omvati told us:

> The children are running around half-naked because we can't afford new clothes for them. And we're eating just once a day because money is so tight. I don't want any more children. But with him [Om Prakash] so ill, I don't think I shall in any case. So I don't think that I'll bother to have the operation. Anyway, no one here would help me with my work afterward. Do you remember how I was talking of having the operation when I was pregnant before? Just see how that baby girl died. And after that, another girl was born. So in this matter, too, my wishes don't prevail.

A couple of years later, Omvati's second child—a daughter by now approaching marriageable age—lost the sight in one eye after she spiked it on a reed in the roof thatch. Then Om Prakash, still not completely recovered from TB, himself had an eye injury. Sometime later, he too lost his sight in one eye. "We absolutely don't want any more children," Omvati insisted. "But neither of us could have the operation. He's sick the whole time. He can't do much work. I have to do all the outside work, collecting fodder and carrying headloads. That's why I can't have the operation."

Their adobe home had still not been replaced, and only one of their children continued to attend school. Om Prakash was clear about the reason—their unavoidable expenses:

I alone would have been responsible for educating the children. Once I became sick, who else would have sent them to school? Even if there isn't enough money for food, we certainly have to spend 100 rupees on medicines for me every month. There simply isn't any spare money, so how could we educate the children? And then that girl's eye became bad, and one boy had polio. In all those ways, lots of money was spent. We've also sold the small amount of jewelry that was Omvati's share of the jewelry for all the brothers' wives.

Omvati felt very aggrieved about her situation. "There are so many brothers here in my husband's place, but no one even gave us a loan when we had to pay for all those treatments," she commented angrily. She was particularly bitter that when she and Om Prakash were married they had lived in a joint household that comprised Om Prakash's mother as well as his four unmarried brothers: Rohtash, Pratap, Sunil, and Punni. And Om Prakash had subsequently taken the responsibility for arranging and financing their marriages. Yet all four brothers separated their households from Omvati's rapidly after their weddings.

There are six brothers. If they'd lived in one place, they could have built a good kiln-brick house. And if they'd cultivated all the land they own together, there'd have been great benefit. But everyone here wants to live separately, and that means not one of them has been able to build so much as a kiln-brick room for himself. The uncle has three sons and they've all stayed together for a long time. Just see how they were able to build kiln-brick homes. They began to live separately only after they'd done that.

By the time Omvati's son contracted polio, Om Prakash and all his brothers were living in separate households and farming their own shares of their father's land. As far as Omvati was concerned, Om Prakash's outlays on behalf of his brothers warranted some return when he himself was in need. But the brothers were managing their separate household finances, and their wives were making no efforts to help Omvati with her work when she was under stress. "Not one of them helps me," she claimed. "But I can't just watch my sisters-in-law when they're in trouble. I always help them out. I'm the daughter-in-law who has remained longest with our mother-in-law. Maybe it's because I'm still living with her that they don't think it's necessary to help me."

So why had Om Prakash's brothers and their wives separated their households from Omvati's so quickly? According to Omvati, they had all done so by their own choice. "I didn't make any one of them become separate," she asserted. The brothers and their wives, however, put a rather different gloss on events.

*   *   *   *   *   *

The fourth of the six brothers, Pratap, was married about four years after Omvati. According to Omvati, Pratap's wife, Promilla, did not give birth even once while living in a joint household with her: "She became separate very quickly. At first, Pratap said that they'd just be eating their food separately when they separated their cooking hearth. He said he'd continue farming jointly with his brothers. But now, everyone's farming is also divided up."

Promilla's lengthy account contrasted markedly with Omvati's brief comments. Promilla explained to us that her cousin had been married to Pratap's uncle's grandson and that she had told Promilla's father about Pratap. Promilla's father visited Dharmnagri to bind Pratap to the match. He was told that Pratap's family wanted to delay the marriage for a couple of years, as they wanted to build a separate house for Pratap's bride. Promilla was married in 1975—the promised house, she commented in 1990, was still to be built. The cohabitation took place six months after the wedding, and Promilla moved into a household with her mother-in-law, Om Prakash, Omvati, and their two children and the other unmarried brothers. Almost immediately, Promilla told us, her mother-in-law and Omvati began subjecting her to daily taunting and criticism:

> My husband had work at a sugarcane crusher near my parents' home in Haldaur, but I remained in Dharmnagri. I did all the cooking and scoured all the dishes. Sometimes I helped my mother-in-law and Omvati with the dungwork and feeding the animals. But mainly it was the cooking. It used to take me till midday to turn ten pounds of dough into bread. It was the cold season, and after cooking the bread I had to clean the dishes. Even so, they used to fight with me. They'd criticize me and taunt me, saying, "Your work is never completed on time, but we could do it all quickly." That used to make me very angry.

Once, when Promilla was visiting her parents, she complained to her father and brother. She did not want to return to Dharmnagri, she told them ominously:

> I told them that if they compelled me to go, I'd certainly die from overwork or from suicide. My husband was in Haldaur. Meanwhile my mother-in-law and sister-in-law were tormenting me behind his back. My father persuaded me to return to Dharmnagri, but my brother told my husband to call me back to Haldaur. My mother-in-law and sister-in-law said I should remain with them in my husband's real home now that I was married, not in my parents' home. But my husband persisted and he

took me away. I'd been in my parents' home for a month when my mother-in-law and my husband's sister arrived. They began insisting that my husband send me back to Dharmnagri. But he asked them how he could do that, since it was my brother who had called me to Haldaur! He told them to talk to my brother instead. Then my brother said, "Since the son-in-law is living in Haldaur, what business does the daughter have living in Dharmnagri?" He also said to my mother-in-law, "You always say she does no work, so what would there be for her to do in Dharmnagri anyway?" So between my mother-in-law and my brother, there was quite an angry exchange of words. In the end, I didn't go back to Dharmnagri with them.

Indeed, Promilla remained in her parents' home for about a year, even after Pratap's job in Haldaur had come to an end and he had returned to Dharmnagri. Pratap used to visit her in Haldaur, but he contributed nothing toward her expenses. Eventually, he took her back to Dharmnagri. But Promilla's troubles there were not over:

Then my mother-in-law began making lots of comments about my dowry, such as, "Your mother and father have given you nothing." About that time, my father took me to his house for the Holī festival. I didn't go back to Dharmnagri for another year. My husband came to collect me many times, but my father wouldn't send me back with him, not even when his mother came as well. Then my mother gave birth to a son, and she died two weeks later. I began caring for my baby brother. I didn't return to Dharmnagri even when my mother-in-law made a condolence visit. But the baby eventually died from a stomach infection. Shortly after that, my husband's cousin's son—the one who's married to my cousin—was attending a wedding at his own in-laws' house in Haldaur. He met my father there and said I should now be sent to Dharmnagri. So, after much flattery, I came back here. But my husband and I immediately established a separate household. We kept the jewelry that had come from my parents, but we left behind the jewelry my in-laws had presented to me.

* * * * * *

Meanwhile, about six months after Promilla's wedding, Rohtash (the second brother) had married. Normally, brothers married in order of their age, but Rohtash had been badly disfigured by an eye injury, and no offers of marriage had come his way. His only option was to buy a bride. Rohtash bought Rajballa, a woman with a tiny daughter already, by paying Rs 800 to Rajballa's brother in Saharanpur (to the west of the river Ganges). It was not entirely clear where Rajballa was from. Several different places were mentioned to us by Rohtash and other family members. It was said to be somewhere very distant, which seems plausible. Initially, we found it impossible to communicate with Rajballa. Even her in-laws (and our research assistants too) had found her incapable of understanding what they were saying, and she herself had to amplify her scarcely comprehensible speech with elaborate gestures and sign language. Apparently, too, Rajballa's notions about the correct way to perform domestic rituals were seriously out of kilter with those of her in-laws.

Largely because of this uncertainty about her origins, Rohtash had Rajballa bathed in the Ganges to purify her before bringing her to Dharmnagri for the first time. From then onward, she lived in Dharmnagri, never once visiting her brother or any other relatives. As with the other brothers, Rohtash initially lived in a household with his mother, Om Prakash, and Omvati. That arrangement lasted barely six months after his marriage. Rohtash explained: "Rajballa insisted that we separate from my mother. When she first arrived, no one could understand what she was saying. My mother used to get angry with her over that. So I took her to live separately from my mother."

Rajballa's son was born after she had separated from her mother-in-law and Omvati. For some years, her house was somewhat apart from those of the other brothers, at the back of the area that they used as house sites. She had very little contact with them and their wives. She did all her housework alone or with Rohtash lending a hand. Indeed, when her son was born by cesarean section in Bijnor women's hospital, it proved impossible to persuade Rohtash's mother or his brothers' wives to stay in the hospital to look after her.[6] Rohtash's sister and a widowed neighbor reluctantly agreed to do so. On Rajballa's return from the hospital, Rohtash—not his mother or any other woman in the connection—did all Rajballa's housework and cared for her and the children.

*   *   *   *   *   *

Sunil was next in line. He was married in 1979. Within a year, however, Sunil and Santosh had also separated their household from his mother's, just a week before the youngest brother, Punni, was married. According to Omvati,

> I tried to persuade Sunil not to separate just before Punni's wedding. I told him that even if he wanted to separate soon, he should at least wait until Punni was married to Pushpa. But he wouldn't listen. You see, at that time we'd all got some money because some of our land was purchased by the government right by where the barrage is now. Sunil

reckoned his share would be spent on Punni's wedding if he remained joint with us. He separated from us because of money.

By contrast, Santosh asserted that her mother-in-law had made her become separate. "We remained joint for only a year, and every day there used to be a fight over something. Omvati wouldn't let me use anything in the house."

"It was almost as if our things were going out of the house in one direction just as Pushpa's dowry things were arriving from the other direction," interjected Sunil.

While Santosh was joint with her mother-in-law, she had to do all the cooking and scouring of dishes, as well as do the work for the animals: "My parents had presented a female calf to me. It was part of my dowry. But we sold it soon after I was married. It continually broke its tether and caused us a lot of bother wandering all over the place. But there were two milk buffaloes that had been presented to Omvati by her parents. I had to do the work for them." According to Sunil, the work became the focus of trouble between Santosh and his mother: "You see, when we were all living together, Santosh used to do her work rather slowly. My mother used to say, 'Santosh doesn't know how to do any work' or 'She's no good.' Santosh used to tell me everything my mother said to her or about her. At that I got angry. Then my mother made us separate our cooking hearth, so we did."

Santosh kept none of the jewelry that had been presented by her in-laws when she was married: "They'd presented a gold ring, a gold-covered collarbone, silver anklets, and two pairs of silver wrist ornaments. But my mother-in-law took them off me right away and kept them to present to Punni's bride. When Punni separates his hearth, Pushpa probably won't get anything either. It'll all be kept by Omvati."

In fact, some years later, the jewelry was divided among the daughters-in-law, and Santosh received a silver waist belt as her share. But at the time of the separation, Santosh felt, they had been unceremoniously thrown out without possessions. They were given nothing apart from one small cot to sleep on. Sunil told us: "My mother gave us nothing at all. We even had to borrow rice from Rohtash for our meal that evening."

In the succeeding years, relationships remained antagonistic and abrasive. For a short while, Om Prakash worked Sunil's land on a sharecropping basis. According to Sunil, this was of "no benefit to us and great benefit to himself," and Sunil ended the arrangement. So little did Santosh trust her in-laws that she used to seal her grain storage jars before visiting her parents so that Sunil would not be prevailed upon to lend rice or wheat to his brothers' wives. "They'd ask him behind my back, but not to my face," she said. Yet on one occasion when Santosh asked to borrow some clarified butter to make her dish of rice and lentils more tasty, her mother-in-law angrily refused: "Ask Sunil for some. You're separate. You're not afraid of anyone. You can do what you like. Just send news to Sunil that you need some clarified butter. He's your husband whether you sleep at the head of the bed or at the foot."

Santosh had little hope of help when she was ill or pregnant. During Santosh's first pregnancy, her parents became ill. She insisted on visiting them against her mother-in-law's express wishes. When she then became ill herself, she received no help, just barbed comments. Santosh would not call her sister to help. She believed that her in-laws would simply be sarcastic about how she was trying to avoid having to give them anything for helping her. Such was the tone of her relationships with her in-laws that Santosh did not eat the clarified butter and unrefined sugar that her own parents sent when she was pregnant for fear that her in-laws would say, "All the world eats after giving birth, but look at Santosh eating before!"

*   *   *   *   *   *

Pushpa, the wife of the sixth brother, Punni, was pregnant for the first time when we first met her in 1982. She was still living in a household with Omvati and their mother-in-law. Over the months we lived in Dharmnagri, Pushpa's relationships with her in-laws often reached a flash point. If Punni tried to provide her with any extra food while she was pregnant, Pushpa told us, he would get in trouble with Omvati and his mother: "It's like that when you're living in a joint household. If my husband considers bringing something, he hesitates because there'll be nothing left for me once it's divided. If he does bring anything for me, Omvati and his mother taunt him, saying, 'He's coming with things for his own wife, hasn't he even a little shame?'"

Worse was to come, however. Pushpa became seriously ill during the seventh month of her pregnancy. She had severe abdominal pains and became very weak from losing blood in her feces. She began finding it hard to move around and do her work. Out of necessity, Omvati and their mother-in-law let Pushpa rest: "But even then my mother-in-law was saying, 'She's just sitting down the whole time and doing no work. She's creating an illness as a pretext for doing no work.'"

Punni's mother sometimes got medicines for Pushpa, but she stopped doing so when Pushpa failed to recover. Increasingly worried about Pushpa, Punni visited her parents. He told them Pushpa was getting no treatment and he had no cash of his own. Her mother and brother immediately rushed to Pushpa's side:

> They became very upset when they saw me. My mother even spent the night in Dharmnagri, and my husband had a big fight with his mother about that. Then my mother decided I should be taken to hospital. She had me admitted in Dr. Nita's clinic even though my mother-in-law was against it. My mother paid all the medical expenses. Five or six women from my natal village came to see me in hospital, and some of the men too. But not a soul came from Dharmnagri. I stayed in hospital for four days, and everyone there was asking, "What, doesn't she have any in-laws?" My mother told them, "Of course she does, there are five other brothers and their wives, their mother, and their sister, but none of them has visited my girl."

Punni slept at the hospital but returned to Dharmnagri every day to work the land. His mother was furious at being overruled, and when Punni asked her for some money, she became even more angry:

> Your mother-in-law took your wife away. She can meet all the expenses. I cleaned up all Pushpa's shit for a fortnight, but you think only of your wife. You've put your wife on your head! And she tells only you about her illnesses, as if she didn't have me or your sister to tell. I have six daughters-in-law, and the only one who's any good is Omvati! Your mother-in-law came and embraced Pushpa and took her to hospital. She's staying with her there. She can pay for everything.

Om Prakash joined in the fray: "It's not our business. Her mother took her away, so she can pay for the treatment. If you want to separate your hearth from us, you're free to do so."

Punni pointed out that Pushpa was seriously ill, as they would have realized if they had visited her in the hospital. His comment provoked outrage. Above the din that ensued, Punni's mother shouted that he could deal with Pushpa's excrement when she came home from the hospital. She would not. "Why should I? Let her mother do it if she wants to." And Omvati yelled that she had washed out innumerable clothes soiled when Pushpa had diarrhea even when she herself had been heavily pregnant. "But Pushpa never noticed the work I was doing, she just went off to hospital with her mother. Just so much work as I did for her, just so many bad things did she say about me," Omvati alleged.

After Pushpa returned to Dharmnagri, Punni tried to separate their cooking hearth from Omvati and his mother. But Omvati was set against this: "Punni will stay joint with us just until his baby's born, and then he'll separate very quickly, like the rest did. Pushpa and Punni are quite ready to separate from me and his mother. Pushpa's pregnancy is nearly full term. If they separated that would be their choice. But the whole village would criticize me, saying that we haven't even helped her through one pregnancy. That's why we've prevented them from separating. Maybe they'll do so after the baby's born."

Thus, Pushpa gave birth while still living jointly with Omvati, though she did so on such a broken cot that the baby fell right through the strings onto the floor. And even then, Omvati's complaints continued because Pushpa had failed to set aside *dhotīs* and other items for presentation to various relatives:

> Lots of expenses have landed on us, since we're still joint with Punni. And there are many expenses when there's a first-born son. Pushpa hasn't got a single *dhotī* set aside, yet one will have to be given to all the women. There's not a single *dhotī* from her mother's house. My parents gave plenty when my first son was born, and I'm one of three sisters. And Pushpa's an only daughter! I was given three *dhotīs* at the last Tījo festival but Pushpa was given only one. There are five sisters-in-law and a mother-in-law and three married women in the uncle's courtyard. And the husband's sister. And the priest's wife is demanding a *dhotī* for herself. We'll need to buy eleven *dhotīs* from the bazaar. If any other relatives are called for the *jasthawn*, then they'll also need to have *dhotīs*.

Yet when the *dhotīs* were bought, no one was satisfied. According to Santosh, there were not enough, and she and Promilla would have to wait until later. "And they were just nineteen-rupee *dhotīs* and the cloth for the blouses was useless," Sunil butted in. His mother turned on him, livid: "What, when your son's born, will you be giving out fifty-rupee *dhotīs*?"

Within weeks of their son's birth, Punni and Pushpa had succeeded in separating their cooking hearth. A short while later, Pushpa mused about her situation:

> My marriage was arranged here because my brother's father-in-law knows the uncle. But my father stayed outside in the men's sitting area when he came to bind the boy. When he got home, my mother was angry that he'd given so little in the binding, saying that I was their only daughter. My mother insisted that clothes, utensils, fruit, and sweets should be given. A week later my father returned to Dharmnagri. So he came here twice before my marriage. Each time he went back home after having seen only the men's sitting area. He didn't even go inside the house to see what sort of building his daughter would live in. And when

he came to bind the boy, my mother-in-law told him about all the land owned together by the six brothers as if it were all my husband's.

Pushpa and Punni were not living separately for long, however, because Punni's mother moved into their household after Omvati's troubles began. "But I'm not joint with my mother-in-law. She's joint with me!" Pushpa explained. "So I have the rights over whatever comes from my mother's house. It's up to me whether I give anything to my mother-in-law. When I first came to Dharmnagri, it was all new. Absolutely everything remained in the hands of Omvati and our mother-in-law. Now, I'm in control."

*　*　*　*　*　*

Pushpa was the only sister-in-law who gave birth while still living in a joint household with Omvati. All Omvati's other sisters-in-law had separated their cooking hearths several years before Omvati's oldest child was struck down with polio in about 1984. Like all the other brothers and their wives, though, Punni and Pushpa had separated from Omvati and Om Prakash in a climate of hostility and mistrust, claims and counterclaims.

It is most unusual—and generally most unacceptable—for a man to live in his in-laws' house, but by 1985, Om Prakash was spending much of his time at Omvati's parents' house, and Omvati and his mother would visit him periodically. Omvati's parents were paying for his treatment and the special foods—milk, fruit, almonds—to help him recover, as well as feeding all the guests who came to see how he was. When Omvati and her mother-in-law both came down with malaria, Omvati's parents paid for the treatment. No one in Dharmnagri would pay for medicines for them. Even after that, Omvati said, her parents wanted "to load me down with grain and other foodstuffs whenever I went back to Dharmnagri."

By 1990, only the help that Omvati was obtaining from her parents and siblings moderated her almost overwhelming sense of hopelessness and despair. Om Prakash was no longer living regularly in her parents' home, but her parents were still providing everything that Om Prakash and his family needed:

We have no income at all. My husband remains an invalid. All our expenses are being met by my parents. My husband stayed with them for several months. Then they provided medicines, food, and drink. They paid for everything. If anyone came from Dharmnagri, all the food and the things presented to them were given by my parents. My husband and my son with polio survived thanks only to my relatives. If they hadn't helped us, then those two wouldn't have lived. My husband's treatment is continuing even now—100 rupees' worth of medicines arrive every month for him. That's why I never get clothes made. There's so little land. We don't even get enough to eat from it and we have to buy from the bazaar. Our clothes come from my parents' house. My husband wears my brothers' old clothes. To this day, I haven't bought any cloth. We don't have the money for it. Even now, if there's any trouble, I send news to my parents. No matter where they manage to find things, they'll certainly send things for me. My oldest brother is very good—he also helps me a lot. And both my sisters are now married into good homes. Their husbands are in service, and they too keep sending clothes for my husband. Yes, there is love and peace in my mother's home.

Notes

1. Other major expenditures, such as weddings, had similar effects.

2. See Jeffery, Jeffery, and Lyon (1989:77-97, 167-176) for more on women's work and access to health care during and after pregnancy.

3. See Chapter 6, note 4.

4. This uncle was the grandfather (FF) of Krishnu: see Chapter 6.

5. Generally, brothers were married in order of age, so it was unusual for Om Prakash to have an older unmarried brother.

6. This is described in more detail in Jeffery, Jeffery, and Lyon (1989:114-118).

11

Should I Become a Pauper?

The dates of the Muslim and Hindu festivals celebrated in Jhakri and Dharmnagri were settled according to lunar calendars comprising twelve months of twenty-nine or thirty days.[1] Islamic festivals shifted backward by about ten days every year in relation to the seasons. By contrast, the "leap month" inserted into the Hindu calendar every third year ensured that Hindu festivals moved within a small range during the same season every year. Thus it was completely fortuitous (and not wholly welcomed by us) that the Muslim Eid marking the end of the month of Ramzān in August 1982 took place on the very same day as the Hindu festival of Tījo.[2] Our frustrated attempts to cover both festivals simultaneously caused a great deal of mirth in both Dharmnagri and Jhakri.[3] As people repeatedly pointed out, the two festivals neatly highlighted married women's links with their parents and siblings. After a month of fasting and practicing other forms of abstinence, Muslims had eagerly awaited the Eid moon, which marked the new month that would begin with Sweet Eid [Mīthi Eid].[4] Special dishes, many of them sweet, were prepared. A Muslim woman—especially one married within the previous twelve months—should be in her husband's home for Eid. There, she would be visited by her male kin, who would arrive bearing their Eidi gifts of cash, clothing, foodstuffs, and especially sweets. For Hindu women, though, Tījo was an occasion for visiting their parents and celebrating the festival by singing Tījo songs at the tops of their voices as they swung on specially constructed swings.

In many important respects, a young married woman would be incorporated into her husband's household. Many a strong-willed little girl who obstinately refused to obey her mother or who put herself forward too much or demanded more food would be reprimanded with the reminder that such behavior would be totally unacceptable in her future home. She would be told to mend her ways quickly, for all too soon, she would have to adjust to the requirements of her in-laws. People would say that their married daughter had gone to "her own house."

Yet a married woman was rarely completely cut off from her parents and siblings. She was entitled to receive clothing and jewelry, foodstuffs, cash, and occasionally milch animals from them, though not land or other productive resources. As with the dowry, her control over the items sent was partial (at best) for as long as she remained in a joint household with her mother-in-law. Thereafter, she might use the foodstuffs as she wished and decide who should wear items of clothing. Among Hindus and Muslims alike, people wanted to give generously to their married daughter and sister. It was a matter of honor and merit. Ideally, then, her parents and brothers should send gifts after the rice and wheat harvests, to mark certain Muslim or Hindu festivals, and when marriages and births took place in her household or in their own. One time a young man arrived in Jhakri from nearby Chandpuri with Eidi gifts strapped on his cycle even though his married sister had been dead for several years. Not for nothing did parents say that "a daughter takes throughout all her life."⁵ As the opening song hints, the continual obligations—here to provide the bhāt *when the sister's child is being married—could indeed become oppressive.*

A woman's relationships with her parents and siblings entailed more than gift exchanges, however. She would expect to visit them from time to time and obtain a break from the rule of her mother-in-law and husband. Marriages and births in her natal home were especially important occasions for such visits, although she would probably also be allowed to visit in the event of illness and death. But the conditions under which she made such visits were largely set by her in-laws, who might resist her request if they considered the occasion did not merit it, if there was too much work for her to do, or if they feared that she would complain about her treatment in their home. Her brother would also visit her in her in-laws' village to check that all was well. But her father would probably visit only if she had no adult brothers; her mother and sisters would hardly ever visit her, if at all.⁶ Nevertheless, they would all be concerned about her protection and security, and a crisis, whether marital or monetary, might spur her natal kin to provide more support than normal.

A Song Requesting the *Bhāt*

"O brother, bring me an ornament for my forehead!
O brother, I'm requesting the *bhāt*, bring it quickly!"
"Sister, have you gone crazy?
What, are you out of your mind?
Should I become a pauper?
Should I heap everything on you?"
"O brother, I'm requesting the *bhāt*, bring it quickly!"

"O brother, bring me a necklace for my throat!
O brother, I'm requesting the *bhāt*, bring it quickly!"
"Sister, have you gone crazy?
What, have you become insane?

Should I make my wife go naked?
Should I heap everything on you?"
"O brother, I'm requesting the *bhāt*, bring it quickly!"[7]

A Father's Worry About Patched *Pājāmas*

Imrana was born in Qaziwala in the late 1950s. Before her birth, four other daughters had died, so she was a much-wanted child. Her father loved her dearly even though she was followed by six more children. She alone among the sisters was taught to read the Qur'ān Sharīf (by the wife of the *imām* [leader of prayers] at the mosque). In about 1973, Imrana was married to Irfan, a middle-peasant Sheikh in Jhakri. She had never experienced any serious financial problems and, indeed, was already living in a kiln-brick house on the edge of the village when we first knew her in 1982. Occasionally, she would sell dung cakes if she had any surplus. Otherwise, like most women in Jhakri and Dharmnagri, when asked about her "income," she told us about the money and other items she received from her parents.

> Even now, after over fifteen years of marriage, my mother has clothes made for me, my husband, and the children. She also gives some grain whenever I visit. When my brother's wife had a son, my brother gave me 250 rupees. He called our other married sister to stay for a while, and he gave her clothes as well as 250 rupees. My mother-in-law has never taken any jewelry or anything else from me. Whatever my parents and brothers give, I'm allowed to keep for myself. And whatever my husband earns, he puts into my hands. I can spend it as I need to.

Nevertheless, Imrana's father tried to ensure that she was living well in Irfan's home. Like most fathers, however, he rarely visited Imrana. That is a task for a woman's brothers:

> In all the years since I've been married, my father's visited me only three times, once when Rabia [Irfan's BD] was being married, once when I had mastitis and he came to ask after my health, and one other time. On that last occasion, he came without telling me beforehand. I was wearing a pair of *pājāmas* that I'd patched slightly. I desperately wanted to hide the patch from him, but he saw it. When he got home again, he had some clothes made and sent them to me. He told my mother to come and talk to me and find out if I don't have clothes made for me by my husband! When my mother came, I told her I have plenty of clothes. I explained that my patched *pājāmas* had been only slightly torn, and my father had seen just a small patch! Then my mother realized that there were no difficulties in my house.

The Plight of Shankar's Sister

Shakuntala had been married to Shankar, a poor-peasant Chamar, in 1980. For a few years, she had been able to rely on her mother-in-law's help. By 1990, though, Shakuntala's mother-in-law was no longer alive, and there was no one readily available to help with her work when she had a baby or when the harvest work became too heavy. Shankar's brothers' wives had their own work to do, and they had no daughters of an age to help. And Shakuntala's three sons were all still small. Another possibility might have been Shankar's married sister, but she was unable to visit Dharmnagri for long. "You see, her husband works away from home at a sugarcane crusher, and he spends whatever he earns on drink." Shakuntala told us. "That's why my husband's sister is so troubled. She isn't comfortable anywhere."

Shankar's sister was an only daughter, so we were puzzled that she had been married to a man like that. Shakuntala explained:

> My father-in-law used to smoke a lot of hashish. He was intoxicated all the time. When my husband's sister was to be married, her three brothers were still small children, like my three boys are now. My father-in-law didn't make careful enquiries. Without looking properly, he arranged her marriage on someone else's advice. Now his only daughter is greatly troubled. There's neither land nor a proper house, and her husband doesn't even give her money for food. She has to cut wood fuel from the scrubland, for her husband is careless and never gives her money for fuel either. She's always short of money. Whenever she comes to Dharmnagri, we give her money. My husband and his brothers get 5,000-6,000 rupees a year from selling sugarcane, so they have ready cash to give her. After every harvest she gets grain, too. Either she comes to collect it or her brothers take it to her. We also provide her with cloth. The three brothers arrange the giving together. It's up to us to give things to her. Partly, it's because we're happy to give. And because it's an act that brings merit, giving to her will create no shortages in our house. But we've also been compelled to give because she's been so troubled. And she is the only sister. If my husband and his brothers had been older when she was married, would they have let their only sister be married into a house like that? But they were small, and their father didn't have much sense.

Fatima and Her Brothers

Fatima's father-in-law was a wealthy Sheikh farmer in Jhakri, the only son of an only son who inherited all his grandfather's land. Yet Fatima often felt that she and her children were living less comfortably than they could.

My father-in-law built this kiln-brick house for us with his money. But it has just one room, and there are many of us. My husband's younger brother isn't married yet, and he has the other half of the house to himself. It's empty! The wheat and rice crops are divided, and we do get our share. But my father-in-law keeps all the cash income from the sugarcane and gives us just 500 rupees or so. I don't have any income of my own. I used to spin, but I haven't done that for a year. My oldest daughter doesn't spin either. I don't sell either milk or dung cakes. All the money remains under my father-in-law's control.

Nevertheless, Fatima's husband, Farooq, had managed to rent some land. Initially, he rented just a third of an acre, the next year two-thirds of an acre. By 1991, he was farming about two and a third acres, rented separately from three men in Jhakri.

If we had any spare grain from our share, we used to sell it. And when my father or uncle came to visit me from Qaziwala, they always gave me some cash as they were leaving. Maybe they'd give ten rupees, maybe five. Anyway, we'd collect all that money together. When we had 500 rupees, we rented some land. Now we have enough land separate from my father-in-law's to look after. We pay 1,000 rupees each year for every acre we rent. We're hoping that one of those men may sell us some land.

Not once since her marriage in the early 1970s, Fatima had suggested borrowing money from her brothers. One brother had been the headman of Qaziwala for a while and had found it very costly to entertain in the manner that he felt he should. Her other brother was cheated by a colleague in the fertilizer warehouse where he worked. Fatima felt she should not pressure either of them to do more for her than they already did:

I still receive the festival gifts regularly, eleven pounds of flour, a coconut, a couple of pounds of sugar and pulses, everything like that. There used to be four festivals when gifts came. Now nothing comes on Muharram, just on the two Eids and on Shabrāt.[8] If my children visit my sisters, they're given clothes and money. That's because my sisters are older than I am. And when I visit my brother in Qaziwala, he gives me clothes and money. My brother and uncle also give me money on Eid. My uncle gave me ten rupees last Eid. When my sister's daughter was married, my brothers presented thirty-one suits and 10,000 rupees in the *bhāt*. Even if my brother the headman has to borrow to do so, he must spend that much to keep his good name in the village.

Yet Fatima seemed worried about her finances. Her older daughter was nearly of an age to be married. A *bhāt* of the size her brother had given her sister would cover only a fraction of the expenses that Fatima would face when providing her daughter's dowry and entertaining the wedding guests. And although Farooq was carefully managing the incomes and expenditures for the land he was renting, they did not have enough to begin saving.

> We're troubled. My father-in-law gave clothes to his sons' children on Eid. My husband's two younger brothers each have three children, and they received two suits each for their children. We were given a suit apiece for our two girls, but there was nothing for the four boys. If my father-in-law would meet our daily expenses, we'd be able to save enough for our daughter's wedding. The income from our rented land is spent on household expenses. My in-laws have been paying for a wedding each year. Last year, it was my husband's brother; this year it was his only sister. There's another brother still to be married. Then, in a couple of years, we'll have to get my daughter married.

Brijpal's Intervention

Brijpal was the younger of two Jat brothers in Dharmnagri. He operated a farm of about six acres. Unlike his older brother—who was renowned for heavy drinking and a brusque manner—Brijpal had never sold land to repay debts. And when we first arrived in 1982, his household had immediately struck us as happy and relaxed. Like his brother's children, his own children affectionately called him *chacha* [FyB], a relative with whom children could expect to have a more easygoing relationship than with their father. We often enjoyed the cheerful company provided by his family. His house was among the first where Roger could go freely into the family courtyard behind the men's sitting area. Some weeks after we arrived in early 1982, we joined the family during Holī, the Hindu festival when people daub one another with powder paints and colored water. Brijpal and his wife, Swati, got into the spirit of things—no doubt helped by the country liquor laced with hashish—and they chased each other through their house, drenching livestock and guests as they went. Another time, shortly after we arrived in 1990, Brijpal summoned us for tea and sweets. With mock pathos he told the tale of how he had won a television in the village lottery. The celebration insisted on by his neighbors had cost more than a new television set, and the set he had won was in any case destined to become part of the gifts for his third daughter's cohabitation. He always seemed ready for a joke, even at his own expense, and appeared to take the cares of life lightly.

But one evening in early August 1990, Brijpal's brother rushed into our home. "We need your jeep right now! Brijpal's oldest daughter,

Priti, has eaten some rat poison in her in-laws' house. She had a row with her husband. She might die. You must take us there now." A rescue mission had to be mounted. Priti would need medical treatment before being brought to her parents' home. Without our jeep, the journey of some thirty miles would take several hours, by which time it might be too late. In local terms, this was definitely men's work. There had to be a show of strength. Who could tell if her in-laws might prove difficult or even violent in defending their honor?

Into the jeep with Roger piled Brijpal and his brother along with five of their eight sons, all strapping young men. Roger drove as fast as the dusk, the roads, and the traffic would permit. At one point, the railway-crossing gates were closed, but it was the final two miles that seemed never-ending, as they bumped along the rutted sandy track to the village where Priti had been married. Roger was wondering what was ahead of them. Would he be able to park the jeep where they could make a quick getaway if necessary?

For two hours after arriving in Priti's house, Roger sat, rather bemused, in the midst of pandemonium. For one thing, Roger thought he recognized Priti herself, right in the midst of the mêlée, energetically voicing her troubles and clearly not at death's door from eating rat poison. But then, Roger had last seen Priti eight years before, when she was visiting Dharmnagri to attend her second sister's wedding. His habit of not looking too closely at women for fear of causing embarrassment was now proving a liability.

Several string beds were brought into a courtyard so that the visitors could sit down. But there were no further efforts at hospitality, and no tea was prepared. Was this a bad sign? Brijpal took Priti to a more secluded courtyard to ask what had happened. Roger and the rest of the guests sat silently where they had been put. When Priti's husband returned from his day's work in the fields, a veritable shouting match ensued. For over an hour, there were rarely fewer than two people talking simultaneously, the men sitting on string beds, the women joining in as they hovered in the background. Several rhetorical speeches were addressed to Roger by Priti's husband. But other people were competing for Roger's ear, and Priti was also shouting her version of events from behind her senior male in-laws, from whom she had to conceal her face. Roger was bombarded by a cacophony of arguments, each drowning the others out. To whom should he listen first? He heard words such as "rat poison," "fault," "beating," and "rage," but he could not create a coherent story from the hubbub. Gradually, the noise abated. Some elderly men calmed things down. Brijpal's nephews took some of the young men aside for conferences elsewhere. Brijpal went to talk to his sister, who was also married in that village and had been instrumental in arranging Priti's marriage some fifteen years previously. Tea and snacks were finally served. The issue appeared to be resolved.

Roger and Brijpal's party returned to Dharmnagri, though without Priti. Roger was still puzzled, but driving home in the dark—mindful of unlit buffalo carts, cycles, pedestrians, and the armed highwaymen reputedly operating in the area—was hardly conducive to obtaining a clear account of the episode. So the next day, Patricia and Radha called at Brijpal's house to find out more.

Brijpal and his third daughter explained their side of the story. The previous day, Brijpal's sister—the one married in the same village as Priti—had sent her son with the news that Priti had swallowed rat poison and was calling for her father. Brijpal's arrival in a jeep with Roger and six other men had taken Priti's husband by surprise. Brijpal continued the tale:

> When I asked him what was the matter, he replied, "What are you asking me for? You should just ask your daughter." But I told him that I was asking him and not my daughter. He then told me that Priti had tried to eat rat poison. He said that if anything had happened to her, we'd all blame him. He said she could easily take rat poison in the future. That was why he'd had me sent for. At that, we became very heated. We began shouting at him that no one takes their own life without reason, and the whole matter was clearly his fault. The people of his village were also saying it was his fault.

"And didn't Priti's mother-in-law also say there was no blame on Priti's side?" interjected Brijpal's daughter.

"So what was the problem between Priti and her husband?" Patricia asked. Brijpal's daughter took up the story:

> My sister came to Dharmnagri with her children some time after the Tijo festival. She had her husband's permission. After a few days here, she went back to her husband's home with the children. She left one of her sons behind because our mother wanted to keep him so that he could attend school here. My sister hadn't made any firm plans with her husband about when he would fetch her. She decided to go back by herself, as her husband was busy with farmwork. She knew she had a lot of work too. But after she'd left, her husband arrived here. When he discovered she'd already gone, he became very angry. He was angry she had stayed so long and then angered again because she hadn't waited to be collected by him.

Priti's husband apparently harangued them about this and then went off furious, taking with him the son who had been left behind. When he arrived home, he began arguing with Priti, complaining that her parents did not care for her properly, that whenever she went there the children got sick and "those people" did not get them treated. Brijpal's daughter continued:

> My sister said, "It's not like that! My parents and brothers and sisters care very much for me. If I called them in the middle of the night, they'd all come running to my side." But her husband continued to say bad things about us to the other people in his house. He also beat Priti on her ankle with a stave. Then Priti herself became angry, and she got some rat poison. But her husband saw her just before she managed to eat it. He snatched the poison away from her and then sent our cousin [FZS] to fetch our father.

Brijpal himself was clearly incensed by his son-in-law's behavior. "My son-in-law said plenty of insulting things about me and my family in front of the people of his village. That made me feel bad. They weren't true at all. When Priti's oldest son got polio, her in-laws got no special treatment for him. Yet whenever he comes to Dharmnagri with his mother, we get treatment for him. And Priti has run a separate household for the past six years. She's very hard working."

Brijpal's daughter agreed:

> No one there has ever seen my sister with a load of dung in a basket on her head. She gets up so early that she's done all that work while everyone else is still asleep. And by the time she had two sons and a daughter, she wanted to be sterilized, but her husband and his mother were both completely against it. They were saying, "There are just two sons and they are both ill," for one had polio and the other always has a cough. "What's the guarantee that they'll survive?" they were saying. That was why they weren't going to stop other children being born. But then my sister had twin daughters, who are both very weak. And the oldest girl is also weak. All three girls look one of a kind. I once asked my sister's husband to give her more money for expenses, but he asked where he would find it. "What, is money found on trees?" he said. Then I asked him why he wasn't getting proper treatment for his children, and he said, "It's not within my control, whether all five children die and their mother as well." He doesn't talk very much, but when he does, he says things that tear the heart. Everyone in his village and all our relatives used to think he was very straightforward, but now we all understand what sort of man he is.

After a pause, she resumed. "My sister's quite sturdy and her husband is thin. If she hit him, he'd be knocked over to one side. But our mother has told my sister that she shouldn't hit him. Our mother said that our sister's honor is in her own hands. That's why my sister remained silent until now."

"But this time," said Brijpal, "we all went to his village and criticized him roundly. We warned him in front of everyone in his village that we wouldn't let him live in peace if anything happened to our Priti. We said we'd have him strung up in a noose. He shouldn't think we're weak. This whole village of Dharmnagri could unite to protect her. And I told Priti that if her husband said anything to her again, she mustn't remain silent. She should send news immediately."

Taslima's Visit to Her Parents

One day in spring 1991 when we were just finishing our day's work in Qaziwala, Taslima's parents asked if they could squeeze into our jeep and get a lift back home to Jhakri. Taslima's father, Akbar, was a poor-peasant Sheikh in his mid-forties. Taslima, his second daughter, had been married into a middle-peasant household in Qaziwala a couple of years earlier, and Akbar and his wife had been visiting her. They asked us to wait a few moments while they gathered their belongings. Some fifteen minutes later, when they had still not appeared, Radha and Zarin went to search for them. Zarin told us later about the row going on between Taslima's parents and her in-laws:

> Taslima was complaining that her sister-in-law (HeBW) was making her go outside and make dung cakes. The sister-in-law was denying it, saying she wouldn't have said such a bad thing. Since the two of them were living separately, she said, they both followed separate lives. She was saying she'd raise her own children and not go outside at all! And she said that Taslima needn't go outside either. But she herself makes twenty basketloads of dung cakes, she claimed, and yet never complains about it to Taslima when she gets back home! Then she told Taslima's mother that she'd talk to her husband. She said he'd be back by the evening. "He's not dead!" she said. Taslima's parents said they'd return in the evening.

Then they came to the jeep with Zarin and Radha and spent the entire journey grumbling about Taslima's in-laws. Taslima's mother told us what had happened:

> Taslima's sister-in-law was fine yesterday evening. When we began to set off for Jhakri, she made us stay overnight. Enough, a good thing has been damaged all because of some rice. Taslima's sister-in-law made some rice cooked with salt and pepper, and then she made a second lot in the same pot. Some was left over, and she began asking us why we hadn't finished it. She complained that she'd have to feed it to the buffalo, for where else

could she throw it? I was angry at that, and I asked her if they never had leftover rice to be fed to the buffalo. I told her she should have been thoughtful enough not to say such a thing until her guests had left. From then on, there was fighting.

Akbar said he had been silent all morning, listening to the shouting and squabbling. "But I'm going to speak out when I go back this evening!"

A couple of weeks later, Akbar was in Qaziwala again, and he wanted us to give Taslima and him a lift back to Jhakri. Once more, Zarin went to collect them. Taslima was reading the Qur'an Sharif inside her house. Akbar was lying on a bed on the veranda outside. Akbar called Taslima to come, but she was not allowed to leave with him. Akbar stormed off along the path, muttering angrily to Zarin as he went: "I've made the trip to collect her fifty times over, but they still won't send my girl back with me. My legs are breaking. I can hardly walk. Am I crazy? Don't I have work to do instead of coming back to Qaziwala repeatedly? Taslima's mother is ill in Jhakri. We'll see. I'll give them a taste of how I feel!" Akbar hardly paused for breath as he clambered into the jeep. "These people won't send her with me. That was the eighth time I'd been there. Now they're saying she can come this evening or tomorrow morning. I'm going to straighten them out." As he got out of the jeep when we arrived in Dharmnagri ten minutes later, he was still expostulating about Taslima's in-laws. "If Taslima ever comes home, I won't send her back to Qaziwala, not even if scores of years go by! I'll show her in-laws who can say when she'll be sent back to them!"

Dealing with Jayavati's Difficulties

A few days after Ritu had been married, Radha and Patricia were talking to Durgi and her oldest sister-in-law, Kusum, about arranging marriages. After Kusum's husband had died suddenly, she had been left with the task of arranging the match for her daughter, Jayavati. Kusum had looked for a boy in a number of places. In several instances, the boy's people began making comments such as, "A boy has become very costly these days." Kusum could not afford to arrange her daughter's wedding in a family that would make demands. Her husband's death had put all the family responsibilities on her and her oldest son, a young man who had just been married and was still a rather inexperienced farmer. Eventually, however, Kusum had found a boy whose family did not ask openly for anything in the dowry, and Jayavati was married there.

But now there was a crisis. Jayavati had returned to Dharmnagri to lend a hand with the arrangements for Ritu's wedding. Jayavati's husband had not been invited to the wedding. Indeed, he had not even been informed about it. When he came to collect Jayavati, he discovered the wedding preparations in full swing. He was furious not to have been included among the wedding guests. Kusum said he had wanted to take Jayavati with him there and then:

> He said there was no reason for him to stay on in Dharmnagri, since he hadn't been invited to the wedding. He made Jayavati get ready to leave with him. But we'd put a lot of Ritu's wedding arrangements in Jayavati's hands, and Durgi wouldn't let him take her away. So the next day, he left without telling anyone. He should have told me he was going, for I should have given him some money before he left. But you know, there's another reason why I didn't want to send Jayavati with him.

Durgi joined in: "Jayavati is having problems in her in-laws' village, and her mother won't send her back to her in-laws. First of all, she's going to summon Jayavati's father-in-law and talk to him. You see, he's troubling Jayavati." We asked what she meant by "troubling." Kusum told us how Jayavati had returned to Dharmnagri for Ritu's wedding in a very distressed state: "Jayavati was almost too embarrassed to tell me what was wrong. With great difficulty, I managed to extract the story from her. When Jayavati's in her in-laws' village and she's inside her house sleeping beside her husband, the father-in-law sneaks stealthily behind the house. He watches everything daily. Jayavati's husband says nothing. He's afraid of his father. It all seems bad to him, but he can't say anything to his father."

Then Durgi took over:

> Jayavati's father-in-law is still quite youthful. So is his wife. They have just the one son and a daughter who's ready for marriage. But the father-in-law looks at Jayavati with leering eyes, and he tells his son not to have sex with her. He also tells them not to lock the door when they're sleeping inside the house. So Jayavati's husband has also told her not to lock the door, for his father would be angry. Jayavati told me, "Auntie, my house in my in-laws' place is adobe and so my father-in-law can go round the back, lift up the thatch with a stick, and see everything." One day the father-in-law even got beaten up! You see, some guests had come and they were all sleeping outside. At that time, the father-in-law went to the back of the house to watch Jayavati and her husband. His foot slipped, and he cried out as he fell. The guests woke up and thought that a thief had come. In the darkness, they began beating him. Then the father-in-law told them his name and said he wasn't a thief. The guests asked, was

it really him? And what he was doing there? Then he lied to them in order to deceive them. He claimed he was searching for something. That's why, before anything else, we're going to call the father-in-law and tell him straight. We'll ask him if we married Jayavati to him or to his son. Kusum's brother organized the marriage, so we'll call him here too and tell him what's going on. Jayavati's husband is also upset about his father's bad habit. He's also said that we should call his father and talk to him straight. He said we should even beat him with our shoes if need be. He told us that he wouldn't consider anything we did to his father as wrong. But he himself can't say a thing to his father. And Jayavati was saying that she'd rather die than live in her father-in-law's house.

A Song Marking a Boy's Birth

Silently indicating with her finger,
The husband's sister asks for the new mother's golden bangle.

Father-in-law stands outside
And remonstrates with his daughter-in-law,
"Give it to her, Queen Bride,
For my daughter is an outsider now."
Silently indicating with her finger,
The husband's sister asks for the new mother's golden bangle.

Brother-in-law [HeB] stands outside
And remonstrates with his sister-in-law,
"Give it to her, Queen Bride,
For my sister belongs to someone else now."
Silently indicating with her finger,
The husband's sister asks for the new mother's golden bangle.

The king [husband] stands outside
And remonstrates with his wife,
"Give it to her, Fair Queen,
For she's my darling sister."
Silently indicating with her finger,
The husband's sister asks for the new mother's golden bangle.[9]

Notes

1. Islamic months begin with the new moon and Hindu ones with the full moon.

2. See Chapter 6, note 4.

3. At that time, the tone of communal politics of the locality was quite different from the tensions and threats of violence that came to the fore during our stay in 1990-1991. People's amused responses to the coincidence of Eid and Tĩjo

in 1982 contrasted sharply with their anxieties over the near coincidence of Eid with the Hindu festival of Holī in spring 1991, when the general-election campaign was beginning in the highly charged climate soon after the first assault on the mosque at Ayodhya. The district magistrate in Bijnor, for instance, was rumored to have said that he could not guarantee the safety of any women out in the streets at this time.

4. Mīthi Eid is so called to differentiate it from Bakr Eid [Goat Eid], when goats and other animals are sacrificed.

5. In Hazrat Nizamuddin, for instance, people talked about the "final gift" [*ākhri dān*], the white funeral shroud in which a woman's body is wrapped before burial. See Jeffery (1979:57).

6. Some women in Dharmnagri had never been visited by their mothers. In Jhakri, since marriages were generally within a close radius and often between relatives, mothers could visit their married daughters, but they normally did not do so very often. Women in Bijnor had less access than normal to their natal kin when they were pregnant and in the immediate postpartum period. See Jeffery, Jeffery, and Lyon (1988, 1989). See also Raheja (1988); Raheja and Gold (1994); and Dyson and Moore (1983) for more discussion of the significance of the links between a married woman and her natal kin.

7. This song is from the *bhāt* genre, sung when women visit their brothers to request the *bhāt* or when the brother brings the *bhāt* to his sister's marital home.

8. Muharram is the first month in the Islamic year. See Chapter 4, note 1. The Shabrāt festival, more correctly Shab-i-Barāt, is the night during the month of Sha'bān when people's fortunes for the coming year would be registered in heaven, and people kept vigil through the night.

9. This birth song touches on the same theme as the first song in this chapter but from the perspective of the new mother in relation to her husband's married sister. Often, women claimed, the husband's sister sets her sights on items of jewelry that her brother's wife brought with her from her own parents' home, usually as part of the dowry.

12

Toasted on One Side

Jabruddin was in his late twenties when we first knew him. He lived in the same Sheikh compound as his second cousin [FFBSS] Nisar and Najma. Khalil and his brother, Khurshid Ahmed, were his first cousins [FyBS]. Jabruddin's parents had both died just a few years before our arrival and so too had Jabruddin's younger brother. Thus, he was the only adult man in his household. In the early 1980s, he was farming the land jointly with his father's three younger brothers and their sons. As an only surviving son, he would come to control more land than any of his first and second cousins once the farming enterprise was divided. Already, his share of the produce was enabling him to live more comfortably than several of the other families in the compound. He and his wife, Jamila, had built a kiln-brick house with two rooms. By the mid-1980s, they had upgraded it by plastering its exterior and adding a tiled facade decorated with Islamic inscriptions praising Allah and the Prophet Mohammed.

Jamila and Jabruddin reflected several common features of family patterns among Muslims in rural Bijnor. The marriage partners of the Jhakri Sheikhs were generally from nearby villages, either exclusively Muslim (as Jhakri itself was) or predominantly so. When we visited other villages in the area, people whom we had not met before would welcome us, explaining that they had heard about us from their relatives in Jhakri. In jest, indeed, people often talked of the area as "chhota Pakistan" [little Pakistan] because of these convoluted and densely interwoven marriage networks.[1] Jabruddin's mother and Jamila [her BD], for instance, had both been born in Islampur Das. Jamila's mother had come from Tikkupur. Jabruddin's sister was married in Burhanuddinpur and her husband's sister Hashmi was married to Haroon, in another Sheikh compound in Jhakri.[2]

Yet in other ways, Jamila's life was unusual. Jamila's mother was widowed young, and she returned to her own brothers' house in Tikkupur, where Jamila was reared. Far from being caught up in the joys and woes and the comings and goings that typified life in such richly dense networks, Jamila experienced herself as utterly isolated. The previous chapter indicated the significance of the

Arranging Kindling at the Cooking Hearth

*links that married women in Bijnor—whether Muslim or Hindu—have with
their natal kin. Jamila's case puts all that into high relief. To have virtually no
contact or support is a serious matter, and it leaves a woman in her husband's
home feeling "toasted on one side."*

* * * * * *

It took a long time to get to know Jamila. When we first arrived in
early 1982, she and her husband, Jabruddin—like many others in
Jhakri—were suspicious about our intentions. Why were we asking so
many questions? What was the point in their answering? What would
they gain from it all? And how would we use the answers? Had we
come to count them so that they could be sterilized? We tried to explain
the purpose of doing research and writing books. Khurshid Ahmed
tried to dispel people's fears by saying our work would result in the
sorts of information that students read about in school. He insisted that
answering our questions would bring them no harm. But for several
months after our arrival, many people in Jhakri remained wary of us.
Jamila herself managed to divert us from our intent by hijacking our
"interview" attempts with her jesting and sometimes abrasive humor.
Only gradually did she become willing to talk to us.

One of our initial aims was to explore the work of rural women in
Bijnor District, particularly the work that pregnant women did at different stages in their pregnancy. Jamila was one of several pregnant
women we hoped would talk to us about this, but we had to content
ourselves with passing comments, grudgingly tossed in our direction.

* * * * * *

We could tell from just watching Jamila and other women in Jhakri
that pregnant women continued with most of their work throughout
pregnancy. One day, Jamila was carrying food to the fields for Jabruddin. He was harvesting sugarcane and had no time to come home
during daylight. She said that she did that every day at that time of
year—but would not stop to talk further about it. A few weeks later, we
again asked her to tell us about her work, but she said that Jabruddin
had told her not to.

"He gave no reason," Jamila told us. "But what will you do once
you've written down all my work? Will you do it for me?"

"No, of course not!" said Swaleha, laughing. "But surely there's no
problem in just telling us about it?"

"My biggest work is going to bed at night, getting up in the morning,
and having a bath."

Jabruddin's cousin's wife, Najma, intervened at this point: "Why are you telling them lies? Whenever do you have a bath each day?"

Jamila ignored the dig and turned to Swaleha. "Don't you have any jewelry to wear, Swaleha?" said Jamila. Swaleha said that she did.

"Then why don't you wear it?" demanded Jamila.

"Because I'm traveling around and it's not safe to wear it. Anyway, it feels heavy," Swaleha added after a pause.

"But if jewelry feels heavy to you, what would a husband feel like? He'd be very heavy! How would you ever lift him off?"

Swaleha was embarrassed. She asked Jamila not to make dirty remarks but instead to tell us about her work. Jamila retorted that she had no time to do so. Swaleha said we would come back some other time. But when we did so a month afterward, Jamila was again resistant to the idea: "Will you provide me with a servant once you've written down my work?"

Swaleha tried to be conciliatory, saying that we could not provide a servant, but we would do some of Jamila's work for her. With a side-long glance, Jamila replied that her biggest job was removing the children's pee and shit several times a day. Swaleha had clearly had other jobs in mind—and we could not persuade Jamila to tell us about her work on that occasion either.

A few weeks later after talking to other women in Jamila's compound, we went to sit with her along with Khurshida, the wife of Khalil, one of Jabruddin's cousins. Khurshida wanted to hear about the snake that had been found inside Jamila's house the previous evening. We again asked Jamila if she would answer our questions. As we sat there, we were joined by Hanifa, a cousin of Jabruddin's who had recently been married to Haqqani, a young man from another Jhakri family. Hanifa had spent the night after her wedding in her in-laws' home but (as was customary) returned to her parents' home the next day to await the cohabitation some months later. Jamila drew attention away from herself by teasing Hanifa.

"Here you are taking your rest while Haqqani is busy in the fields cutting cane!"

"What else should I be doing?" asked Hanifa.

"Take water out to the fields for him. He must be thirsty!"

Hanifa was embarrassed. "You go yourself. I'm not going!"

"But you're Haqqani's wife, so you should go! Why should I go? You should take it for him. You ought to take care of him. Can't you even take water for him to drink?"

"The people of his house will take care of him."

"Have you seen Haqqani since the wedding night?" asked Jamila, thoroughly enjoying Hanifa's embarrassment.

"No!"

"But your cousin Gulshan has seen her husband! She hid behind a dung-cake stack when she saw him coming. But he raised his hand at her and asked how long she was going to keep *purdah* from him![3] You know, Hanifa, you should go up on the roof when we all go up to sight the Eid moon and take a look at Haqqani from the roof!"[4]

"We can't see anyone's roof from our house," mumbled Hanifa.

"Hanifa should be sent to her in-laws' house for Eid. Haqqani's heart must be wanting to catch sight of her!"

Hanifa was exasperated. "You go there yourself on Eid and see him! Do stop teasing me like this!"

"But Haqqani's my husband's younger brother and I'm his older brother's wife. I'd be embarrassed to talk to him!"[5]

The banter faltered and Swaleha repeated our request that Jamila tell us about her current work. Jamila retorted that she had not been doing any, since her eyes had been inflamed and swollen. Could she not tell us about what little she had been doing, Patricia asked. But Jamila refused further talk.

We saw Jamila again about a month before her baby was due. We were talking to Gulshan and to Jabruddin's aunt Latifan when Jamila came into the courtyard. Latifan nodded in her direction and commented that Jamila was still carrying food each day to the field where Jabruddin was working. Jamila came to sit beside us.

"I'd like you to get some of those pills to stop children coming so quickly," Jamila announced to Patricia. "I don't want any more children."

"I'd like some too," added Latifan. "I don't want any more children either."

Patricia said they would have to get the pills themselves, but Jamila insisted that we would have to do the job for them. Patricia said they would need a checkup. "The thing is this, you have to get them from a doctor. But I'll come with you if you like."

"Don't you like having a lot of children?" Swaleha asked them.

"I have eight and that's plenty," Latifan replied.

"But Jamila doesn't have so many," commented Swaleha.

"But Jamila's already had four children," Latifan replied.

Gulshan explained Jamila's situation to us. "Only two of her children are still alive. That's what counts," she said. "And now a third will soon be born."

Only after the birth of this child did Jamila begin to talk more freely to us. Throughout the pregnancy, she had been ill with a recurrent fever that persisted, despite treatment from various places, until her baby son was some six months old. On one occasion, when the baby was two months old, she went to the Dharmnagri dispensary for treatment. When she returned, no one in her compound even stopped their work to ask what had happened to her. She just carried on with her own work for a while and then went inside her house alone to lie down and rest. It was much the same six weeks later. She was still feeling very unwell but had to finish making dung cakes before she could fetch medicines from the dispensary. She suddenly became much more serious and forth-coming than ever before about her work.

> Because of my work, I never get any rest. I get up in the morning and wash my face and hands. Then I cook the food and take it to the fields. When I get back home, I wash the night clothes that have been soiled by the children. After that I take the animals outside and retether them; then I collect the cattle dung and bring it right here, where we women make the dung cakes. After I've made the dung cakes, I go back to the house and make the evening meal, sweep the house and courtyard, wash the dishes, and water the animals. There are all sorts of separate tasks. Some-times the baby stays hungry, as I can't take a break to breast-feed him. Just tell me, with all that work, how could medicines succeed? I do all my work alone and never rest. I sometimes feel like lying down—but who'd do the work? Everyone just does their own work. No one in the com-pound helps me. I don't get help from the unmarried girls either. If I feel unwell, I might lie down. But I still have to cook the evening meal. No one has ever cooked it for me and fed it to me.

When she had finished making the dung cakes, she picked up her baby son, who had been asleep across her lap as she worked on her haunches. She lifted the basket in which she had collected the dung and the bucket that she had filled with water to dilute the dung before making the dung cakes. On the way to her home, as if to underline what she had been saying, we found her toddler daughter fast asleep, draped over the shaft of a cart near the men's sitting room. Jamila scooped her up and handed her—still asleep—to Patricia. We carried both sleeping children back home, where she left them untended while she went to get medicines for herself from the Dharmnagri dispensary. The ice was broken. Thereafter, Jamila's sense of being alone became a common refrain in our conversations.

*   *   *   *   *   *

In spring 1972, Jamila had been married to Jabruddin, her father's sister's son. The cohabitation took place about three months after the wedding. Jamila's mother-in-law had had several children who had died before Jamila's marriage. Jamila said she had no idea about them.

So when she began living regularly in Jhakri, she was in the same household as Jabruddin's parents, his younger brother, and his unmarried sister. About two years later, Jabruddin's sister was married and she moved to her husband's village, Burhanuddinpur. Soon after this, according to Jamila, her mother-in-law had a loop inserted by the ANM, but she had terrible pains and eventually became very ill and died. Subsequently, Jabruddin's father died, and in mid-1981 Jabruddin's younger brother also died.

Now, Jamila's household consisted only of herself, Jabruddin, and their children. As she saw it, she had no real relatives in her husband's village—and Jabruddin had only one sister, who belonged to her "own house" in her husband's village. As Jamila put it, Jabruddin's sister could visit Jhakri only if her in-laws gave their permission. She usually did so briefly two or three times a year, generally for weddings but sometimes just to see Jamila and Jabruddin or if Jamila was ill and needed help.

When Jamila had her first child, her mother-in-law was still alive. Jabruddin's sister was not yet married, and she was on hand to help out. By Jamila's second delivery, though, her mother-in-law was dead, and Jabruddin's sister came from her in-laws' village to help. The next two times Jabruddin's sister could not come (once because she was pregnant herself), and Gulshan took over Jamila's work. After her fifth pregnancy, Jamila commented that a pregnant woman should get rest, especially near the end: "But rest isn't obtained. I don't go many places. I generally work just in the compound. I go out to make dung cakes and take food to the fields. I carried on doing that right through pregnancy. Lifting dung and making dung cakes and going to the fields, these are jobs that are difficult toward the end. But I didn't get any time off at all—there was no one else to do the work."

This had not really been remedied by the arrival of Jabruddin's sister a month before the delivery. She did just a little of Jamila's work until the baby was born—and stayed only a short time afterward: "I had scarcely any rest. I don't have so much power over anyone in my in-laws' village that I can make them work. She did my housework and outside work after the birth. But her husband collected her five or six days after the birth, and then I did it all myself. No one in this compound helps anyone else out. They all just do their own work. Men can work together, but women are incapable of living together harmoniously."

The only person who had helped Jamila after her deliveries was Gulshan, but even that had become impossible after Gulshan's own marriage. And once Jabruddin's sister had children of her own, it was even harder for her to visit Jhakri often.

Generally, women in rural Bijnor would not call on their own mothers and sisters to help during their pregnancies and deliveries, as it would be shameful for a woman to give birth in front of her mother.[6] Help should be provided, if at all, by a woman's female in-laws. Only under extraordinary circumstances would a woman call on her natal kin. In 1985 during her sixth pregnancy, Jamila became very ill. By seven months, her body and legs swelled and she could not walk. She needed to have all her work done for her and even had to be carried to the latrine. No one in Jhakri was available to do that for her. Jamila persuaded Jabruddin to fetch her cousin [FZD]—but then, as this woman was Jabruddin's cousin [MZD] too, she could not unequivocally be counted as one of Jamila's natal kin.

Jamila felt her position would have been very different if Jabruddin's brothers had lived. Then she would have had real sisters-in-law rather than merely the wives of Jabruddin's uncles and cousins. "Then I could tolerate their criticisms because they'd be real sisters-in-law. Sometimes I'd have to do their work, and they'd have to do mine. That's why real relatives are different from the others."

Jabruddin did not work alone as Jamila had to. Farming entailed expenses that were more easily met when men operated their land together, sharing draught animals and equipment and working with one another in the fields. But in Jamila's view, Jabruddin was overburdened by the other men, his father's brothers and their sons. Unlike all of them, Jabruddin was the only adult male in his household, and there was no one to do his share of work if need be: "Some of the men go away for weeks at a time, but he can't even stay away overnight. If he even visits his sister in Burhanuddinpur, the other men get angry with him. His own father's no longer alive, and he has no brothers. He's alone, so people can say what they like to him."

Jamila also felt they had been poorly treated regarding the debts that had been incurred in order to pay for the dowry and other expenses when Jabruddin's sister was married. At the time of that marriage, Jabruddin's father and three uncles [FB] had still not divided their father's land. In addition to the loan, the interest payments had mounted up, but no one paid off the loan. Only after Jabruddin's father died and the land was divided was the loan repaid by Jabruddin himself—by selling most of the jewelry that had been presented to Jamila by her in-laws when she was married. Jamila was left with some small items and a few pieces of gold jewelry. Everything would have remained with her had it not been for the debt.

There were those, however, who did not have a great deal of time for Jamila's complaints. After chatting to Jamila, one woman reported that

Jamila was crying and yet again saying that she had no relatives at all. Another commented: "What's the benefit of her crying? When Jabruddin's brother was alive, Jamila never used to do much for him. And when she did, she used to say that she was doing him a special service."

From the viewpoint of other households in the compound, too, Jabruddin's finances compared favorably with their own. The land that belonged to Jabruddin's paternal grandfather was divided into four equal portions for his father and three uncles. Two of those uncles had two sons each, and the third had six. Since Jabruddin had no brothers, he would get a quarter share of the land, but his uncles' land would be further divided among his male cousins. Moreover, Jabruddin had only one sister to be married. Those very factors of life and death that made Jamila feel so alone in Jhakri had substantial economic implications. Jabruddin had been able to invest in a tubewell engine, buy more land, and build a larger house for his family. As Khurshida pointed out, Jamila could sell some of the grain that came into her household; Khurshida could not, as her identical share of the crop had to feed more people. If Jamila complained about having no sisters-in-law to help her, others envied her because she did not have to spread household resources so thinly. Indeed, this much was conceded by Jamila herself when talking about her diet during pregnancy: "As there are few people in my household, the grain easily lasts all year, and we can sell some grain in order to buy other things. And I was also able to have milk to drink during my pregnancy."

Unlike some of her neighbors, Jamila did not have to sell dung cakes or milk to raise cash for minor purchases. The sugarcane cultivated by Jabruddin raised enough income:

> I make only as many dung cakes as I need for one year. I throw the rest of the dung into the midden for manure. If I sold dung cakes, the money would just get spent on household things. And anyway, the fertilizer that we buy is not as good a manure as dung. What's the point of selling dung cakes and then putting fertilizer of inferior quality on the fields instead of midden manure? And I've never sold milk. Just at present, we don't have a buffalo that's giving milk, but when we do, I don't sell milk. Since we do so much work for the buffalo, should someone else drink the milk while we don't get the benefit of the work? I put some milk aside for drinking and use the rest for making clarified butter. Then I put the clarified butter aside, and all of us in the house can eat it.

Not only that, but Jamila had considerably more control over the day-to-day management of the household than many other women.

Since his parents' death, Jabruddin had certainly had to abide by what his elders decided about purchasing jointly owned animals because he was the youngest man heading a household involved in the combined farming. But he consulted Jamila about when to buy livestock separately for their own household. Moreover, Jabruddin had put the household purse in Jamila's hands: "Whatever is earned from the farming—grain and money alike—it all remains with me. I proceed according to my own wishes and buy what I want. All the income is spent on household things. Why should I spoil my peace and my food because of money? If there's too much grain and we need money, only then do I sell it. And that too is for the benefit of all the people in the house and when there's some need to sell. I don't sell grain for the benefit of myself alone."

Yet Jamila set the positive features of her married life against the burden of the work that she faced alone. By the mid-1980s, three of Jamila's first four children had died. Even by 1991, her oldest child was a boy of just thirteen. Thus, she had no immediate prospect of a daughter-in-law even though she had been married nearly twenty years. And her daughter born in 1986 was not yet old enough to be much help in the house. Moreover, Jamila was keen to get her children educated:

> I send them all to school. He [Jabruddin] pays no attention to the children's education. I'm trying my hardest to encourage them with their education, but he pays absolutely no attention to it. I send the boys and the girl alike to the *madrasā* in Begawala. The boys don't like studying. Sometimes they go to school, sometimes they don't. But the girl goes every day. I shall have her taught the Qur'ān Sharīf as well as Urdu and Hindi. If the boys don't study, they can still do farming. But the girl will go to another house later on. She should be somewhat capable. Her in-laws should find nothing lacking.

Jamila's enthusiasm for educating her daughter, however, would mean that she would continue to be deprived of help with the housework. During our first research visit, Jamila had talked of being sad at bearing more children because so many of her children had died, two before we arrived and a third during our stay. Yet Jamila had continued to have children. Jabruddin had never suggested that she use any contraception, and she was afraid to do so without his permission. By her ninth delivery in Ramzān 1991, however, she had six living children, four sons and two daughters. She was saying that she would be prepared to get some medicines without Jabruddin's knowledge. Indeed, in 1991 she was making much the same complaints as nearly a decade earlier:

I'm alone in my in-laws' village. I have to tolerate everything alone. Just before my youngest child was born, Khurshida had a fight with Gulshan's mother, who'd said to her, "Whenever your children were born, I alone kicked you!" She said that in anger. She meant that only she had helped Khurshida. My pains began a little while after that, but I said nothing to anyone because of the argument. I had pains the whole evening and right through the night. I was still having them in the morning. Then I cooked the food and put it aside. I made all the arrangements for the fasting. In the evening, when it was time to break the fast, the pains became stronger and then I called two of the other women. Just at that moment, this girl was born. They said I should have told someone earlier. Then the *dāī* was hurriedly called and she came and cut the cord.

* * * * * *

In rural Bijnor, a married woman's visits to her natal village provided relief from her in-laws' village. A woman would go to her parents' house to relax, to throw off the requirements of veiling to which she was subject in her husband's village, and to meet at least some of the people with whom she had spent her childhood. As Jamila once put it, "Women survive in their in-laws' village only with great intelligence, for they must heed and obey their in-laws to the letter. It is possible to refuse to do something once for your parents but not for your in-laws."

But Jamila felt just as much without support in the place where she was born, nearby Islampur Das, as in Jhakri. Her feelings of isolation in her in-laws' village had been compounded by her mother's early widowhood, which compromised Jamila's access to such easy familiarity. Jamila had no one in her natal village except her paternal cousins, and "they never even ask how I am or invite me to visit them." As she commented after one of her deliveries, "I don't have parents or brothers and sisters who would have to be informed after I've given birth. I suppose someone must have told my mother's brother about the baby. But there's no one else to tell."

Jamila's father used to farm in Islampur Das with his father and older brother. They owned twelve acres and they and their wives and children all lived and ate together. Jamila's mother was married very young, and so the cohabitation took place some four or five years later, once Jamila's mother had reached puberty. Jamila was the first-born daughter.

When I was very young, between one and two years old, my father died. He got cholera. My mother completed the four months and ten days of seclusion after being widowed. That's done in the in-laws' house. My grandmother [FM] served my mother's food with her own hand. She used to give very small helpings, and she caused my mother lots of trouble. When the seclusion period was over, the widow's weeds came from my mother's parents in Tikkupur. There were eighteen or twenty suits. My grandmother kept them all and locked them all away. She gave my mother only one suit.[7]

Jamila said that her mother was very young and could not understand all that was going on around her. Jamila's grandmother [FM] was apparently thinking that they should not remarry Jamila's mother into another family.

Some people were telling my grandparents that they should marry my mother to her husband's older brother so that the honor of the house would remain there. Hearing that, my aunt [FeBW] began crying and saying that people were removing the thatch from over her head, that they were creating competing heirs. Because she was so young, my mother just thought that "thatch" meant the roof of the house, and so she asked her sister-in-law, "Why are you crying, sister-in-law? You have one roof overhead and no one's taking it away." Then the other women began telling my mother what was being proposed. As soon as she understood, my mother returned to her own parents' house in Tikkupur, and she took me with her. But didn't my father have any land? When he died, my uncle and grandfather took it all. They never gave me anything. My uncle died a few years later, and my grandfather registered all the land in the names of my uncle's three sons. He didn't think that he had another daughter-in-law and a granddaughter. If some land had been put into my mother's name or my own, my mother would have stayed in Islampur Das. And my cousins have never called me, thinking that their "sister" might want to visit them there.

Jamila had no connection with her father's people and virtually never visited Islampur Das, the village she would normally have expected to regard as her *māykā* [natal village]. Consequently, as Jamila put it, Tikkupur had effectively been both her *māykā* and her *nanihāl* [mother's mother's village].[8]

Jamila's mother did not remarry—so Jamila had no brothers or sisters—nor had she any work that gave her an income of her own. She just helped with the work of her brothers' home. This meant that her brothers were housing her somewhat under duress, and (according to Jamila) she could not put much pressure on them, for instance, in relation to Jamila's education and marriage.

My mother had read the Qur'ān Sharīf. I don't know about my father, as I was so young when he died. Possibly he hadn't learned to read. But if there had been a school or *madrasā* in Tikkupur, then what? My mother was living in someone else's house. She couldn't educate me by demanding that her brothers provide money for a slate and reading primers. I didn't go to school, nor did I go to anyone else's house to study. So I've had to live out my life uneducated. These days, people want educated daughters-in-law, but not when I was married. I'm upset about not having studied just because my mother was living under such constraints. Not to study is harmful. I'm like a blind person.

The decision to marry Jamila into her father's sister's house in Jhakri was made by Jamila's mother and older uncle [MB]. Jamila's younger uncle, however, did not want the marriage to take place. He was, Jamila told us in 1991, still angry about it: "He used to say, 'Those people [Jamila's mother's in-laws] gave my sister nothing. They put her out of the house. Could Jamila's mother-in-law not have said to her own father that Jamila and her mother [her BD and BW] also have some rights?' My uncle says I shouldn't have been married in such a place as this."

Jamila's mother, however, wanted to honor a decision that had been made with Jabruddin's mother shortly after Jamila was born, that Jamila would be married to Jabruddin. Other offers of marriage certainly came for Jamila, from Islampur Das, and from other places too. As Jamila put it, "People come to *ber* trees laden with fruit and use sticks to knock the fruit off [meaning that they would come only to houses with girls when they were searching for a bride]. But my mother said it was better to marry me to our own people than to marry me to strangers some distance away. And my older uncle [MeB] also said, 'Those people [Jabruddin's parents] are our own, and a childhood engagement shouldn't be broken.' My opinion wasn't asked, of course. No one at all asks a girl's opinion!"

The decisions about how much to present in the gift exchanges that accompany a marriage and about what to give in Jamila's dowry were also made by Jamila's uncle [MeB] and her mother: "But my mother was living in her brother's house, so she didn't want to lean too heavily on him. And there's some difference between your own daughter and your sister's daughter. That's why there wasn't much dowry."

* * * * * *

In Islampur Das, then, Jamila had only her father's older brother's sons. Tikkupur was not her own natal village but her mother's. By 1990,

Jamila's mother and one of her mother's brothers were no longer alive, so now there was just one uncle and his sons, one of whom was married and had small children. This remaining maternal uncle sometimes invited Jamila to stay, and then only would Jabruddin take her there.

> There's also my mother's sister in Qaziwala, but she's very poor, so what would I do, having gone to see her? A woman just goes to visit her parents. That's why I don't ask my husband if I can go to Tikkupur, for who's there for me to visit? It's been like this almost since the time I was married. It's not that my husband prevents me from going. I would never go without his permission. It's not right to go without asking. But in any case I just don't go, so why would I seek his permission? Since my parents aren't alive, what would I do once I'd got there?

That was why she visited Tikkupur just occasionally, every "two to four years." She said she could not really say how often she went there, sometimes as often as twice a year, but sometimes well over a year would pass and she still had no opportunity to go. Generally, she went to attend some wedding or engagement, and she had also been to help her cousin's wife after she gave birth. One time, too, she went because her uncle's infant son died. But she did that out of "necessity" because of the death and returned home hurriedly, since she was pregnant and would not ordinarily have gone at all in that condition. Otherwise, her relatives did not ask her to stay often, nor did they press her to extend her visits beyond the time that had been agreed with Jabruddin. And they rarely visited her in Jhakri.

The items sent to a married woman by her natal kin are another barometer of her relationship with them. But Jamila had received far less than she would have expected had her father lived. Her paternal cousins in Islampur Das had not established any regular pattern of sending things to her. Her maternal relatives in Tikkupur did not send grain after the wheat and rice harvests, nor did they usually send sweetmeats and other foodstuffs to mark the main Muslim festivals. She received little from her relatives, and she rarely received the clothing for herself, her children, and Jabruddin that she would expect after staying with them.

In 1991, Jamila told us that she simply spent every day in Jhakri without any hope of a change of scene or some respite from the daily routine. It was over a year since she had been to Tikkupur to see her mother's relatives:

> I used to go there while my mother was still alive. But now I go less often. I have to take all the children with me. I don't like going with so many

children. I feel ashamed to take so many extra mouths to be fed at my mother's brother's house. Even when my mother was alive I rarely went. You see, my mother was herself dependent on other people. She wasn't in charge there. My heart wants to go to my mother's place, but I don't go. I just stay here. And if you leave bread to toast on just one side beside the cooking hearth, doesn't it burn?

Notes

1. This was especially characteristic of the early phases of our work in the area. Later, with the communal antagonisms associated with the Ayodhya affair, few Muslims put things in these terms to us.

2. Haroon and Hashmi were also key informants through our research, as were Haroon's younger brother, Irfan, and his wife, Imrana. See Jeffery, Jeffery, and Lyon (1989) for more on them. Their oldest brother was married to Mehbuba (see Chapters 1 and 3).

3. Gulshan had also been married within Jhakri. While living at her parents' house, she should have been free to move around without veiling herself; but now that Jhakri was also the village of her in-laws, she had to be careful to veil herself when likely to be seen by her father-in-law or her husband.

4. Muslims eagerly looked for the new moon, which marked the end of Ramzān and indicated that they could celebrate Eid the next day.

5. Jabruddin and Haqqani were "village brothers" rather than close relatives.

6. In Bijnor, Hindu and Muslim women alike avoided giving birth in their natal village. In some other parts of north India, women routinely returned to their natal village to deliver, especially for the first time. For more details, see Jeffery, Jeffery, and Lyon (1989:257-258).

7. Immediately after being widowed, a Muslim woman would be secluded in order to establish if she was pregnant by her late husband. The widow's weeds were another example of the gifts that a married woman's parents or brothers provided for her.

8. *Māykā* [literally "the mother's village"] was used by Muslims to refer to the village into which a woman's mother was married and in which she herself was born and raised. We have usually translated this as "natal village." The equivalent term for Hindus was *pīhar*, meaning "the father's village," but again implying that a woman had been born and reared there in her father's house. Jamila, of course, was born in Islampur Das but raised in Tikkupur. The word *nanihāl* derives from the words for the maternal grandparents, *nānī* [MM] and *nānā* [MF].

13

Why Have You Married Me So Distantly?

In the song that opens this chapter, the women of the bride's household sing from the bride's point of view. Despite the accusation, though, not all brides in Bijnor were married "so distantly," at least not in a geographical sense. In the space of one week in early May 1982, some half-dozen marriages took place in Jhakri. Just as among Hindus in Bijnor, most Muslim marriages entailed village exogamy, although the distances involved were usually less. Gulshan's wedding presented a logistical problem, however. Gulshan was born in Jhakri. She was to be married into a home that backed onto the house of one of her uncles, which itself faced Gulshan's across the courtyard. But a wedding, people said, necessitated something a bit more dramatic than having the men of the groom's party simply clamber up the steep stairway onto the roof of the groom's house, walk over the rooftops, and descend into the courtyard of the bride's home. A real barāt *ought to travel rather more than twenty yards, and it ought also to arrive in style.*

The solution was for Roger to take our jeep to the groom's house. The groom and six other men piled into the front; eighteen others crushed into the back. Roger drove across the deeply pitted cart track to the north of Jhakri to the metaled road about half a mile away with little or no chance of changing gear or applying the handbrake. The jeep was followed by more men on a tractor and trolley and yet others on a buffalo cart. The procession followed the road as it described an arc around Chandpuri and Dharmnagri, and then it turned off the road onto another cart track that approached Jhakri from the south. Patricia, Swaleha, and the womenfolk (of course) adopted the rooftop route. Although Gulshan's was to be a "within-village" marriage, a sense of separation between her natal place and her marital home were acted out through the two miles that the groom's party traversed—even though Gulshan always resorted to the rooftop route thereafter to move between her husband's and her parents' homes.

If a woman was married at no great physical distance, however, there should still be some social distancing between her and her relatives, just as there would be if she had been married into a more distant household. Some separation should be maintained, though not to the extent experienced by Jamila (in the previous chapter) or Parvati (in this chapter). Excessively close contact between a woman and her natal kin would be problematic and even dishonorable. If a woman's relatives interfered in her daily marital life, there would almost certainly be conflicts. She might find herself caught on a battlefield between her parents and her in-laws, as happened to Maqsudi during one of her pregnancies, when her parents (from a nearby village) and her in-laws (in Jhakri) argued about who should be responsible for treatment for the serious swelling in her legs.[1] Even when in considerable difficulty, many women would hesitate to draw their parents into such an imbroglio.

For these reasons, many people in Jhakri considered within-village marriage particularly problematic.[2] How could the separation be created if the geographical distancing was absent? How could a woman conceal her marital problems from her parents? Surely they would learn about every minor argument, let alone the major ones. And how would they handle the delicate balancing act of looking out for their daughter's welfare yet not intervening in matters that should not concern them?

There was, of course, no inevitability about any of this. Within-village marriage could provide no absolute guarantee of close contact between a woman and her natal kin. And most parents with married daughters living at some distance would try to keep themselves informed about their situations. Sometimes, too, parents might feel that their married daughter's situation had reached the point where they felt impelled to intervene, maybe even to insist that she return to their home to live. But women who returned to their natal village to escape difficulties in their husband's place generally found their new situation problematic in other ways. Drawing the line between excessive separation and excessive interference was not always simple or uncontested.

A Wedding Song

Why have you married me so distantly?
Listen-look, O my father!

Father, I'm just like your tethered cows,
Wherever you drive me,
I have to go.
Why have you married me so distantly?
Listen-look, O my father!

Father, I'm just like the birds in your courtyard,
Having gleaned some grains,
I'll fly away.
Why have you married me so distantly?
Listen-look, O my father!

Your brothers' daughters have been married close by,
I'm wretched in my exile.
Why have you married me so distantly?
Listen-look, O my father![3]

Parvati's Father and His Land

Parvati was one of the most educated women in Dharmnagri. She had been married into a middle-peasant Sahni household in about 1987.

> I don't have any brothers or sisters. My mother died when I was about twelve. My father never remarried, so I was brought up by my grand-mother and my father's sister. My father allowed me to study as long as I wished. I enjoyed it, so I studied to BA. Then a relative told my father about these people [Parvati's in-laws], and he arranged my marriage here. There are no shortages here. My husband is also BA pass, and he and his father are both in service. All the land is sharecropped, so I don't work in the fields or collect fodder.

There were no draught animals, and Parvati's mother-in-law did the work for the milk animals. Parvati herself just did the cooking and other housework. "I've been married five or six years but I've never seen our fields," she said with pride. And the other women in the compound, all completely uneducated, had created no problems for her when she arrived: "They don't talk to me any differently from the way they talk to one another. And they don't taunt me about being educated. I just talk to them like they talk to me. When my husband's sister's engagement was being arranged, my parents-in-law even asked my opinion, but they didn't ask the other women."

Often, too, the children in the compound would seek her help with their schoolwork. She seemed well settled and well respected in her in-laws' house. But for her relationship with her father, Parvati would have been completely happy: "My father arranged a good marriage for me. But afterward, he didn't keep up the coming and going. I don't know what's the matter."

Parvati's husband's grandmother [HFM] commented that there never had been much coming and going between Parvati and her father. "And when Parvati visited her father recently, her father turned his face away. He didn't even look to see who'd come," she added darkly. Parvati shot her a disapproving glance, but nevertheless she elaborated on the point:

> You see, my aunt [FeBW] has made him think I go to his house only because of his wealth. The thing is, my father owned about an acre of

land. Now a small settlement is growing up there, and the price of land has greatly increased. At the time of my wedding, my father sold just under half an acre for 70,000 rupees. He spent about 25,000-30,000 rupees on my marriage and he gave the rest to my aunt. There's still some land left, and my aunt's trying to persuade him to sell it too. My aunt used magic to turn his heart away from me. It does happen. In truth, some-one's heart can be turned against another person. In just that fashion, my aunt turned my father's heart toward her because she's greedy for his possessions. Last time I went to visit him, it was my own decision. I hadn't been called. I went with my husband and the children and in-tended to stay for a few days. But when I greeted my father, he didn't answer me. He didn't even ask if we were all well. He just turned his face away from me. My aunt also didn't talk properly to me. I felt very bad about that, so I came back to Dharmnagri that same evening.

Fortunately for Parvati, her in-laws were being sympathetic:

My husband and his mother have never said anything critical about my father. But I'm very upset that I can't go anywhere. All I can do is stay in my in-laws' place. True, my mother had brothers and sisters, but visiting them is different from going to your parents' home. Anyway, what uncles and aunts [MB and MZ] would call me? I'm very sad about this because I'd be able to have a change of scene like other women if my mother were still alive. But at least my husband cares for me. He takes me shopping in Bijnor and we sometimes see a film too.

Zebunnisa Returns to Jhakri

Zebunnisa was the daughter of Najma's older sister, who was also married in Jhakri. In 1987, when she was about seventeen, Zebunnisa was married into another Sheikh household in a village to the west of the river Ganges. Her in-laws were no strangers to her, however. Zebunnisa's grandmother [FM] had come from that village, and Zebunnisa's aunt [FZ] had been married there. It was the safe kind of match much favored in Jhakri.

When Zebunnisa visited us in 1990, it was the first time we had met her since her marriage. She was greeted with an excited barrage of questions from Radha, Swaleha, and Patricia about when she had come and how long she would stay with her parents. But something was clearly wrong. She was solemn and glum, not like the girl so given to laughter whom we had known before. Zebunnisa deposited herself gloomily on a chair. "I'm living in my mother's house these days," she explained. And then she launched headlong into the story of her marriage:

My in-laws are bad. My husband used to beat me a lot. He's even attacked me with a penknife. There were nineteen suits in my dowry, but his mother took them all. She's got all my jewelry too. I've returned to my mother's house, and I'm not going back to my husband. He says I'm a bad character. He's only ever given me one suit of clothing, but my mother's just had four suits made for me. When my son was born, my mother sent clothes for everyone in my husband's household. My husband's sister has just been married, but I haven't given her anything. Why should I, since my mother-in-law has taken everything of mine?

"But didn't your parents know those people's character before you were married?" asked Patricia.

"My husband's grandmother [HFM] was my father's real sister. It was she alone who arranged the marriage. But she's dead now. If she were still alive, she wouldn't have allowed all this to happen to me," she added.

"So what happened?" asked Radha.

When my son was a few months old, he became very sick. Even so, my mother-in-law told me to cook. My husband's sister had always been very kind to me, and she asked how I could cook as my baby was so ill. But my mother-in-law didn't listen. Then my baby became even sicker. I told my husband's grandmother I was going to take him to the doctor, since my husband wasn't at home then. She told me I shouldn't go, but I didn't obey. I went alone. Just as I arrived at the doctor's place, the child died. My husband arrived home shortly after that. He asked what had happened and why I was crying. I told him our son had died. He became very angry. He asked why I'd gone alone to the doctor; why hadn't his mother gone? I told him she'd had a headache. At that he began swearing at his mother, saying that if his offspring tasted so bitter to his parents that they couldn't take the baby to the doctor, he and I would no longer have any relationship with his parents.

Zebunnisa paused briefly. "Yes, he used to treat me properly at first. But now he beats me a lot at his mother's say-so. And my mother-in-law keeps telling him to leave me. My mother-in-law prefers living alone. I've told my husband that if there are no more children after two years or so, he should marry again. I told him I'd lift his cattle dung like a servant, but he shouldn't send me away. I asked him to wait a bit longer before getting married again, for some women have long gaps between their children."

"Is that the main problem between you?"

My parents have always given generously to us. My older sister, Nusrat, was married well, too. When I was married, my parents gave 3,000 rupees in a steel tray, a cycle and watch, a bed and bedding, a stool, a small trunk and a large trunk. They gave everything. And they also gave plenty when I had my son. Even so, my husband says no good things were given in his marriage. Nusrat's husband beats her because she doesn't have any children. But her parents-in-law are good to her. When their younger son and daughter were married, they gave Nusrat a suit worth 450 rupees. But my parents-in-law haven't given me a single suit to this day. When I came back to Jhakri, I brought just two suits and some pieces of jewelry, my silver anklets, gold earrings, and a gold nose ring. It was my mother alone who had four suits made up for me.

"But what made your husband turn against you?"

My mother-in-law told me to help my husband's uncle [HFyB] with the fodder chopping. He'd been widowed and had no one to help him. So for a few months, I used to feed the bundles into the chopping machine for him. Then my mother-in-law began telling people I had bad habits and I'd developed a relationship with my husband's uncle. She even said I was going to marry him. But one of our other relatives there heard this rumor being spread about me, and they told my parents. Then my brother came. He wanted to take me back to Jhakri. In order to persuade my in-laws, he lied. He said our father had fallen underneath a cart and that he'd come to fetch me. When I heard the news, I was very upset. But my mother-in-law complained that I'd just sat down crying and hadn't done the cooking or done any other work. Then my husband said he'd go and see how my father was. He told me to stay and do my work. So he went to Jhakri with my brother, and he found my father was fine. When he got back home, he began swearing about how the *susrā* [father-in-law, but used insultingly here] hadn't died. When I heard what he was saying, I felt very upset. I said, "Allah-mian [Lord God] has done well in letting nothing happen to my father. If something had happened to him, who'd feed his small children?" Then I asked my mother-in-law what had happened to my father. She retorted, "Nothing—but your uncle's son has died." "But my uncle has only one son," I replied, "Why are you using his name to swear?"

Zebunnisa took a deep breath and then continued:

"At that, my husband kicked me. Then he beat me with the iron tube used at the cooking hearth to blow air onto the embers. He said I was fighting his mother with my tongue. Then he beat me some more. I went and lay on my bed. I ate and drank nothing for two days. I just lay like that. After two days, my husband told me to wash his clothes. So I washed his clothes as well as those belonging his mother and sister. I also began sweeping the house. But his mother told me not to do any work in her house, and she snatched the broom from me. As I fell, the electricity from a switch low in the wall caught me, and my hair was set alight. My husband's younger brother saw me, and he shoved me away from the electricity with a stick. He said, "You should go back to your parents' house. With all the people in this house causing you trouble, what's the point of staying here?" But I remained silent.

By now, Zebunnisa was in full spate.

That evening, my husband told me to call him brother. I was crouching on the floor. I begged him with my hands joined together not to ask me to do that. I'd been married to him. How could I call him brother? He repeatedly told me to do so, but I always refused. Then he hit me twice across the head. I became unconscious and my teeth were clenched together. But my mother-in-law didn't even look to see what had happened. Eventually, a neighbor found me. She poured some water into my mouth. When I recovered a bit I got up. Straightaway, my husband told me to go and cut fodder with his father. The neighbor said I was in a bad state, but these people were telling me to work. Even so, I went out with my father-in-law and began chopping fodder. Then my husband's younger brother began saying I couldn't put the bundles into the chopper properly. I said, "I've a fever, so how can I work?" And at that my mother-in-law pushed me out of the way and began chopping fodder herself. But then my father-in-law became angry. He slapped his own wife and said, "Zebunnisa's husband has beaten her. Now you want to beat her too. If you beat her or get our son to beat her, that wouldn't be right. What if she were to die and her husband spoke up in her favor and told everyone his parents had beaten his wife? What answer would you be able to give then?

"What did they do then?"

That was when my husband's grandfather brought me back to Jhakri. For two months after getting here I was very ill. I had lots of treatment from the ANM. I'm fine now. Everyone there was causing me problems, so how could I stay? Do you know, my father-in-law used to complain that I'd eat seven or eight pieces of griddle bread at a meal. And when anyone from my parents' house visited, my mother-in-law didn't feed them good food. She'd just give them pulses and rice and she wouldn't cook anything else. But when my mother-in-law's own brother and nephews visited her, she'd cook tasty dishes for them. My in-laws haven't been once since I came back to Jhakri to see how I am. I've heard that my husband is telling people that I called him brother—which I didn't do—so how can he fetch me back to live with him?

She stopped for a moment. "Since they've caused me such unhappiness, bad prayers are rising in my heart."

"Hasn't anyone from your parents' house gone to talk it over with your in-laws?"

My father says we should wait for another couple of months. Then, we'll either send a letter by hand or my father will go to discuss it. He'll do some straight talking. He'll tell my in-laws that if they're going to keep me, they must do so properly or not at all. And if not, they must give all my jewelry and other things back. Until a divorce has taken place and everything's come back here, my husband can't remarry. And I can still say that I have rights and that no one else can marry their daughter to him.

"What do you think will happen then?"

My aunts here in Jhakri are saying I should go back to my in-laws and I shouldn't be eating food in Jhakri. There was even a fight about it a fort-night ago. My aunt [MZ] Najma is married here to my father's cousin, and I sometimes help her with her work. But then her sister-in-law [HyBW] accused me of eating food that belongs to their hearth and not eating at my parent's house. I replied, "The food that's cooked in your house is very tasty. And nothing at all is cooked at my parents' home!" And now we aren't talking to Najma's sister-in-law.

"Do you think you'll return to your husband's village?"

"I'm the only one who knows how much sadness I've endured," she said. "For as long as I could, I said nothing because of my parents' honor. I tolerated it for the sake of their honor. But it's not good to give sadness to someone else's daughter."

"Yes," agreed Radha, "if such a man's sister or daughter were unhappy in her in-laws' house, he'd understand how bad it is to cause sadness to another person's daughter."

That's right. You know my husband's sister, who was married recently? She's living happily in her in-laws' house, and she has no troubles. She always helped me before she was married, and now her husband doesn't like the way I've been treated. He's saying, "I'll abandon my wife in her parents' house for a time, and then they'll learn some wisdom." If those people were the offspring of human beings they might learn some sense. But they're the devil's own children, so how can they? They'll do just as they wish. Do you know, my father-in-law's land used to give them twenty or twenty-five hundredweights of grain, but after this recent wheat harvest, they got only seven. That's the upshot of causing misery to someone else's daughter. Allah-mian has done the sweeping. But I've suffered unhappiness without having done wrong, and bad prayers still come from my soul.

Life in the Natal Village

One day in 1985, Om Prakash's sister, Mamta, told us that her younger daughter, Rani, had been married a short while before into a Dhimar household in Bijnor. Rani's situation in her in-laws' home was proving to be difficult, however. Rani's mother-in-law had taken back most of the jewelry she had presented to Rani (some of which had turned out to be silver-plated brass). The family's claims that the groom was in government service had proved to be deceitful. When the first Ti jo festival after the marriage came around, Rani's in-laws had initially refused to send her back to her mother's house in Dharmnagri. And they collected her back again with so little warning that Mamta could provide no more than a single *dhotī* for Rani. Rani's husband had regarded this as insultingly little, and he refused to accept the Rs 5 he was being offered as a parting gift. Mamta was dismayed that she had been unable to honor her son-in-law properly: "If we'd had more time to prepare, we'd have given him not just money but a whole coconut. And we'd have fed him something sweet and put a spot of vermilion and rice on his forehead to honor him."

Within a few days of our arrival in 1990, we heard that Rani was now living in Dharmnagri with her husband, near her mother's house though cooking at a separate hearth. In the five years she had been married, Rani had never once become pregnant, and her mother-in-law had repeatedly told Rani's husband to remarry. Rani had apparently been advised that she could have children if she had treatment and stopped taking "heating" foods or those that caused flatulence, since they would prevent conception or increase the risk of miscarriage. "But she didn't have any treatment or practice any avoidances," said Mamta's brother Sunil, "so where could a child come from? And Rani and her husband both chew tobacco as well [also 'heating']."

Moreover, Rani's mother-in-law used to beat her. But Rani's husband told his mother that he would not remarry and that even if he were to die, nothing must happen to Rani. "That's why they're both living here, and my son-in-law is a laborer in the fields," Mamta explained. According to Sunil, Rani's father-in-law sometimes helped the young couple by giving them money without the mother-in-law's knowledge.

The move to Dharmnagri enabled Rani to escape her mother-in-law, but it did not result in a totally peaceful life. When married women returned to their natal villages, their arrival did not always meet with approval. In Rani's case, for instance, her demeanor was criticized for drawing attention to her married and sexually active status, in contrast to the asexual status of a visiting daughter. As Brijpal's youngest daughter put it,

In the villages here, a girl shouldn't wear a vermilion spot on the forehead when she's in her natal village. If she does, she's taunted and asked whether she's in her parents' village or her in-laws' village. Wearing a vermilion spot is fine in the husband's place, but not in the parents' home. Rani lives here and she wears one and also a lot of vermilion in her part. She has no sense of shame. Even the young married women in Dharmnagri don't generally wear vermilion spots or vermilion in their parts. Yet Rani just retorts, "I'm a daughter, and they're daughters-in-law!"

With some differences in detail, Rani's history replicated her mother's, for they were both living as married women in their natal village. Mamta was born in about 1946, and she was the only surviving sister of Om Prakash and his brothers. When she reached puberty, her father had initially wanted to arrange her marriage to the son of a man from whom he had taken a loan. "He reckoned that if he married me there, he wouldn't have to repay the money. But my mother wouldn't let that marriage take place. She said she'd take me by the hand and we'd both throw ourselves into the Ganges if he tried to settle that marriage."

Then, despite being warned against a second match by the barber who was acting as go-between, Mamta's father insisted on getting her married when she was about sixteen. "I was visiting my aunt [FZ] one time and my future husband was also there. Later, I told my parents he had hips like a buffalo. I said I didn't want to marry him. Even so, my father didn't listen to me. He asked why I shouldn't be married there. 'What, will you be able to marry the son of some king or grandee if we don't marry you there?' he asked. My father didn't like girls at all. He loved only the boys."

Apparently, Mamta's husband would argue with anyone. He sold the wedding jewelry presented to Mamta by her in-laws. Mamta said that even his own mother did not like him. "She used to swear at him, and she'd say, 'Why can't that sonless one die?' My mother-in-law told me he was born after a seven-month pregnancy, but even then he didn't die. And now she'd brought someone else's daughter into her house and spoiled her destiny. One time, my husband fought with his mother, and he separated our hearth from hers. But he did no work. And if his brother gave me food for the children, my husband would fight with his brother too."

After an argument with her husband, Mamta returned to Dharmnagri only to be followed by him. This would have been in the late 1960s. Mamta's father had just died, leaving her mother with several small children. Mamta's mother was still quite young. Seemingly, people began gossiping about her, alleging that men kept visiting her.

According to Omvati, Mamta had no wish to remain in Dharmnagri even if she went hungry in her husband's house. Yet Mamta was prevailed upon to stay so that people would be convinced that the rumors were false. Mamta and her husband have been living in Dharmnagri ever since. They built a house near Mamta's brothers' houses. In the mid-1980s, they bought a couple of acres of land. For Mamta, however, all this had provided no solution to her marital problems:

> What happiness is there in a man who can't even give his own wife and children a good house and food? When he makes a little money, he drinks it. Then he sometimes hits me and the children and fights with anyone for no reason at all. It'd be better without a man than to have one like this. I'd be satisfied if he died. But he's a live snake. You can neither spit him out nor swallow him. If you swallow, it'll bite you from the inside. If you spit it out, it'll bite you on the outside. I'm tolerating all this only because of my parents' honor. Other women would have left him. He's the sort of man to whom you'd like to feed poison and then pat him gently to sleep for ever. What's more, he says he's tolerating me only for the sake of my parents' honor!

Raisuddin and His In-Laws

Among the marriages that took place in Jhakri in May 1982 was that of Akbar's fifteen-year-old daughter, Rihana, to her cousin [FBS] Raisuddin. At the time, Raisuddin and his parents were living in Najibabad, a major town some thirty miles away. After spending a few days at her in-laws' home, Rihana had returned to her parents' house in Jhakri.

Shortly after this, Rihana was called back to her in-laws' place for a few days because her mother-in-law was unwell. Criticism was heaped on Rihana's mother, for there had been no protracted and tearful sending off such as there should have been for a new bride returning to her in-laws for the first time after the marriage. One young man asked Rihana's mother if he and his family lived in a different village, for they had not been informed of Rihana's departure. And Afrozi's mother commented, "Rihana simply flew away as if she were a black crow."

For this reason, when Raisuddin came to collect Rihana from Jhakri the next time, Rihana's mother was resolute. "No, not now. She'll go with you on the twenty-fifth of Ramzān, like the rest of the new brides," she asserted.

"Ramzān's still a long time off. Send her now for just five days."

"We've already sent her for ten days when no other new brides were going back to their in-laws," she replied.

"There's no need to delay sending a bride to her in-laws. They don't do that in the city. Village women only do it because they have no sense," he added. Then he unwrapped a black *chotī* [decorated threads] for braiding into Rihana's hair. "Look, I bought this yesterday for her, and women have been criticizing me. They're saying a new bride ought to wear a scarlet *chotī*. In that case, hair should be scarlet too! Why else is hair black?" he scoffed.

"It's nothing to do with black *chotīs*," said Rihana's mother. "I'm not sending her with you now."

Then Rihana began complaining that she had not been allowed to go anywhere after Raisuddin had arrived a couple of days earlier. She had wanted to watch a fist fight involving people in a neighboring compound, but Raisuddin had threatened to break her legs if she went.

"Are you going to quarrel with him about that?" asked her mother. "What if you'd got hurt yourself? Then he'd say you'd gone even though he'd forbidden you to."

"Oh, why did you get me married?" exclaimed Rihana.

"Marriage is essential," her mother insisted. "And if we'd got you married elsewhere, we wouldn't have known the boy's character. It's better to marry among one's own. Because of our relationship with him, we can understand him."

To other people in Jhakri, however, there often seemed to be misunderstandings between Rihana and her parents and Raisuddin and his. A few months after the marriage, Raisuddin and his parents returned to live permanently in Jhakri. There was too little income from their land for them all, so Raisuddin began working as a cycle rickshaw puller in Bijnor, like his older brother. Rihana's marital home now abutted her parents' house. Within weeks, neighbors were commenting adversely about the situation. During a visit from Begawala, Afrozi began discussing the situation with her mother, who reported that Rihana had been complaining about her in-laws: "Rihana's mother is no good. She's not telling Rihana the proper way to behave. Rihana told her mother she wanted a divorce—and then Rihana's mother told Raisuddin. Raisuddin went back to his parents' house, and he wouldn't eat for a couple of days until his father asked who had upset him."

Afrozi was clearly annoyed:

If Rihana had a marital home like mine, she'd be unable to stay there for even a couple of days. My husband listens to his parents. He pays no heed to me. He's afraid of his parents. I've been married for eight years, and they still haven't given me a single suit. I got twenty-five from my mother when I married and twenty-five from my in-laws. I'm still wearing them. Or else my mother gets new ones made. What would happen if

Rihana were married in such a place? You know, the other day Rihana's sister-in-law said she'd scour the dishes while Rihana ground the spices. But Rihana's mother wouldn't let her. Rihana's mother doesn't want her girl to do anything. Rihana took only four suits from her parents when she was married, but she speaks up even so.

Afrozi's mother nodded in agreement. In her opinion, Rihana had not been taught how to do housework properly. "And now, if Raisuddin asks Rihana to do anything, she doesn't know how. Rihana's mother is the one who didn't teach Rihana anything, and she alone gets angry. Such a mother shouldn't get angry."

Within a year of her marriage, Rihana had a stillborn baby, born after only seven months of pregnancy. Before a couple of years passed, Rihana insisted on separating her hearth from Raisuddin's parents. According to Raisuddin's mother, both Rihana and her mother were constantly criticizing her: "They said we weren't looking after Rihana properly. There's been no further pregnancy since that stillbirth when you were here the first time. After that, my Raisuddin got a lot of treatment for her, but there's been no benefit and no pregnancy. Even so, Rihana's mother kept saying we weren't getting proper treatment for her."

Raisuddin's brother's wife was sitting close by, listening. She was also critical: "Raisuddin is getting so much treatment for Rihana. He cares greatly for her, but she doesn't understand that. Any other woman would love her husband greatly for what he's doing."

Afrozi's mother pursued the issue. As far as she was concerned, the key problem was Rihana's mother:

It's better to marry among strangers and some distance away. Just look at Rihana. She was married right next door. As a result, her mother speaks up at every point. If Raisuddin says anything to Rihana that her mother doesn't like, she won't allow him to continue, and she begins to fight with him. Rihana certainly benefits from being married close to her parents. But Raisuddin doesn't. Rihana's mother doesn't even acknowledge her daughter's faults, and she keeps saying bad things about Raisuddin's parents even though he's separate from them now. If Raisuddin talks to his parents, Rihana gets angry and her mother fights with him. If he says anything in favor of Rihana or her mother, his own parents get angry with him. He has to listen to everyone and stay silent. He doesn't want to swear at his parents, but how can he speak? It's something that remains hidden in his heart. He can say nothing to anyone. And yet Rihana keeps telling him he's doing nothing for her and her parents are doing everything. If a daughter has trouble in her in-laws' place, honorable parents say nothing. If the girl fights with her husband or he fights with her, they'll make up again. After all, the daughter has to live in her husband's house. That's why her parents should say nothing.

Kavita's Silence

Brijpal's youngest daughter was not convinced that girls benefited greatly from being educated. "Surely," she argued, "you have to cook whether you've studied or not. So, what's the benefit?" Her cousin's wife, Kavita, also considered her education had brought her no benefit, but for a very different reason: "There's no point in studying. I could have got a job, but my husband wouldn't let me. He told my parents to prevent me. My parents listen to him more than to me. They do exactly as he says. What's more, my husband is not my own, so what has been the benefit of all my education?"

She explained that her husband had been having an affair with his older brother's wife—with the full knowledge of his parents and brothers—since before he was married. Once Kavita arrived, the sister-in-law often incited him to beat Kavita and would do it herself if Kavita complained about the affair:

> Hearing things from someone else is one thing, for you can imagine them to be lies. But things you've seen with your own eyes can never be lies. Everyone in the family is afraid of her. She says there's no man prepared to refuse an offer of sex. He [Kavita's husband] still gives her all his money. He goes straight to her when he gets back from work in the evening. I tried to stop him, but he used to beat me. Now I can't tolerate the beating. That's why I remain silent. If I say he can't have sex with me if he continues to go to her, he says I can get a divorce. She's teaching him to divorce me. My husband doesn't follow my wishes at all. He believes everything my sister-in-law tells him. She even persuaded him to take my watch and silver necklace presented by his parents and give them to her. But I don't say anything, so at least I don't have the beatings anymore.

In the late 1980s, when Kavita's father was arranging her marriage, he was told that the boy had passed the intermediate examinations [twelfth class]. The boy's family were middle-peasant Jats, and Kavita's father hoped his future son-in-law would be able to bribe his way into a good job. Failing that, there was the land to farm. "But he wasn't Inter pass. He'd failed!" Kavita told us. "He learned doctoring work with a local practitioner, and just now he's had to pay 1,000 rupees [as a bribe] to get his license. If my people had known he was having an affair with his brother's wife and that the land was mortgaged, my marriage would never have taken place here."

Apart from the affair, Kavita's parents now knew all these matters. According to Kavita, her husband had persuaded her father that he was being unfairly treated by his brothers over debts they had incurred and that he was not going to receive a share of their father's land. Already, Kavita's father had helped financially—to the tune of Rs 15,000—for building Kavita's new house. Now, Kavita's father was preparing to put about five acres of land into her husband's name.

> My father would never think to register land in my name. And my husband won't be taking me there to do so! The last time I visited my parents, my husband complained to them that I fight with him a lot. So my mother asked me why I fight with him. She told me to remain silent and not interfere with him whatever he might do. But how could I tell my parents about my husband's affair and the beatings? I've never said a thing about it to my father when he visits me here. How could I tell him about such a wicked matter? I couldn't tell my mother either. Even if I got the courage to do so, my mother wouldn't be able to say anything to my father. So what would be the point?

A Wedding Song

"O brother, stop the palanquin!"
"O sister, the palanquin won't stop,
You must go to your in-laws' place,
Leaving your father's alleys behind."
"O sister's husband, stop the palanquin!"
"O wife's sister, the palanquin won't stop,
You must go to your in-laws' place,
Leaving your father's alleys behind."[4]

Notes

1. Maqsudi was another of our key informants. See Jeffery, Jeffery, and Lyon (1989:95).

2. This contrasts sharply with the situation in Hazrat Nizamuddin, where women were explicit that within-village marriage ensured that their parents and brothers could protect them from marital problems. See Jeffery (1979).

3. This *bannī* (sung at the bride's house) represents a bride complaining to her father about being sent away so distantly in marriage.

4. In this *bannī*, the bride asks her male relatives in turn to stop her being taken away, but they all say that she must leave the lanes and alleys of her father's village.

14

If My Uncle Saw
the Situation I'm in Now

In Dharmnagri and Jhakri, people talked about "taking a bride for a price"
[bahū mol lenā] when a man paid—anywhere between several hundred and
four or five thousand rupees—for a wife. Most villages in Bijnor had a handful
of bought brides, some of them relatively local, some from the foothills of the
Himalayas or from further east in Uttar Pradesh and Bihar (all areas of greater
poverty than the relatively wealthy part of the Gangetic plain in which Bijnor
is situated). It was certainly not an approved method of marrying. There were,
indeed, only about a half-dozen bought brides in Dharmnagri and Jhakri. Yet
their experiences highlighted important issues for married women in rural
Bijnor.

Sometimes a man who had been widowed or deserted by his wife could not
arrange another conventional marriage, maybe because he was considered too
old by parents with young marriageable daughters, maybe because his first wife
had accused him of mistreatment. Other men had some social or physical dis-
ability, such as stammering or disfigurement as a result of injury, or they were
extremely poor. Bought brides themselves were generally women whose first
marriages had ended in widowhood or separation. Without any means of their
own, their future rested in the hands of their in-laws or their own relatives, who
had proved unwilling or unable to take responsibility for them. So they were
sold, maybe by a brother who needed cash or by in-laws who did not want an
extra mouth to feed.

Our research assistants were very critical. "What, have women become like
goats that they can be bought and sold?" Radha commented to us one day. The
villagers' critiques emphasized other contrasts between the bought bride and
other married women. The typical bride would have come with a dowry, but
bought brides did not. Bought brides were completely cut off from their natal
kin, and they received neither the gifts nor the other forms of support available
to other brides. Their husbands' relatives and neighbors often voiced suspicions
about their origins, and bought brides were very poorly placed to protect them

Gossiping at the Handpump

selves from taunting and censure. Not surprisingly, bought brides were often reticent (even if their neighbors and in-laws were not), and we often first learned that a woman was a bought bride through probing an otherwise unexplained hiatus in her maternity career.

This story tells of Lakshmi's early widowhood and how her subsequent eventful life culminated in her becoming the bought bride of Lalit in Dharmnagri. Lalit was a poor-peasant Sahni some fifteen years her senior who bought her from his cousin [MBS], who lived in a village near Bijnor. Lakshmi's tale illustrates several features common to the lives of bought brides. It also points up some of the difficulties of doing "oral history."

*   *   *   *   *   *

Lakshmi's first baby—a girl—was born in Dharmnagri one afternoon in July 1982. Lakshmi told us later that she had been aware of contractions since the previous evening, but she had told no one about it. She had cooked the food in the morning as usual. She had even gone to the fields to weed the rice, but she came back around midday when the pains became stronger.

The sequence of events thereafter was somewhat confusing. Lakshmi herself told us she was alone when the baby was born. Lakshmi said her husband, Lalit, and his brother were not at home and Lalit's brother's teenage daughter was visiting a nearby house. Lakshmi said that the carpenter's wife from next door found her a few minutes later, and she called Lalit's niece and sent her to summon Lalit. According to the carpenter's wife, however, she had been called by Lalit himself when the delivery seemed imminent:

> Lakshmi had no one with her. It was very difficult for her. Lalit came to my house and told me to go straight to his house, as Lakshmi was having her pains. Then he went to Chandpuri to call the *dāī*. When I arrived, Lakshmi was squatting on a pair of bricks on the ground beside the bed. She was clinging to the bed and writhing in great pain because those were the final contractions. I held on to Lakshmi to steady her. I'd hardly arrived and asked how she was when the baby girl was born onto the floor! So I wiped the baby with some old sacking that was lying there to stop the dirty blood from getting into her mouth. I massaged Lakshmi's belly, and the placenta was delivered immediately. Then I helped Lakshmi onto the bed. And then I came right back home and washed myself thoroughly. Lakshmi was alone, so what else could I have done?

The *dāī* arrived over an hour later to cut the cord. She buried the placenta—either in the midden (according to Lakshmi) or in the house (according to the carpenter's wife).

Our first research in Dharmnagri focused on childbearing. In Lakshmi's case, what we had regarded as a fairly straightforward attempt to picture the events surrounding her delivery drew our attention to some salient features of our other dealings with her over the years. Lakshmi was completely cut off from her natal kin. She was also extremely isolated from other women in Dharmnagri and subjected to derision when she did mix with them. But throughout, our attempts to piece together her story were hampered by divergent versions of how her life had unfolded. How could we make sense of it all?

*   *   *   *   *   *

Lakshmi first became pregnant just a few months after she had arrived in Dharmnagri in about 1980, but Lalit had been so angry one day (she told us) that he beat her hard on her belly and she miscarried. Within a couple of months, Lakshmi conceived the baby who had just been born. Throughout the pregnancy there had been domestic disputes. Lalit's parents had died many years before. There was no other woman in the house to help Lakshmi apart from Lalit's niece, who proved to be uncooperative. Perforce, Lakshmi did all the housework, cared for the cattle, collected fodder and worked in the fields alongside the men if need be. Lalit's brother sold his share of the rice harvest to raise some cash with the result that food was short. Throughout Lakshmi's pregnancy, grain had to be bought time and again from the bazaar in Bijnor. She ate the normal pulses and bread diet, for nothing special was available. She had a particular craving for meat, but that was ignored because money was tight: "When the man doesn't want to do something, the woman can do nothing. He wouldn't buy meat for me. That's why my baby dribbles so much, for my craving wasn't satisfied."

The carpenter's wife told us later that she was hearing angry voices through the adjoining wall yet again, before the day of the delivery was over. Lakshmi herself later claimed that the very day she had given birth, Lalit's brother denied her food:

> I was happy when I realized I was pregnant, as this would be my first child. And my husband and his brother were pleased, too, because the brother has just one girl and his wife is dead. My husband didn't complain that I had produced a girl. But his brother didn't want another girl in the house. He wanted a boy. "Why was a girl born?" he demanded. He began swearing at me and saying that he wouldn't feed me. "If you'd had a boy," he said, "I'd be giving you a lot of wealth to eat. I'd be giving you clarified butter and milk. But it's a girl, so I won't give you anything!"

The cow was bought by him and it will go with his daughter when she's married. That's why he won't even give me milk. But anyway, I wouldn't drink it if he gave it to me, for he said it would be as if I were drinking his urine.

At first, she had to drink black tea. She was unable to have *harīrā*, a preparation of various items considered "strengthening" and "heating," to replenish her strength and to ensure that the "dirty" blood would be properly expelled. Instead, she took powdered ginger and *ajvāyn* seeds [both "heating"] in her palm and swallowed them with hot water.

What else could I do? There's nothing else in the house, not even clarified butter. My husband's brother says that if he has to pay for anything now, he won't pay for the *jasthawn*. My husband doesn't have any money to buy food for me. All the money and the things in the house are under his brother's control. He keeps all the money himself. He padlocked the grain store the day the baby was born so that I wouldn't be able to take anything to eat. Everything's kept in the grain store.

And Lalit's niece cooked for herself, her father, and Lalit but refused to cook for Lakshmi, saying that Lakshmi was just lying on her bed, so why should she cook for her? Only after Lakshmi complained about severe afterpains and the *dāī* advised her to begin taking solid foods did Lalit borrow some money to buy clarified butter and cook pulses and bread for her. Because of her "polluted" condition, Lakshmi could not cook for the rest of the household, and she had to eat the food prepared for her by Lalit out of dishes separated from those used by the others. She also had to be bathed daily by the *dāī*, squatting on a plank placed over a pit newly dug in the floor so that the warm water poured over her by the *dāī* would drain away. Lalit's niece refused to clear the cloths soiled by the mother and new baby. All told, the *dāī* was paid some Rs 15 and about five pounds of grain and unrefined sugar.

It was inconvenient having Lakshmi unable to work around the house, however, so the *jasthawn* ceremony was arranged quickly, on the eighth day after the birth. The temple priest was called to cook a meal for the family, perform a ceremony to cleanse the house, and consult his almanac of birth signs so that the appropriate name could be selected for the baby. Lalit's brother had provided money, but Lalit failed to give it to the priest. The priest stormed off, swearing at Lalit and leaving his tasks uncompleted. When Lakshmi demanded to know what had happened to the money, Lalit lost his temper in a flash: "I've got a fever, and I spent the money on medicines. But I gave the priest eight rupees and still he didn't do the work."

Lakshmi butted in angrily: "Would the priest really have left without giving the baby a name if you'd paid him like you're claiming? The priest said he'd consult his almanac only once the money's been paid. You'd better sort it out." But Lalit did nothing—and his daughter remained unnamed.

To add to her problems, Lakshmi told us, a few days later Lalit pounded her chest repeatedly. "He's a very cruel man," she concluded. Lalit intervened to defend himself. "This woman's mad," he claimed. "I'll explain what happened. When I came back from the fields yesterday, the house was in darkness. I asked her where the hole in the cooking stove is so that I could pour some kerosene into it. But she didn't answer me. She just sat there silently. So I got angry and beat her."

This time, Lakshmi could not stay silent. She was seething with anger herself: "If you had to sit on my chest for two hours, that was because I managed to stay alive for two hours!" Then, turning to us, she asked, "Which of these two is the better man? His brother beat me one time right outside the temple. Both brothers are bad. Whichever one sees me, beats me. And the girl answers back too." And the stream of accusations continued.

*   *   *   *   *   *

Lakshmi had to resume most of her normal work around the house right after the *jasthawn* ceremony was abandoned. She began cooking for the rest of the household again because Lalit's niece now refused to do even that: "She does nothing in the house except pick up the baby sometimes. She takes the food to the men in the fields and does some fieldwork too, like weeding and bringing some fodder. But just a couple of days after the *jasthawn* ceremony, I had to load three baskets of cattle dung and tip them into the midden."

A woman whose pregnancy was proceeding without any serious hitch would not expect to obtain much help with her work around the house and outside. But after delivery, she would be considered weak as well as polluting to her family members. She should be allowed some rest from her usual round of duties, especially the heaviest tasks such as carrying headloads of cattle dung or fodder for the livestock. Lakshmi's mother-in-law was long since dead, and so was Lalit's brother's wife. But was there no other woman to help out? What about Lalit's sister? Why did she not come to celebrate the birth of her brother's first child? Why were no gifts presented to her? And could she not have taken over Lakshmi's work for a while? "My husband has just one sister who's a lot older than he is. But she's never visited Dharmnagri the whole time that I've been living here," Lakshmi told us. "There was a fight between her and the two brothers. That's why she didn't come to help me when I had my baby. My husband's brother refused to call her."

The hostilities had begun several years before, when Lalit's niece was just a toddler. Lalit, his brother, and his sister-in-law [BW] went to live in their sister's village and began working there. Lakshmi recounted what she had heard:

> That woman who was my sister-in-law [HBW] was no good. She didn't live decently in Dharmnagri. That was why the brothers left the village and went to live with their sister. They began doing laboring work there. But even then, that woman didn't live properly. She began having an affair with the man who's married to my husband's sister. At that time she had one daughter and was a few months pregnant with her second child. But the affair was discovered by my husband's sister's son, and he became very angry. One day, he followed that woman to the fields when she went to weed the rice seedlings. He strangled her with some cloth around her throat, though he lied and said someone else had abducted her and killed her.

In the furor that ensued, Lalit and his brother returned to Dharmnagri. There had been scarcely any contact with the sister ever since: "She used to visit Dharmnagri. But she's not been here since her son murdered that woman. Because of that, no one here calls her for a visit. And she doesn't come uninvited because she's afraid. I've met her only once. We'd gone to Shukarthal, by the Ganges, for my baby's head shaving. That's the place where she's married. While we were there, she presented five rupees for the baby."

Nor did Lakshmi have any support from her natal kin: "No one comes here from my natal place, and no one here even knows where that place is. Anyway, there's no one there to inform about the birth, so no gifts were sent here to mark the birth."

*   *   *   *   *   *

Lakshmi's relationships with other women in Dharmnagri did not provide her with much support either. On a day-to-day basis, neither did she offer to help the women married to Lalit's relatives and neighbors nor did they help her. In her dealings with them, she was often subject to barbed comments and criticism about her relationships with Lalit and his brother, about her habits, and about her origins.

One day, the carpenter's wife came into Lakshmi's house and, without further ado, launched a barrage of allegations—that Lakshmi slept with both Lalit and his brother, that the whole neighborhood knew that to be the case, and that she herself could hear the arguments every night when Lalit tried to sleep with Lakshmi and she refused him. After she had gone, Lakshmi told us that Lalit's brother had never remarried after his wife's death. According to Lakshmi, Lalit was jealous and would accuse her of having a bad character if she so much as talked to his brother. But, she said, she had once slept with Lalit's brother without Lalit's knowledge because he had forced her to. This had been after the last menstrual period before her pregnancy, so she did not know who her baby girl's father was.

Then, during the Tījo festival in 1982, Lakshmi visited the carpenter's house.[1] Two of the carpenter's married daughters had managed to come for a visit. When Lakshmi came into the courtyard carrying her tiny baby, they began commenting about her.

"Why aren't you wearing new glass bangles to mark Tījo?" asked one. (Lakshmi said she had no money.)

"In any case, you shouldn't be going out and about everywhere like this. You're a new mother, and your baby is hardly ten days old," added the other. (Lakshmi made no attempt to justify herself.)

"And just look how dirty Lakshmi is," responded the first. "Even in this heat she's not bathing, and she has a handpump in the yard!" (Lakshmi hung her head and went back home.)

The same themes echoed through the years. One time in 1990, Durgi chided Lakshmi for not keeping herself and her child clean: "Your shirt's filthy. Why don't you wash it?"

This time Lakshmi rose to the bait. She lifted her shirt right up in front of her face. "If I wash my shirt, I'll be naked like this," she shouted angrily. "I have only this one shirt!"

"But your children are small, and the baby's drinking your milk," said Durgi. "When I breast-feed, I wash all my clothes every third day. Otherwise a bad smell of milk comes from the shirt. Your baby's filthy, too. Can't you bathe the child in some water? Go away and wash yourself and the baby!"

*   *   *   *   *   *

Lakshmi was particularly vulnerable to this sort of disdain, for both she and Lalit had had rather checkered careers. By 1982, Lalit was in his mid-forties, and yet he had never had an orthodox marriage. He was an object of ridicule in Dharmnagri. He stammered, and he persisted in using bullocks to thresh the wheat long after everyone else had begun having their crops threshed by machine. He was poorer than his relatives, and not someone they could recommend as a husband. No offers of marriage had ever come for him. Thus, several times he had paid money in exchange for a woman who would live with him—six times, indeed, before he had bought Lakshmi. According to Lakshmi, Lalit's widowed brother had also slept with the various women brought into the house by Lalit. Some of these women had stayed for only a few days before vanishing. One had disappeared with all the jewelry. Another had thrown pepper into Lalit's niece's eye. As Lalit himself admitted to us,

> I've never had a proper wedding. All the other women stayed for just a few days and then went away. One of them took all the utensils when she left. And the woman before Lakshmi ran away with the money and silver from the house. She stole all the stuff. Then I went crying to my mother's brother's house near Bijnor. His son told me not to be sad. He told me I could take Lakshmi and he'd marry someone else. First I had to get the 2,000 rupees together. Then my cousin let me take her.

Usually, a bride would arrive in her husband's home with a sure reputation. Her in-laws would know where she came from and what her caste was. They would have enquired through their kinship network about the bride's family's wealth, honor, and standing in their village. They would have met members of the bride's close family and known what sort of people they were. But the bought bride would come with none of this aura—and she would have no relatives ready to defend her reputation. Like the other bought brides in Dharmnagri and Jhakri, Lakshmi was very aware that her obscure origins left her open to derision, accusations, and innuendos. The people of Dharmnagri had only her word. They could not check her story out. Might she not claim to be one thing but really be another?

> I very much regret that I wasn't educated. If I had been, I could write to my relatives and call them here. Then I could stop talking to all the village women who keep insulting me—like my neighbors. They're always slandering me, saying things like, "Who knows who she is. Is she a Hindu or a Muslim? Nor do we know what caste she is. And no one has any idea about all the houses she's lived in before she came to Dharmnagri." But what can I do? My mother's brother came as far as Bijnor. But those people there [Lalit's MBS and family] told him that I'd caught cholera and died, not that they'd placed me in their cousin's house. And now my uncle thinks I'm dead. He doesn't know I'm right here in Dharmnagri.

Sometimes, too, Lalit himself was quite prepared to add his doubts to those of their neighbors. After all, he said, he merely bought Lakshmi from his cousin, and no one had ever visited Dharmnagri from her natal village. "I don't even know where she's from—and her people don't know where she is. So how could there be any coming and going or any gift giving? I don't know whose daughter she is or to which caste she belongs. I couldn't bring her straight back to Dharmnagri. She had to be purified before I could place her in my house, so I had her bathed in the Ganges."

*   *   *   *   *   *

Most married women in Dharmnagri and Jhakri were visited by their relatives from time to time, and they would often be brought to meet us. Sometimes, too, we visited women's natal villages because of a wedding in the family or a medical emergency. In some cases, we recognized their brothers; in others, we had maybe drunk tea in their parents' house.

Lakshmi's origins, however, were still as mysterious to us as to her neighbors. We too had no more than Lakshmi's own account of her life. And just the barest bones of the story she told us seemed to hang together: She was married very young to a man with whom she had never lived and she was taken in by her uncle's married daughter, whose husband later sold her to Lalit's cousin in Bijnor, who in turn sold her to Lalit himself. Like other bought brides, her core theme was that she had been a victim of fateful events, and had come down in the world through no fault of her own. She presented herself as a woman who was really better than she seemed to her Dharmnagri neighbors. Perhaps her stories remained her best hope of self-defense against their effronteries. But over the years, as she elaborated on her history to us, several details in her various accounts were impossible to reconcile with one another.

Lakshmi's father was apparently from a village in Moradabad District, the district that adjoins Bijnor to the south and east. Lakshmi—his first child—was born in the early 1950s by cesarean section. Her mother never recovered, and Lakshmi was just over a month old when her mother died. Her father cared for her until she was about twelve years old, when he arranged her marriage to a young man in a village near Najibabad, a town about twenty-five miles northeast of Bijnor.

That, at least, was how one version went. In another account of the same period, Lakshmi told us her parents had both died when she was three. In yet another rearrangement of events, Lakshmi said she was reared by her grandmother for a few years, and then her father had begun living with another woman. Some six months later, however, this woman had fed poison to Lakshmi's father because she was angry that he had never presented her with any jewelry: "But there had been none to give her. You see, my mother's brother had been just a small child when my mother married. He came with her to my father's home, and she reared him. And when he was married, she gave him all her own jewelry to present to his bride. So the people in my father's house were very angry that this woman had poisoned my father. They vowed they wouldn't let her live. And they killed her and buried her inside the room."

After Lakshmi's mother's brother was married, he moved back to his own parents' place in Mathura District (some 100 miles southwest of Moradabad). According to this recasting of events, Lakshmi had spent the rest of her childhood there after being orphaned. Her uncle arranged her marriage when she was very young—maybe eleven or twelve she thought—to a young man in a village near Gajraula (a small town about forty-five miles south of Bijnor)—not Najibabad, as she had told us on another occasion. "When a girl's parents aren't alive, who asks her what her wishes are or seeks her opinion about the boy? I didn't even know my husband's name. But my uncle arranged a good marriage for me. The house where I was married was very good, and the boy was physically mature."

Wherever this was, and whether it had been her father or her uncle who had arranged it, Lakshmi's first marriage was apparently very short lived. Because she was very young, the cohabitation did not take place immediately. Thus she did not even see her husband, let alone sleep with him:

> For one thing, I was very young; for another, *purdah* is much stronger in villages than in the towns. My father came to collect me two days later. My husband tried to persuade him not to take me away so soon, but he eventually let my father take me. But we'd hardly got back home when the news came that my husband had died. He'd gone out to the fields and been bitten by a snake. He died right there in the fields. My husband's place was very good. There was a huge kiln-brick house. And they gave me one hundred items of silver and gold, whereas my father had given me just ten things.

It was after her husband's death—in this permutation—that Lakshmi's father died of grief. Her mother's brother took over her father's job in the army, and only then did Lakshmi go to live at his house.

But then, we were not at all certain that Lakshmi's husband had died, and according to Lakshmi's later account, her uncle had arranged her marriage. After all the ceremonies had taken place, her in-laws came to collect her:

> That day, my husband went to the fields. There he was bitten by a snake, and he died. He was brought back home and a snake-bite healer was called. The healer came and gave my husband back his life. The healer

recited sacred words in my husband's ear and blew into it. When my husband revived, he just said the name of God, "Rām Rām." And then he said he didn't belong in that house anymore, he belonged to the man who had given him life. And so he went away with the snake-bite healer. His parents tried to stop him. But he insisted on going with the healer, so his father eventually said, "Let him go."

Another glossing of these events added a further twist to the saga: "My mother-in-law was my husband's stepmother. She wouldn't let my husband sleep with me. At that he became very angry. He never used to go out to the fields. But that day, he went out in anger, saying he'd never return. 'Today only some news of me will return,' he predicted. When he got to the fields, two snakes bit him. A snake-bite healer brought him back to life—but didn't return him to his home."

Lakshmi said that her mother's brother had given everything necessary for her dowry, but her in-laws returned it all, along with the jewelry they themselves had given her, when she went back to live in her uncle's house. In this shuffling of the details, however, Lakshmi's uncle's wife kept all the jewelry.

Her uncle apparently moved to Delhi about a couple of years after Lakshmi had begun living at his house. She did not go to Delhi with him but went to live at the home of her cousin [FBD], who was married and living in Chandpur (about twenty miles south of Bijnor). The cousin was expecting a baby. Lakshmi went to help, according to one version, because the cousin had fallen out with her mother-in-law and needed someone to do her work.

Lakshmi stayed there until the baby was several months old, when her cousin's husband took her to a village near Bijnor. When Lakshmi's cousin found out, she was furious. But it was too late to do anything. Her husband had apparently arranged a *karāv* marriage for Lakshmi, when there was no circling of the couple around the sacred fire, no priest or other trappings of a normal Hindu wedding, for Lakshmi had already been married once before.[2] But did her cousin's husband give her some jewelry by way of a small dowry, as Lakshmi claimed on one occasion? Or was it he (rather than Lakshmi's uncle's wife) who had kept all Lakshmi's jewelry?

Lakshmi stayed with this man for a while (though was it one year or two, or even four?), but he became dissatisfied with her when she failed to produce a child for him. He told her that since she was not going to have any children, he would not keep her in his house any longer. Lakshmi told us: "His sister had put him under some magical influence. She told him to discard me, as I wasn't going to have children. She promised she'd bring him a woman with a child already, one who could call him Dad. But someone else's piss-child can't call another man Dad. What's the benefit of forcing a child to do that?"

At that very time, though, Lalit was in need of another woman:

> Earlier, he had brought a woman to his house. She was beautifully fair skinned, but she wasn't the sort of woman to stay. She'd been married already somewhere else, and she'd run off with the jewelry. So everyone in the family and all the neighbors told him [Lalit] not to give her any jewelry, for she wasn't a woman who would stay. But he began asking his aunt to give him some jewelry for her, for her arms and throat didn't look nice without jewelry. So he got some things from his aunt. He gave them to this woman, and she put them on. Then she told him she wanted to go to the cinema. So he took her to Bijnor. On the way home, she said that she wanted to go by way of her parents' place. Some policemen were standing by the roadside outside the police station on the main road. She told him [Lalit] to stay put and not to go anywhere. She said she'd be coming shortly, and she went inside the police station. But she didn't return. After some time, he began searching for her. He asked the police where she'd gone. But he couldn't find her. Then he went to his cousin's place—the village where I was married—to see if they knew where she'd gone. He began to weep, and he told them how she'd run away with all the jewelry. His [Lalit's] cousin-brother began laughing and teasing him, saying, "Decorate her some more, and give her some more jewelry to put on!"

By that time, Lalit's cousin [MBS] had already taken in another woman for whom he had paid Rs 3,000. He offered Lakshmi to Lalit provided that Lalit give him Rs 2,000 in exchange. So Lakshmi was brought to Dharmnagri: "When I arrived here, I found I had to live in this tumbledown hut. I was so angry that I began banging my head against the wall so hard that I bled. I was thinking about the fine two-storied building that my first in-laws lived in. And here I was in this shack. My fate's turned out bad. But what can I do now?"

* * * * * *

Lakshmi regarded herself as tied to Dharmnagri. She had to think of it as both her natal village and her marital village. Sometimes she claimed never to have left the village at all since she had first arrived with Lalit. Her parents were both dead, and there was no one to visit in her real natal village: "No one calls me to visit them. My first husband died and then my cousin's husband sold me to a man near Bijnor. Then this man [Lalit] gave some money for me, and I came to live in Dharmnagri—where I've been ever since."

But another time, she told us she had made a couple of visits to her father's brother's house: "I stayed there for a fortnight each time. They didn't invite me to visit them. I just went of my own accord because I wanted to see them. My husband didn't stop me going. I went there by myself and returned by myself. But I haven't been since the baby was born."

If this had been so, however, would Lakshmi not have told her uncle where she was living? Might he not have found out how much her fortunes had declined? Similarly, it was not clear what contact there had been with her cousin [FBD] married in Chandpur. Initially, Lakshmi said that she had not met her cousin since she was married to Lalit. The cousin had neither invited her to Chandpur nor visited her in Dharmnagri. Lakshmi would like to meet her cousin, but Lalit did not let her go. But it was all rather baffling. Was the cousin still there in any case? Had the cousin died, and had her husband failed to invite Lakshmi to the funeral? Or had the cousin been repudiated by her husband?

> My cousin had a very bad character. When I went to live in her house, I discovered she was having an affair with her husband's younger brother. Even in front of me, they were doing wrong. One time, I was lying on a bed in one room, and they began making love in the next room without even closing the door. They weren't in the least embarrassed about my presence. My cousin's husband knew what was happening. He came upon them making love one time, and he beat them up. In the end, he sent my cousin away and made another marriage.

And Lakshmi's mother's brother had apparently managed to trace her only as far as Bijnor: "My caste is Jat and my husband is just a Sahni. I used to wear very good clothes, but now look at my condition. If my mother's brother could see the clothes I'm wearing, he'd be terribly upset. My cousin's husband arranged my marriage in Bijnor, and now my uncle doesn't know where I am. If my uncle saw the condition I'm in now, he'd cut my throat and bury me."

Notes

1. See Chapter 6, note 4.
2. See Chapter 15 for more on remarriage among Hindus in Bijnor.

15

A Woman Should Die
Before Her Husband

Several widows have been prominent in South Asian political life—among them Indira Gandhi, "the widow" of Salman Rushdie's novel "Midnight's Children"—but their powerfulness has been in marked contrast to the experiences of widows in rural Bijnor.[1] In Dharmnagri and Jhakri, a woman with adult children and daughters-in-law living in her ambit would expect to be at the peak of her powers, able to exercise control over aspects of her own daily life as well as over other household members. In large measure, though, these capacities would be derived from her husband's control over productive resources and household income. Almost certainly, his death would result in a series of changes that would be evidenced by declining powers for his widow. An able-bodied widower in his middle years, still able to control household resources, would probably not experience this decline so soon.[2]

Given our interests in childbearing, our research in Bijnor was not explicitly focused on widows, who were expected to be celibate. Nevertheless, we knew several widows in Dharmnagri and Jhakri quite well, sometimes because they were the mothers-in-law of our key informants, sometimes because they had become dāīs as a means of earning their keep. And the issue of widowhood often came up in conversation. Roger's mother had been widowed some years before we first lived in Dharmnagri, and Patricia's shortly before we arrived in 1990. They both continued to live independently. When Patricia's mother— then in her early eighties—came to stay in Dharmnagri for a few weeks, her ability to negotiate the journey from Britain to India alone was a major topic of conversation throughout her visit. Why did our mothers not live in the households of our older brothers? Could they cope with all the affairs of a household? How did they manage financially? People's comments were often double-edged. They admired our mothers' independence yet hinted that we and our brothers were seriously failing in our filial duties. Ideally, an elderly or middle-aged widow should be housed and cared for by her adult sons and their wives—though the ideal was not always met.

245

What, for instance, if she had no sons? What if she had antagonized her daughters-in-law and was only grudgingly granted support in old age? Or what if her sons considered their own finances so tight that they refused to support her? If there was land, she would be unable to cultivate it without men's help, and she would rely on them to ensure that she received her entitlements. If there was no land, she would face a cheerless future. Almost certainly without education or training, she would probably be compelled to seek employment in lowly and ill-paid work, as a domestic servant in a wealthy household, as a farm laborer working in the fields or herding livestock, or as a dāī.[3]

Widowhood, of course, could come at any age. A woman widowed in her twenties or thirties—with sons still too young to work the family land or seek other employment—faced rather different issues. How would she provide for her children and settle them in marriage? Could she retain control over her husband's land and ensure that her sons' rights were not usurped by their father's brothers and nephews?[4]

Moreover, whereas the older widow would probably face fewer restraints on her movements than before, the young widow would have to be constantly mindful of malicious gossip about sexual liaisons. An older widow would be unlikely to remarry and would hope to rely on her adult sons. A young widow would almost certainly be encouraged, if not required, to enter into another union both to avert rumors about her sexual behavior and to provide her with economic support. Few women—whether Muslim or Hindu—who had been widowed before menopause had failed to remarry. A young widow's in-laws might "seat her beside" her husband's younger brother so that control over her husband's inheritance would not be lost.[5] *Or if she returned to her parents' home, they and her brothers would probably arrange another match for her, either a marriage with a dowry or as a bought bride, rather than have to support her indefinitely. Among Muslims, women could make second marriages (whether after divorce or widowhood) with the same ceremonies as for first marriages, and there were proportionately rather fewer widows—and widowers too—in Jhakri than in Dharmnagri.*[6] *Among Hindus, however, a second union would generally be termed karāv or satāv rather than shādi or byāh (the terms used for the first union) and the ceremonies would be simpler. Nevertheless, the woman would be referred to as a "wife" [bahū] and her children would be the man's legitimate heirs, just as among Muslims. Often, we came across such remarried widows through collecting maternity histories, just as we had the bought brides.*

With the childbearing and the worries about getting children married or the juggling of relationships between their in-laws and their natal kin, women often found married life problematic. But most feared being without a husband even more. Widowhood underlined the special vulnerabilities of the woman without a man on whom to depend. Even allowing for the risk of dying in childbirth, women were more likely to outlive their husbands because men were generally married to women some years their junior. Thus, widowhood was a plight that most women could expect to strike them at some stage.

A Widow and a Widower

Siddharth was from a middle-peasant Sahni family in Dharmnagri. He had long had a reputation for heavy drinking and violence. Neighbors had often reported warning him about the dangers of drink; others had told us of providing a haven for his wife, Seema, when he beat her. Then, within days of arriving back in Dharmnagri in 1990, we heard about Siddharth's death a couple of years previously. His mother told us how Siddharth had returned home after a drinking bout during the Holī festival and gone inside his house and locked the door.

Seema, his widow, picked up the story when Siddharth's mother could no longer bear to continue: "He'd sleep the entire day and go out drinking in the late afternoon or evening. Then he'd come back home, just before dawn sometimes. And again he'd sleep all day. After Holī, he'd drunk a lot, and he went inside and put a rope around his neck. When he didn't open the door the next morning, the men of the house sent someone to call the big landowner. He came and had the door opened in front of him. We found my husband dead."

After Siddharth's mother went to do some housework, Seema continued the story with her voice lowered: "He used to beat me a lot. Sometimes, he beat me so much that I had to have stitches. One time, he came home drunk and angry, and he beat me with the bed knob. That time I needed stitches in my back."

Seema was married in 1980, when she was about seventeen years old. Because of these marital problems, she decided to be sterilized at the Bijnor women's hospital when her third child was some three months old, just five years later.

> What would I have done with more children? If there had been five or six and he'd died, I'd be spending my whole day looking after the children. And then what would happen to the farmwork? How could I do the housework as well as the farmwork? My husband also used to beat the children, and he did no work. Now, I have two and a half acres of land. My husband's older brother is sharecropping about half of it for me. I myself work the remainder. I'm not educated, but I am intelligent. If I weren't, how would my mother-in-law let me carry on living here? I'm relying on my own courage. If it weren't for that, my mother-in-law could put me out at any time. She's already tried a few times. If I didn't use my intelligence, who would provide for my children?

So had her in-laws not helped her since she was widowed? Seema was scornful: "What help do they give? On the contrary, they want me to help them! My husband was very bad. He spent whatever cash income there was from the crops on drink. And when that was spent, he used to take grain from the house and sell that. Then nothing remained in the house for us to eat. He finished off a lot of grain and a lot of cash. While he was alive, I was always worried. Now he's dead I'm still troubled. But my parents are well off, and they help me a lot."

Seema was not alone in having problems. The wife of Siddharth's brother (the one who was sharecropping Seema's land) had died a few months before our arrival. Seema's mother-in-law, still grief-stricken by this second episode, told us that her daughter-in-law had been pregnant a couple of years earlier and had wanted an abortion and tubectomy at the same time. But the Bijnor hospital was closed because two or three women had apparently died during operations. The pregnancy was not terminated:

> Then, very soon after that baby was born, her period was late again. She wanted to obtain some medicines from a private doctor in Bijnor. She paid the consultation fee of twenty rupees but didn't understand that the money wouldn't cover medicines. We don't know what happened then. She didn't tell anyone here what she'd done. Maybe she obtained some medicines from someone in the village. Anyway, she became very ill with malaria and then a severe fever. She asked us to call her brother, and he took her back home for treatment, along with my son. Soon, she seemed to be recovering, and her brother suggested that my son return to Dharmnagri to plant his sugarcane. He and all the children were in Dharmnagri. She died three days later. Her corpse was returned to Dharmnagri for cremation.

By this stage, Seema's mother-in-law was weeping. She wanted to recount what had happened but could hardly continue: "There are six children, two boys and four girls. The youngest was just a year and a half when her mother died. My oldest daughter sent her daughter to cook for them, but she's gone back to her parents now. Now, sometimes, I cook their food; sometimes it's prepared by my second daughter's daughter. When she goes back to her parents, I'll have to do it all myself."

At this point, she could carry on no longer, and she retreated, sobbing, into her house. Once she was out of earshot, Seema began whispering that her in-laws had been talking of getting her married to her widowed brother-in-law:

That way, one set of children would have a mother again, and the other would have a father. At first, everyone was prepared for that to happen. My husband's sisters were also in favor. And my brother-in-law and I were both ready too. But then everyone became silent on the matter. My brother-in-law's wish is to marry me, but he says nothing in front of anyone because he's embarrassed. His children are running around, troubled the whole time, and I'm very upset about that myself. But I can't help them out. If I do any work for the children, everyone will say I'm doing it only because I want to be married to my brother-in-law.

Seema told her in-laws to talk to her father because she would marry again only if her father permitted it. But when her father visited Dharmnagri, none of her in-laws mentioned anything to him. According to one of the other young married women in the family, Seema's in-laws had been trying to find another bride for Seema's brother-in-law. "But no one suitable has been found," she told us. "What father would willingly marry his daughter into a house where there are already six children?"

Rohini's Difficulties

Rohini's widowed mother arranged Rohini's marriage in the mid-1940s, when Rohini was about nine years old. The cohabitation took place two years later. "In those days, boys and girls were very simple. If anyone said anything to them or hit them, they'd never answer back. In those days, too, people used to arrange marriages without even seeing the boy or the girl. The marriage took place wherever the parents had fixed the match, whatever the boy was like, and whether the girl was black or blind. There was no question then of the boy's or the girl's wishes."

When Rohini was married, her in-laws asked for nothing in particular in the dowry. This was especially fortunate, since Rohini's father had died when Rohini was a small child, leaving Rohini's mother in a perilous state. She had returned to Dharmnagri, her own natal village, to live with her two little daughters in the midst of her Sahni relatives there. But she lived independently. And without any land, she could not have afforded to give more than the seven utensils and seven *dhotīs* and shirts she managed to present in Rohini's dowry.

People used not to think badly about having daughters. But these days the dowry has grown huge, and even so the boy's people's stomachs aren't satisfied. It's for that reason alone that people have begun thinking that just one or two girls are enough. People reckon that they'll be able to give something to all their daughters if there are just a few and that their daughters will be comfortable in their in-laws' place. These days, people want more dowry. If the bride doesn't bring much with her, her mother-in-law will either make her do more work or constantly complain to all her neighbors that nothing at all came from the bride's house.

For reasons that were never justified to Rohini, her father-in-law had allocated land to all his sons except Rohini's husband. Consequently, her husband worked as a permanent farm servant on a large farm near Bijnor. Rohini was never allowed to live there with her husband, however, because there was so much work to be done on his father's farm.

My mother- and father-in-law and my husband's older brother often used to beat me. My husband never beat me, but he never stopped the others beating me either. These days a mother-in-law can say nothing to her daughter-in-law. No son will tolerate any criticism of his wife. If he hears any he'll be quite ready to fight. That's the reason that people separate their cooking hearths more rapidly than in the old days. But people were very simple then. And now, of course, the bride arrives from her parents' house knowing everything. Previously anyone could beat a daughter-in-law, but the daughters-in-law of today are ready to beat other people. That's why a mother-in-law just keeps silent these days. She says nothing in order to protect her own honor. The wives of today have climbed onto their masters' [husbands'] heads. Previously, no young man would so much as open his mouth to say anything in favor of his wife. In those days, a bride would cry all the way from her parents' house to her in-laws' house. These days, there aren't even a couple of tears!

Thus, despite the beatings, Rohini remained joint with her mother-in-law for some ten years. But then, one time while Rohini's husband was home, some money was stolen from his mother's trunk:

My sister-in-law [HeBW] took that money, but she told everyone I'd taken it. If my husband hadn't been there at the time, he'd never have known about the accusation. He was very angry and said he wanted to separate our hearth then and there. So that was how I became separate from his mother. It was certainly the case that he and I both wanted to separate. But only one of us could say anything. Otherwise his parents would have been angry because the two of us were of the one opinion.

Rohini used to visit her mother in Dharmnagri every year or so, sometimes staying with her for several months at a time. By the time that Rohini's hearth had become separate, her mother was blind and in need of care, and she asked Rohini and her husband to move to Dharm-nagri. Rohini's husband refused to become an "in-living son-in-law," but he permitted Rohini to stay with her mother while he continued working as a farm servant and cooking his own food.[7]

But then Rohini's husband died. Rohini was summoned back to her in-laws' place. She remained there for some years, doing various labor-ing jobs such as rice weeding and harvesting and cutting fodder that she sold in the bazaar. There was also a large landowner in the village, and Rohini used to fetch water and wash the dishes when weddings were taking place in his house.

> But my in-laws wouldn't let me do that throughout the year. They thought that I was young and it would be dreadful if anyone dishonored me. That was why I helped only at weddings. I used to be given forty to fifty rupees and a new *dhotī* in addition to being fed. In fact, I did rice weeding and harvesting only a couple of times because my in-laws didn't like me doing laboring work. After my husband died, the farmer where he'd worked had been keen for me to work for him. He said he'd pay me one and a quarter rupees for every one that he used to pay my husband. He wanted me to bring both my children with me so that they could also work for him. But my in-laws wouldn't let me do that.

Soon, however, Rohini's situation in her in-laws' home became more and more difficult, to the point that she could remain there no longer:

> By the time my husband died, he'd managed to save quite a lot of money. He'd put it in a trunk in his mother's room. Then, after his death, his mother asked me if she could borrow some money. So I gave her the key. Without telling me, my mother-in-law took all the money out. I didn't realize that it was empty until I looked inside some time later. For another thing, my brother-in-law [HeB] wanted to take me into his house even though he already had a wife. And my father-in-law was talking about selling me to someone on the other side of the river Ganges. That was when I returned to Dharmnagri for good.

Once back in Dharmnagri, Rohini did whatever laboring work came her way, for she had no other source of income. For a time, she worked in the big landowner's house, helping to prepare food and clean the dishes in the kitchen and also working in the garden. At one point, however, she was asked to put the quilts and pillows on the beds every night:

> But I refused. That's not a suitable job for a woman. I told them they should ask one of the men servants to do it. At that, they told me there

wasn't enough work for me to do in the kitchen, and so they sacked me. After that, I sometimes did rice harvesting in this village and in others nearby. But there wasn't much laboring work for women in this area. There was plenty for men, and it was throughout the seasons. But I did get some money from the government three times a year because I was registered as having no source of income. I collected it from the post office right here in the village. These days, I get 180 rupees each time.

Rohini's problems were compounded when her only son, then about ten, was hit by a speeding car as he was playing in the village street. The driver picked him up and took him to the hospital, but he was dead within the hour. "Those people gave me ten rupees for shroud and burial [*kafan-dafan*, though as Hindus, the boy would have been cremated]. But I gave it back. I said that since my son was worth 100,000 rupees what would I want with ten? That man should have thought, 'Who will there be now to earn for her?'"

Thus Rohini was left landless and without a regular income. And her growing daughter would soon need to be married. When the girl came to marriageable age, Rohini asked her in-laws to help. But her husband's brothers said that they could not do so. She herself would have to arrange her daughter's marriage:

And the people here in Dharmnagri also didn't help me find a boy. Rather than repeatedly asking people to help me, I thought it was better that I, a poor widow, get my daughter married and keep my self-respect. That's why I ended up using a go-between. I made the engagement without seeing the boy. I didn't even see him once before the wedding. When he arrived on the wedding day, I saw that he was very black, whereas my daughter was very beautiful. Everyone in the village began saying I must have "eaten money" [been paid to accept the match]. I just closed my eyes and got on with the wedding.

Since Rohini did not have enough money to pay for the marriage feast for the *barāt*, people in Dharmnagri contributed some rice. But it was of poor quality and was reduced to a mush during the cooking. "If that rice hadn't been given, I'd have made other arrangements, and the men in the *barāt* wouldn't have laughed at me," she said. Rohini's in-laws had contributed nothing toward the expenses of the marriage. Indeed, they were apparently not even planning to attend, but Rohini insisted.

I asked my mother-in-law to come and perform the goddess prayer ritual, which has to be done by one of the household elders. She refused, so I got angry and threatened to get it done by the priest. I told her I'd tell everyone that any shortcomings in the arrangements were not my fault but hers. I pointed out that the girl was her own son's child. At that she became afraid, and she came to the wedding with one of her daughters. But none of her sons attended. And when my husband's sister saw the groom, she said, "There's no oil in these sesame seeds," meaning the boy was no good and my daughter wouldn't be able to live in her in-laws' place. She asked me what I'd looked at before the wedding. At the very least, I should have looked at the boy, she told me. I told her that would have been fine, but it was now too late to do anything about it. But my daughter had heard what her aunt said, and she began crying and saying that she didn't want to be married. I thought that she should go out and find a boy she did like for herself if she didn't like someone else's choice. But I just kept silent and made everyone else quiet down. I told them all that it was fine as it was. But then, when the groom stretched out his hands when we were warding off the evil eye, we all saw that his palms were badly cracked. Everyone began saying this was a sign that he was suffering from heat, and my girl wouldn't be able to stand living with him. Then later, at the time of the bride's farewell, the groom's people sent the jewelry for my girl into the house. It was all old and had been borrowed! At that, my husband's sister said that my girl shouldn't wear the jewelry. She said that they weren't going to let the wedding take place. I said to her, "I'm arranging this wedding out of happiness, and time and again you're finding something to be unhappy about!" I told my girl to get dressed to go. And my husband's sister put the jewelry on her and seated her in the vehicle. My poor girl was crying as she left.

Rohini's daughter refused to allow her father's brother to collect her from her husband's house a couple of days later. She insisted that she would go only to the place from where she had been married. And when she arrived in Dharmnagri she began telling Rohini that she did not want to be sent back to her in-laws' village. Rohini was furious with her.

I told her I'd cut her into little pieces myself and put the pieces in a sack and throw them into the Ganges. I said I'd hire a horse-drawn buggy from her in-laws' village so that they'd know I was tipping her into the river. My husband's brother also threatened to beat her till blood flowed out of her eyes. He told her that I'd been widowed at a very young age, but I'd never looked lustfully at another man. He insisted that my girl go back to her in-laws' house. He said, "You must tell us if there's any trouble. But this is the world and there'll always be something to complain about." So she went back soon afterward for the cohabitation.

Rohini returned all the jewelry that her daughter's in-laws had borrowed for the wedding, saying that her girl could do without. Her daughter's in-laws were clearly not at all well off. There were hardly any utensils in the house, for instance.

> But my daughter just said, "It doesn't matter. This is how I'll have to live." That was over twenty years ago. If I manage to save any money from what I earn doing laboring work, I send it to my daughter. Just yesterday, I got someone in Jhakri to sew a petticoat for her. It cost one rupee. My daughter's very capable. That's why her husband takes notice of what she says. And she's got five children of her own. I'm telling her to get at least one of the girls married while I'm still alive. So for my sake, she's searching for a boy. My husband was very simple. That was why I decided to fulfill all his obligations. I decided not to remarry. I'd bring up my children alone, for there'd be no way of knowing whether a second husband would care for them properly. It caused me a lot of worry, and it took a lot of time to care for those children. But I never spread out my hands [begged], and I never looked lustfully at another man. And now, far fewer days remain to me than I've lived already.

Anisa's Means of Support

When we first met Ahmed—a rich-peasant Sheikh in Jhakri—he was married to Asghari. She was very weak and had taken a long time to conceive their first child. By 1985, it was clear that Asghari was seriously ill with pulmonary tuberculosis, but even so, Ahmed was obtaining no medicines for her. The ANM in Dharmnagri got a short course of treatment for her, but it was to no avail.

By the time we returned in 1990, Asghari had died. Ahmed's mother told us that Asghari had realized she was dying and had asked Ahmed to marry again so that their daughter's care would be ensured. Thus Anisa, who had previously been married in Qaziwala in the mid-1970s, was married to Ahmed in spring 1987, about six months before Asghari died.

In 1991, we met several women in Qaziwala who had known Anisa during her first marriage. Anisa's sister-in-law [HBW] told us that Anisa had a lot of fertility treatments and she had been pregnant with her first child after some eight or nine years of marriage, when her husband died of tuberculosis. She was about four months pregnant, and she had a miscarriage. Apparently, Anisa became "mad with grief over her husband and the child" and she began running away from home. Another woman married into the same connection put a different gloss on events, however. She claimed that Anisa was unhappy that her first husband had tuberculosis, so she spent very little time living with him in Qaziwala. That alone was why there were no children. And when he died, Anisa refused to be married to his younger brother. For that reason, this woman commented dryly, Anisa's parents had married her in Jhakri, into a house "where there was already a double bed."

Anisa had not been consulted about her first marriage, but her mother did ask her about her marriage to Ahmed. "But I didn't know then what my destiny was," she told us ruefully. "I didn't know I'd get such a bad man. Now everyone here taunts me. My mother-in-law and my sister-in-law [HyBW] both say I can't survive without a husband. But no one's parents live forever. Parents can look after their daughter when they're alive. But what happens after that? There has to be some means of support for her. That's why my parents married me here. And that's why my in-laws taunt me."

Then she bared her arms to show the bruising and the scars where she had been cut by her glass bangles when Ahmed beat her.

> He beats me daily. There's no such day when he doesn't beat me. His parents also beat me. My sister-in-law beat me too, and I've had constant pains in my lower back and in my belly ever since. They won't let me visit my parents. It's over a year since I've been. If anyone came from my parents' place, my parents-in-law would insult them. That's why my brother doesn't come any more. It's over a year since my mother came. My father was butted by an ox a few days ago, and he was badly hurt. Even then, they wouldn't let me visit him.

She began sobbing and bemoaning her fate:

> If I didn't think of the children, I'd just die. But then I realize there's no one who would care for my children. They'd end up running from one place to the next being beaten. I don't want any more children. There's no consideration shown to these two. It wouldn't be right to have more. They aren't provided with proper clothes or with medicines when they're sick. I'll take those pills to stop children. Can you get them for me? Neither I nor the children are treated with any consideration. I have constant pain in my lower back, and still my husband beats me. I can't stand being beaten now. Tell me how to put these beatings behind me! My first husband never even slapped me with his four fingers, but this one beats me daily. One time, I told him to abandon me and take another woman if he doesn't like me. But he said he wouldn't. He said, "I'm going to carry on beating you, just like I used to beat Asghari and my cousin's wife too! No one intervened then to stop me. No one can obstruct any of my actions!" He's even put his hands round my throat to strangle me a number of times. On occasion, I've considered taking poison. But then I think about the children. Anyway, the villagers would say it was an unlawful death.

But what was she to do? Could she get out of this situation? She had virtually no contact with her parents and felt there was little prospect of rescue from that quarter. If she died—either by suicide or murder—her children's future would be even more perilous. "So how can I escape?" she asked. "All the young wives in Jhakri are troubled too. Just now, Dilshad has divorced Dilruba and thrown her out." Swaleha reminded her that Dilruba had returned to Jhakri because of her children. Anisa was scornful: "She shouldn't have come back. She went away, so she shouldn't have returned. If I ever went away, I wouldn't return like that."

A Widow's Worries

Udayan's father had been quite seriously ill before he died. Udayan's mother put it all down to his having been sterilized in the mid-1970s, for he had been very weak since the operation.[8] He had a lot of pain in his abdomen and was unable to do heavy work. In autumn 1982, after some weeks of various treatments, he died from the effects of kidney stones. He was then in his mid-fifties.

Udayan's father was a poor-peasant Sahni, relying on his own land and the land he sharecropped for income. Udayan, however, had refused to help his father on the land, so he and his wife, Urmila, had been made to live separately from his parents. Udayan had been compelled to seek employment. But Udayan was the only adult son, so he had to give up his job and turn to farming after his father's death. The land was all in his mother's name, and Udayan had to organize the farming with his two unmarried brothers. In the longer run, he would be responsible for arranging their marriages and finding husbands for his two unmarried sisters. At times he seemed overwhelmed by the responsibility, and he was becoming weak from the heavy work to which he was not accustomed. Udayan reestablished a joint household with his mother and his unmarried siblings, and his siblings helped him in the fields. Urmila herself sometimes had to help out as well, though she was kept busy with the extra cooking and animal work in the larger household. Urmila said she hardly had time to comb her hair and plait it. Her four children, all still very young, made it hard for her to keep up with all the work. Things had been all the more difficult because Udayan's father had died during the rice harvest, when all the able-bodied household members had to be out in the fields.

In the midst of all this disturbance, Udayan's mother was unwell. She had been having some treatments locally but was very weak and had no appetite. A few weeks after being widowed, she told of how she had been dreaming about her husband, seeing him busy at work and stopping to ask her for the torch so that he could go out in the dark to check that the cattle were safe. She was sorely missing him and the care he gave her. Perhaps it was not surprising that her preoccupied children's neglect aggravated her grief over her husband's death:

> My husband didn't consider money to be money. I've been troubled for a long while by pains in my arms. Whenever and wherever I asked for treatment, he'd get it for me. He took me to Meerut, to Shanpur, to Nehtaur, and even to Lucknow. He borrowed money if necessary. But I got relief only from a doctor in the Bengali village right here.[9] And now I have bloody stools and a persistent cough. I can't face taking anything except tea. But Udayan can't take me for treatments like his father could. He's far too busy with the farming. My husband cared greatly for me.

She elaborated on this theme. She explained how her parents-in-law had both died when her husband was still a small child. She told of how her husband's four older brothers had taken all the land and livestock for themselves and given none to her husband. She talked about how her husband had arranged his marriage to her, in about 1948, and how he had met all the expenses himself because his brothers had not helped. Everything they now had—land, animals, and house—had come from his efforts. And she recounted how his brothers had tried to wreck their marriage:

> During my first pregnancy, I began bleeding at seven months. My husband got me plenty of treatment. I didn't really understand what was going on, as I was so young. For a long time after that, I didn't get pregnant again. My husband's brother told him to sell me, and he would find another bride. But my husband refused. He said he wasn't very worried about having children, he was only concerned that I should be in good health. He refused to take another wife. He was very understanding.

In any case, she conceived shortly after this. Udayan was born early, looking "like a little rat," and people began commenting on the weak babies she was producing. Then, once more, she did not conceive, this time for five years, and her husband's brother again suggested that she be sold and replaced. Her husband refused and insisted that one son was enough for him. Five years later, she had a girl, followed by a second, then two more boys and the two youngest girls. She was bitter about her in-laws but had nothing but praise for the protection and care her husband had given: "This world is very bad. Anyone can have a long gap between children. That's not under their control. And if a woman has children too quickly, people gossip about that too, saying, 'Look she's having a baby every year!'"

Perhaps, too, now that she was widowed, Udayan's mother was aware of the shift of power within the household. Without her husband, her position was weakened, especially if she remained unwell. She was concerned about how hard it was for a woman to find any paid work in the village. And indeed, a neighbor alleged that Urmila was complaining about how much time she had to spend cooking for everyone in the new joint household and about how much they were all insisting on eating.

Within three years, the household had split again. Udayan's mother began living with her remaining three unmarried children, although the farm was still jointly operated. "People these days aren't willing to cook for others," she commented. "When a lot of people live jointly, there's a lot of work. That's the main reason young women these days want to separate from joint households as quickly as they can. And their husbands say nothing against it. In the old days, young men used to do as their mothers wished, but now they listen to what their wife wants. A woman should die before her husband because there are lots of worries if she's still alive when he dies."

Notes

1. In 1995, out of eight prime ministers and presidents in India, Bangladesh, Pakistan, and Sri Lanka, four were women, two the widows and two the daughters of assassinated politicians.

2. For more discussion of these issues see Drèze (1990); and Chen and Drèze (1992). Wadley (1992) presents an account of a woman who managed to overcome some of the difficulties of widowhood. Vatuk (1990) discusses widows' fears of dependency on their sons.

3. For further on this see R. Jeffery and P. Jeffery (1993).

4. The young widower would not face identical economic problems, but he would almost certainly remarry because having no woman to do household work (including caring for children from his first marriage) or having no male heirs would generate enormous problems for him.

5. See Kolenda (1987) for further discussion of the pressures on widows to "marry" their late husband's brother.

6. In 1991 there were twenty-five widows and eighteen widowers in Dharmnagri, five widows and two widowers in Jhakri. The rates were much higher in Dharmnagri than in Jhakri. Widows made up approximately 12 percent of ever-married women in Dharmnagri and 5 percent in Jhakri; widowers were 10 percent of ever-married men in Dharmnagri and 2 percent in Jhakri.

7. See Chapter 6 for more on the "in-living son-in-law."

8. Many people believed that sterilization made a man "weak," one of the symptoms of which is impotence.

9. In the 1970s, four villages were established in the environs of Dharmnagri for Hindu refugees from Bangladesh.

16

Allah Gives Both Boys and Girls

Bashir was one of three Sheikh brothers who had been among the most wealthy farmers in Jhakri. Bashir was first married in the mid-1940s and had two sons, Razaq and Suleiman, and two daughters. Then, on being widowed, he married again.

Bashir and his second wife, Bilquis, were among the forty-one couples we initially selected for our research, but they had proved very difficult to deal with, giving wildly contradictory accounts and blowing hot and cold in their relationships with us. We were never entirely sure of why this was—but we were somewhat consoled by the knowledge that they dealt with other people in Jhakri in the same way.

Bashir and Bilquis were married around the time that Razaq and Suleiman themselves were married, yet Bashir had denied them access to his land. Razaq and Suleiman were in extremely difficult economic situations. Throughout the 1970s and 1980s, they watched helplessly while their father sold land to pay his debts, and their youthful stepmother continued to bear sons who would be entitled to share what might remain of their father's land. Being the son of a wealthy farmer was no guarantee of economic security, and Razaq and Suleiman were compelled to seek other sources of income. The relationships between Bilquis and her stepdaughters-in-law were also abrasive. For Suleiman's wife, Sabra, Bilquis was living proof of the unflattering stereotypes of the stepmother and the mother-in-law, in this instance combined in the same person.

For Suleiman and Sabra, the issue of security in old age loomed large not just because of their financial situation. From the time we first met them, they were acutely aware of the importance of having sons who would support them when they were old and infirm. In many ways, their concerns echoed those of Durgi and Devinder (in Chapter 4). Not only did Sabra have no sons, but the line of daughters born in the quest for a son created worries about arranging their marriages, anxieties that were seriously exacerbated by Suleiman's disinheritance. By the time we returned in 1990, however, the significance of these themes that had so dominated Sabra's life had altered in ways that we had not at all expected.

Displaying the Dowry Jewelry

* * * * * *

Many people in Jhakri had initially suspected that we were somehow associated with the government family-planning program. From the start, though, Sabra had given us a friendly welcome. She would often come through the fields from Jhakri to the Dharmnagri dispensary where we were living. There was frequently some reason for seeing the doctor. And when she had finished, she would generally take a few minutes to chat with us. Sometimes, too, we would talk to her while she worked at home.

On the first sunny day for a while during the 1982 monsoon, Sabra wanted all the clothes to be dried before nightfall, so she carried on pounding her laundry as she chatted.

"You haven't been in Jhakri for a while," she complained, though with a smile.

"We've been going to other villages and getting women to fill out forms for us. And do you know, the people there haven't been as frightened as the people in Jhakri!"

"I've filled out one of your forms without worrying about it. But I can't say why other people in Jhakri are afraid," she replied.

Indeed, not only did she willingly respond to our requests for information but she was more tenaciously curious about life in Britain than many of the other people we met. One time, Sabra wanted to hear about marriage ceremonies in Britain. Before Patricia could get a word in, Swaleha said that weddings in Britain were very simple and that the bride and groom simply exchanged rings. Sabra's response was instant:

> That sounds like a good custom. For us a girl seems burdensome. Her parents have to give her a dowry with jewelry, utensils, and so on. They have to give several pounds of silver and gold. And when the girl goes to her in-laws' house, her parents have to fill a whole trunk with clothes. It's a dreadful thing how much has to be given to get a girl married. Nowadays, people want to arrange their son's marriage only into a house from which they'll get a splendid dowry. Meanwhile, who knows how a girl's people will be able to marry her? They just have to get the dowry and jewelry ready. There ought to be a law that dowry should neither be given nor taken.[1]

Another day when Sabra was visiting us, the ANM came to confirm that we would take Bhagirthi to the hospital in Bijnor in our jeep. Bhagirthi had been married into a rich-peasant Rajput household in Dharmnagri. In 1979, she had had a stillbirth because she was given three labor-accelerating injections by the dispensary compounder. She was now about to give birth again, and the ANM had told her that the baby's head was large. The ANM did not want to be held responsible for any further calamity, and Bhagirthi was anxious enough to want a checkup in Bijnor. Sabra asked who we were talking about. The ANM retorted:

> Whoever it is, I don't want to be blamed for any problems. Nor do I want people to think I get women dragged off to hospital to be sterilized by compulsion. Have I ever told you to be sterilized, you with your four girls? And haven't I had you treated for TB without any pressure for sterilization? And aren't you all right now? And didn't I get treatment for Asghari for TB so that she'd become pregnant? And didn't I help Dilshad's sister Gulistan when she nearly died in childbirth?

At each of these assertions, Sabra nodded rather sheepishly. Then the ANM asked Patricia to make sure that Bhagirthi had clean cloths prepared for her baby. She turned to Sabra again: "Do you know, when I went to help with Zubeida's delivery, there wasn't even a piece of cloth the size of a pocket handkerchief clean enough to wipe the baby off."

Sabra again assented, and the ANM departed, leaving Patricia and Sabra exchanging rather bemused grins as she went. Yet Sabra was a good deal more prepared to seek the ANM's services than many others in Jhakri. She had, indeed, obtained considerable relief from TB, though it was not completely cleared up.

Some time later, Sabra again came to the dispensary, this time to obtain some medication for her daughter, whose head was covered in boils. As we chatted, we were once more joined by the ANM, who began asking about various pregnant women in Jhakri. She then launched into complaints: "Jhakri women are so unwilling to have prenatal tetanus injections. I give the injections free before the birth. That's much better than having to pay for them afterward. I give freely what comes here free from the government. But I don't give anything from my own pocket. People would become suspicious. But people don't listen to me."

"That's because people are afraid of you," said Sabra.

The ANM pursed her lips. She had no answer to that. As she started to leave, Sabra began asking about tetanus injections. Sabra said that she was in the fourth month of pregnancy. Some months later, in early 1983, it was Fatima who told us about Sabra's delivery: "She's had another girl, poor thing. That's the fifth."

*   *   *   *   *   *

When we talked to Sabra about her childbearing career, it became very clear why she was so vocal about the problems parents faced in providing dowries for their daughters. Sabra was married to Suleiman in about 1969. Her first pregnancy had ended in a miscarriage. Sabra thought she must have been three or four months pregnant, though she was not sure. She had missed three periods.

> But I was young and I didn't know what that meant. I didn't know why periods stopped coming. Nor did I ask anyone. I'd been spreading wheat out on the roof to dry in the sun with my sister-in-law. But in the afternoon, clouds began to appear and we collected the wheat into sacks in case it rained. Then we put the sacks in the grain store in the house. That night I was tired and slept heavily. In the morning, I had stomach pains and bleeding began. I told my sister-in-law that I hadn't had a period for three months and now suddenly one had begun. She said that I must be pregnant and she called the *dāī* who was living in Jhakri then. The *dāī* said that the bleeding had started because I'd been lifting heavy weights. She gave me some pills and told me to eat pulses without chili pepper or spices. But even so, I still had pains and the blood continued to flow. In the evening the baby itself came out. It was just a ball the size of my fist. We called the *dāī* again. She said it was hard to stop that happening, as I'd been lifting heavy things, so she gave me some medicine to clean me out properly. The *dāī* told my husband the names of the things he had to bring from the bazaar and she ground them and gave them to me to drink.

We asked what had happened in the next pregnancy, but true to form, Sabra reprimanded us for not going on to ask her what food she had eaten after the miscarriage or what she had paid the *dāī*. We obediently noted down the details and then asked what had happened in her other pregnancies. "Well, after that baby fell, I had a girl without any trouble," she told us. "But the next time, because I had so little sense, I caused an abortion at five months."

We were astonished at her willingness to mention such a sensitive subject and hardly dared to press her for more details. But after a few moments, we asked—somewhat diffidently—if she would tell us about it. Sabra told us what had happened with hardly any further prompting:

> You see, it was partly that I was lacking in sense, partly that my mother-in-law and my husband's sisters didn't explain things to me. Five months had been completed and sometimes I had spotting like at the end of a period, when just a small amount of blood comes out. At that time I was fighting with my sister-in-law [HeBW]—we weren't speaking to one another. So I talked to a neighbor about the spotting, and she said the

baby certainly wouldn't stay in place, it would miscarry. So having listened to that woman, I went to a doctor and told him that I wanted an abortion.

What doctor had agreed to do such a late abortion, when surely she could have died? Did the doctor not even ask why she wanted an abortion? Did he not suggest that Sabra bring her husband with her?

No, he didn't ask me anything. He simply gave me the medicines—just tablets, nothing else. And I took them to my mother's house. My husband didn't know anything about it. You see, a man wouldn't like the idea of an abortion. And also, I was very young at the time, and I just panicked. Now I have five children, and I could cope with another baby, but I didn't think I could then. So I was afraid of my husband, and I took the pills to my mother's house. It was there that I ate them. I didn't tell anyone there first. I just ate them, and the baby was cleaned out. No one was with me at the time. I got pains in my belly, and so I went outside to crap. It was then that the baby fell, and I became unconscious. Sometime later my mother found me, and she carried me inside.

The baby was a boy. Sabra's mother wrapped him up in cloth and buried him. Sabra herself became very weak. Her mother was furious with the doctor and said he should not have done such a dangerous thing. For as long as Sabra's husband was still alive, she told him, he was not to do another abortion for Sabra or he would have to face the consequences.

And out of fear of my husband, I stayed with my parents for a week afterward. But someone had told him about it before I got back to Jhakri. He was very angry. When I got back from my mother's house, he asked me why I was lying down. He said, "Go outside and do your work!" I managed to walk slowly out into the courtyard. But I couldn't work or even sit. So I went back inside. He said some more angry things, and he swore at me. But then he became silent. Having an abortion at five months is dangerous. It's also a sin. It's wrong to kill something with life in it. But I was young, and didn't know any better. Now I'm able to think. Now I'm afraid. I worry about what will happen after I die.

After that, Sabra had given birth only to girls. And yet, when we asked her after the fifth girl was born if she had ever taken medicines to procure a son, she was adamant: "I've never taken any medicine like that. If Allah wants to give me a boy, He'll do so without any medicine. Allah gives both boys and girls, so what's the point of taking any medicine?"

She had not been altogether happy when she had become pregnant again, however, though she had felt she should do nothing about it: "I caused an abortion once and was very troubled after that. And now my health is not what it was then. Anyway, I'm afraid of Allah. Previously, I didn't understand so much."

On balance, even though she had no son, she did not want any more children. It would be hard enough to bring up the five girls she now had. "My health is bad. We don't have enough to eat because we don't have enough land from which to obtain grain. These children are too many. It's hard to feed the children and ourselves. Five children are a lot." Not surprisingly, she and Suleiman did not organize any celebrations in 1983 to mark this latest arrival.

* * * * * *

Sabra's situation in Jhakri was in marked contrast to that into which she had been born. Her parents and three brothers lived in nearby Badshahpur, where her brothers shared the operation of a farm of over eighteen acres. There was, as Sabra put it, no need for them to seek jobs elsewhere, as the farming kept them fully occupied.

> My father arranged my marriage. My mother also agreed to it, but it was my father who'd seen the boy. I must have been eighteen or so at the time. There were other offers of marriage for me—I can't remember how many—but my father liked only this one. The go-between was a Julaha [weaver] from Chandpuri.[2] He used to go to Jhakri and Badshahpur selling cloth, and he told my father that if he wanted to get me married, he'd show him a boy in Jhakri. The Julaha told my father-in-law about me, and then an offer of marriage was sent to my father. Parents don't ask the girl anything about her marriage. And out of embarrassment the girl doesn't say anything. The parents alone make the decision.

At the time, Suleiman's father, Bashir, operated about thirty acres jointly with his two brothers. He had two adult sons, of whom Suleiman was the younger. Sabra's parents gave her a dowry consistent (as Sabra put it) "with their own standing and the expectations of the time": some fifty-five pounds of brass and copper utensils, eleven pieces of jewelry (silver and gold), thirteen suit lengths for herself and eighteen for the people of her in-laws' connection. There was also a cycle and watch for Suleiman and the customary bed and stool. Sabra's in-laws had presented her with twelve pieces of jewelry and fourteen suits. Further items of clothing and foodstuffs came from her parents when Sabra went to Jhakri for the second time after the marriage. A year later, her parents sent a buffalo. The clothing and foodstuffs were rapidly used up, as was to be expected. But Sabra was soon forced to succumb to her father-in-law's financial demands.

> There were utensils in my dowry, but I can't remember how many separate items. You see, my father-in-law sold the lot. He also sold two pieces of the jewelry that my parents had presented to me. That was before I'd been married for even a year. My father told him that it had not been his right to sell the things. My father asked him to say where he'd sold the things so that he could get them back. But my father-in-law just asked my father to say how much everything had cost and he'd repay the sum. He still hasn't done so. I even told my mother-in-law that I'd give some other jewelry to them if they'd return the utensils from my parents' house. But they didn't. Then a little later, my father-in-law forcibly took the jewelry that he himself had presented me—apart from two pieces that I hid. At that time, we were still living jointly, and one of the bullocks died. So he [her HF] sold my things and bought another bullock and made all the arrangements to cultivate the crops. And even those two pieces of jewelry that I managed to hide didn't remain with me. My husband's brother needed money one time and he asked for them, and I've never had them back. And the jewelry from my parents' house got broken, so I sent it to the goldsmith for repair; but he disappeared with it all. So nothing has remained with me.

Bashir's propensity to cheat his relatives and cause them financial worries was widely commented upon in Jhakri, and several people told us about the bad blood it had caused in Suleiman's wider family. No one in Jhakri expected that we would get a straight story from Bashir— and, indeed, we did not. According to Bashir's two brothers, he was caught up in disputes with them and their children. We heard several convoluted tales of money that Bashir had borrowed from his brothers but never repaid. And when the land was divided among the three brothers, Bashir got control of the tubewell, so his brothers had had to sell land—and also some wedding jewelry belonging to Maqsudi, one of their daughters-in-law—in order to pay for the installation of their own tubewell. There was plenty of antagonism toward Bashir.

It also seems that Suleiman and his brother, Razaq, were hardly paragons themselves. They had reputedly been involved in several thefts in the village. One man alleged that this had prompted Bashir to oust them from his house and refuse them access to most of his land and its produce. Suleiman and Razaq received just one acre between them. A different—though not wholly incompatible—account was given by Sabra. Just before Sabra was married, Bashir had made a second marriage to a woman much younger than himself. Sabra believed that Suleiman's exclusion from his rightful dues had been instigated by his stepmother, Bilquis, who wanted to preserve the land for her own children:

> We were all joint with my parents-in-law until after my first daughter was born. But then my mother-in-law made us separate. That was about three and a half years after my marriage. You see, my mother-in-law is a stepmother-in-law. She'd been fighting with me from the day I was married. She didn't want to have her daughters-in-law with her. She began saying that even more often around the time my husband's two sisters were being married. And then my father-in-law joined in all the squabbling, and he made us separate.

This had had several consequences. For one thing, Sabra was deprived of help that she might otherwise have expected, particularly after childbirth:

> My mother-in-law gave me no help with my first baby, and that was when we were still living jointly! She hasn't helped me with any of my other children either. And I can't call my husband's married sisters, since my mother-in-law gets angry that they're helping me. It's a father's job to call his daughters, but my father-in-law rarely calls the older one and he never calls the younger one. His wife doesn't want them to come. And I have nothing to give them, so how could I call them myself?

Sabra had found this particularly trying before and after the birth of her fifth daughter. For most of the pregnancy, Sabra was severely incapacitated with a fever and chest pains (almost certainly TB), yet she was compelled to work right up to the end: "Women should stop lifting heavy loads or making dung cakes, but I had no respite at all. The girl was born at night and I'd worked right into the evening. If I'd had someone to help me, I'd have stopped working, for I wanted to lie down and rest."

Such little help as she had after the delivery came from Razaq's daughter and from Sabra's oldest daughter, then eight. Suleiman's sister happened to be in Jhakri but could help for only a day in the face of her stepmother's ire.

Perhaps more serious than this, however, were the implications of being cut off with hardly any land. For some time after her fifth daughter's birth, Sabra ran a fever and had pains throughout her body, especially in the pelvic region. After a couple of weeks of treatment from a private doctor in Bijnor—costing Rs 120—Sabra felt somewhat better. But she still had the sensation of "ants walking all over the body." Over the next two months, the medical expenses had mounted to Rs 1,500, and Suleiman had had to borrow money to pay the bills. "My medical treatment is consuming money that should be spent on food. Sometimes we've had to stop the treatment because we were short of money. But then we get medicines when the pain gets too bad again."

Suleiman's brother, Razaq, had not been so short of resources. His mother-in-law in nearby Chandpuri told us she had not wanted her daughter married to Razaq, but her husband had given his word and would not break his promise. After the marriage, her husband frequently gave Razaq financial help for the sake of their daughter. This had enabled Razaq to save some money, and he had bought about two-thirds of an acre of land on his own account before his father cut him off. Razaq's wife died in 1980, according to her mother during premature labor after Razaq had beaten her severely. Even after this, Razaq's father-in-law continued to provide for his grandchildren's schooling and other expenses.

Suleiman, however, had not had such comprehensive support from his in-laws. Sabra's parents continued to send her the customary gifts of clothing and foodstuffs on festivals and after she gave birth, but they did not send substantial cash gifts. According to Sabra, "Our girls see children in other compounds with toys, but we can't afford to buy things like that. We can afford to eat, but not much more. My father-in-law hasn't given us our share of land, so my husband has to do laboring work."

Was Suleiman not able to rent land or take some land on a sharecropping basis? "He [Suleiman] doesn't have enough money to buy land at 20,000 rupees per acre," Sabra told us. "For one year, he rented nearly two acres from someone in Dharmnagri. That cost 900 rupees for the year. But then we didn't have enough money for the rent, so we'd sharecrop and get half the crop instead."

What was going to happen that year? Did people in their own compound not give out land to people who wanted to sharecrop?

> We haven't been able to get any land that way this year. The people of our compound won't help anyone. They prefer to get work done by laborers if necessary. That way they can keep all the crop themselves. We used to have a buffalo that gave ten pints of milk a day. But the children got none of it to drink because we used to sell all the milk. With that income and anything my husband could earn from laboring sometimes, we could manage to buy our food. I had to breast-feed the girl older than this baby for longer than I wanted, as there was no other milk in the house to give her. But that buffalo died last year. So now we're very

worried about money, as we used to rely greatly on the income from the milk. My three brothers and my father have nearly twenty acres. It's a matter of fate that there's nothing for me in Jhakri.

Suleiman's rights to his father's land and Sabra's control over her dowry had been seriously infringed, with the result that Sabra had grave worries about the future: "Whatever a girl's parents give and whatever clothes and jewelry come to a daughter-in-law from her in-laws belong to her alone. But my in-laws left me with no jewelry and they even sold the utensils that my parents had given. Now I have five daughters, and I'm very worried. If I even had utensils and jewelry, they'd be of use to me. But my parents-in-law left us with nothing. We're just like rats in an unused water pot."

*   *   *   *   *   *

Suleiman and Razaq, however, were not content with such a position, and they decided to go into business together. They began buying tree plantations—mostly eucalyptus, a cash crop introduced a few years earlier. Then they would fell the trees, sell the wood, pay the debts incurred in buying the plantation, and use the profit to meet their families' needs. Slowly, the business began to flourish: "Whatever profit they earned from the business, the two brothers put to some other use," Sabra explained in 1985. "They saved some money and bought some land. They bought nearly two acres from their own income. We get grain from it; but we also have to buy grain, since we can't be fully fed from the grain that comes from our own land."

By the mid-1980s, things seemed to be promising. Sabra was not so constantly short of money, though they were still living in a single room in the corner of Bashir's courtyard. But the children were still a worry. The girl born in 1983 had died, but another one had come to take her place. And there was still no son. As Suleiman put it,

> I don't want any more girls—we already have more than enough. I'd like a little bit of a boy. But it's not good to have too many. Two boys are enough; otherwise they'd fight over their shares of land. I can't say that large numbers of children are necessary. In any case, there's a big difference between boys and girls. A man with twenty acres might like a lot of children, but a small person like me needs only two boys and a girl. Then I could give my girl in marriage, and my two boys would each bring in a bride. The boys would be able to help one another, but the land wouldn't be split up too much. God has chosen to give me five girls, and there was one other who died. Parents love boys and girls the same—but a girl goes to her own house after she's married. Boys stay with their

father. They do cultivation and animal husbandry, so their father can get some rest when he's old. Girls are fine, but the name of boys is greater. This is the reason: Boys make money for their father.

* * * * * *

Every time we returned to Jhakri, new houses had sprung up. People were shifting from cramped quarters in the center of the village to new sites on the outskirts, where they were constructing kiln-brick houses with higher walls than the older-style houses and with flat roofs instead of thatch. On our return in 1990, one such house was nearing completion. It consisted of a line of three sizable rooms beyond the pathway that had earlier marked the edge of the village. It had yet to be plastered, and several of the windows did not have their wooden frames and shutters. The boundary wall had not been built, and one room was currently being used to house some livestock. The building turned out to be Sabra's.

Our immediate supposition that Sabra's life had changed for the better was dispelled as soon as we met her again. Suleiman had died in a road accident about two years earlier. "He was on his way to Bijnor on his Vikki [motorcycle]. He was hit by a minibus at the crossing with the road to the Ganges barrage. The bus didn't stop. Later a police vehicle came past and they saw him. They took him to hospital but he died later. And now I have six girls and a boy. The boy was in my belly when my husband died. He was born three months after his father died."

Even without being widowed, Sabra would have had great problems in settling six daughters in marriage. Now, there was not enough land to feed the family, and Sabra herself could not cultivate it. Nor could she contemplate engaging in Suleiman's tree business. Without the goodwill and generosity of others, she and her children faced a bleak future.

Razaq had remarried shortly before Suleiman's death. Immediately after, he and his wife established a joint household with Sabra.

> My father-in-law never gave his two sons by his first marriage their proper share of the land. But they'd managed to buy land. They'd bought nearly three acres altogether. They used to work it separately. But since my husband's death, the land has been operated jointly, and the cooking hearth is also joint. We also had the Vikki mended, and we sold it. My brother-in-law has bought a new one. My brother-in-law has also taken over my husband's work in Bijnor, checking the men who fell trees.

Since then, Razaq had taken full responsibility for Sabra and her children. In order to lighten the task, his first wife's father had arranged and paid for the marriage of Razaq's daughter by his first marriage. Razaq's daughter explained what had happened one time when she was visiting Jhakri:

> I've been married now for just over a year. My grandfather [MF] paid for my marriage. He married me from Jhakri and gave me a very good wedding. There were twenty suits for me and twenty for my in-laws. He gave all the things in the dowry. And the bed was a double one. When the wedding party was departing with me, my grandfather gave my husband 10,000 rupees and told him to find himself a job. My husband is studying in tenth class at the moment, but he's also searching for employment. After my uncle died, my father began caring for my uncle's children. There are six girls and a boy, so my father couldn't have paid for such a wedding as I had.

Meanwhile, Sabra's oldest daughter was now about seventeen. She had studied only the Qur'ān Sharīf, for when she had suddenly reached puberty, Sabra had stopped sending her to the *madrasā*, where she might have learned some Urdu and Hindi. The girl herself commented that she had been unwilling to attend the *madrasā* since she was the only "big" girl going. She had remained at home for several years, helping with the family's work. But now she had reached the age to be married.

Razaq had taken the matter in hand. He viewed a boy in a nearby village and decided on the match. There was land in the boy's family, but the boy did not work on the land. He had studied to about fifth class, but he was also Hafyz Qur'ān [able to recite the Qur'ān Sharīf by memory] and he was teaching the children in his village. Given Sabra's daughter's education, it was a good match.

The marriage was to take place during the month after Eid, in late spring 1991. Sabra, however, had no jewelry to present to her daughter. "A few years ago my younger sister died, but my father had already set aside jewelry for her marriage," Sabra told us. "My father gave all that to me because I had nothing left. I presented that jewelry to my husband's brother's new wife—but that too got stolen. When my husband's funeral procession was waiting at the cattle byre and everyone was there, there was a theft at our house and all the jewelry was stolen."

Fortunately, Razaq also took responsibility for all the details of the marriage arrangements, including the dowry. Sabra's brothers also played their part, for this was the first of Sabra's children to be married and it was incumbent on them to provide the *bhāt*. Sabra received Rs 3,000, fourteen suits (two for the bride herself, one for the groom, and the rest for Sabra and her other children), and three pieces of jewelry for the bride—a gold nose stud and nose ring and a silver necklace. This was all a great relief to Sabra, who proudly displayed all the items to us on the wedding day.

The wedding party from the boy's village was being received by the Jhakri men at Sabra's new house on the village outskirts. The bride and her female relatives were inside the village, waiting in one corner of the compound of Bashir, Sabra's father-in-law and the bride's grandfather. But when we asked if Bashir was making any contribution to the marriage expenses, Sabra denied it vehemently. "My mother-in-law," she told us, "made a curse that these children of mine would end up in a desolate place with no one to care for them. But did Allah forget them?"

"A person who has killed off someone else's money and land cannot live happily," commented Razaq's wife.

"Yes," said Sabra nodding, "just look how much land our father-in-law has sold. And still one or another person who has lent him money is standing up and demanding his money back. Stealing someone's entitlement isn't right. He'll never be able to live properly. He didn't even give two acres to us out of the ten or twelve acres he used to have."

*   *   *   *   *   *

Bashir's behavior caused no surprise in Jhakri. The role taken on by Razaq, however, was a source of wonder in the village. One young man reminded us of the thefts that Suleiman and Razaq had perpetrated years back and commented that Razaq was transformed. Maybe the deaths of his first wife and his brother had chastened him; maybe he was afraid of what punishment Allah might bring him next. Gulshan reported that Razaq had not let his niece sit on the ground during the seclusion before her marriage but had insisted that she sit on a bed. Another young woman told us that Razaq had responded to his niece's tearfulness by saying that he would make good directly any shortages she felt there were in the dowry. But she also added a note of caution: "Sabra has six girls, and her brother-in-law has arranged the marriage for one of them. There are still five others. I don't know if he'll do all the other weddings. Uncles like that are rare. But his second wife is from the town, and she's very good."

The future, then, was uncertain for Sabra and her children: "The younger girls are still studying. I want them to study reading books as well as the Qur'ān Sharīf. But then that'll be enough. What, are they to be made to go out for employment? If there were a school or *madrasā* in Jhakri, I might let them study more. But no one in Jhakri teaches children. I'd like them to be married into farming families so that they can eat from their own land. But beyond that, it's a question of their destiny what sort of husband they get."

As for the boy, Sabra would also like to see him educated: "There's so little land. What can come from it? If he's willing to study, I'll send him to the *madrasā* in Begawala to become Hafyz Qur'ān. Then I'll send him to the government school in Dharmnagri. If he wants to continue further, I'll send him to Bijnor. If he studies, he could get an educated wife, somewhat schooled, too. I want him to study and then get service. But beyond education, Allah is the master."

Notes

1. As we noted in Chapter 3, there is such legislation, but it has been ineffective in combating the rise in dowry in north India.

2. Many castes were associated with occupations. Julahas were generally associated with weaving, although they did not necessarily earn all their income that way. Chandpuri was a mixed Hindu-Muslim village near Dharmnagri and Jhakri, and many of the Julaha homes had working looms.

Afterword

In Sabra's story, we saw shifts in fortune and shifts in mood, hope and a sense of unpredictability, agency as well as endurance and victimhood. Here were preoccupations with matters of birth, marriage, and death and with the present and future well-being of the household. Sabra's story leaves a bittersweet taste—the "sadness and happiness" that people in Dharmnagri and Jhakri so often alluded to in conversations with us. Through the accounts of Sabra and the other women who feature in these pages—and our own overarching narrative structuring the book—we have aimed to illuminate the complex conditions within which women in rural Bijnor could exercise their capacities for agency.

What life dealt Sabra and how she responded made her story uniquely her own. Other women, of course, handled their situations in different ways. Durgi and Kamla, for example, generally used their agency within permissible bounds, putting their efforts into raising their children, organizing their children's marriages, and managing their household affairs as best they could. But in opting to be sterilized, the normally compliant Najma broke ranks—and was roundly criticized for doing so. When Omvati was in grave difficulties, she presented herself as an innocent victim let down by her ungrateful sisters-in-law—yet they thought she had abused her position and was getting no more than she deserved. Dilruba's reward for unwarranted assertiveness over the years was divorce and lack of support from other women. Jamila complained about the lonely fate she had to endure—while often tormenting other women instead of building supportive relationships with them. And as for Lakshmi, her elusive past made it impossible to evaluate her portrayal of herself as a victim of cruel mishaps.

Many women in Dharmnagri and Jhakri seemed to appreciate the opportunities to narrate their experiences to us, to make sense of their pasts and their presents. For ourselves, too, there has been an element of therapy—sifting through our fieldnotes, piecing things together—as we have struggled to grasp what our attachment to Bijnor means for our own biographies and how our experiences there have influenced our understandings of the various social worlds we inhabit. Of course, as readers, your own biographies will have brought you to these narratives with your own preconceptions, and you will make your own sense of these stories.

Clearly, our own agency is evidenced in our reworkings of the women's narratives. We may have created misleading impressions of finality. Some threads we think we have tied up may yet become unravelled. Indeed, every time we have returned to Bijnor, unpredictable changes have taken place and people's lives have been diverted, whether by pleasant surprises or terrible shocks. These narratives, then, should not be read as account books with a final tally providing a sense of closure, but as the unfinished and unresolved stories of people still working out their lives in conditions of ambiguity and uncertainty.

Glossary

Auxiliary Nurse Midwife (ANM). A government female health worker, with responsibility for maternal and child health services for a population of about 5,000.

bannā, bannī. Bridegroom, bride; also the name of genres of songs sung by female relatives and friends of the bride and groom.

barāt. Marriage procession of bridegroom and his male relatives and friends to the house of the bride; the groom's female relatives do not usually participate in a *barāt* but await the new bride's arrival at home.

bhāt. Gifts presented by a woman's brothers when the first of her children is married. For a daughter, the gifts may be included in the dowry; if the oldest son is married later on, *bhāt* may be provided for a second time.

byāh. Marriage (see also *shādī*).

chathī. Muslim purification ceremonies normally carried out about six days after a birth, when festive food is cooked (see also *jasthawn*).

compounder. Local term for a pharmacist, sometimes offering a wide range of medical services (injections, for example).

Copper-T. An intra-uterine contraceptive device.

dāī. A traditional birth attendant, nurse, or midwife.

dahez, jahez. Dowry (cash, clothing, domestic goods, jewelry etc.)

dhotī. A cotton *sārī* worn by married Hindu women in Bijnor round the lower body with one end pulled up over the head (and concealing the face when a woman observes *purdah*). Also the shorter cloth length worn by Hindu men as a wraparound lower garment (see also *lungī*).

dupattā. A shawl worn by Muslim women to cover the head (and face when observing *purdah*) ànd draped over the shoulders to cover the breasts. Also worn before marriage by Hindu girls.

Eid. Muslim festivals, especially those marking the end of Ramzān (Mīthi Eid) and commemorating Abraham's willingness to sacrifice Isaac, at which goats are slaughtered (Bakr Eid) (more correctly, *īd*).

gaunā. Cohabitation, the ceremonial bringing of a new bride to her husband's home, which symbolizes the start of her married life; cohabitation may take place at the same time as the marriage or some months later.

ghar jamāī. A man who lives in the house of his father-in-law.

Hafyz Qur'ān. Person who can recite the Qur'ān Sharīf from memory.

hakīm. Practitioner of Unani (Greek or Arabic) medicine; usually Muslim.

Harijan. The name given by Mahatma Gandhi to outcastes or members of untouchable castes and tribes.

Holī. The Hindu spring festival, marked with water-fights, sprinkling of powdered colour, singing, dancing and a bonfire.

imām. Islamic religious specialist, usually the leader of prayers at a mosque.

jasthawn. Hindu birth ceremony at which a *pandit* (priest) removes birth pollution and names the baby (see also *chathī*).

karāv. A second marriage, or the remarriage of a widow.

lungī. A cloth worn as a wraparound for the lower body by Muslim men (see also *dhotī*).

madrasā. Islamic school or academy, taking children from about age five to eleven or twelve for girls, and to fifteen or sixteen for boys.

mahr. A marriage portion settled on the wife (among Muslims only).

maulvī. A learned man, teacher of Islamic law.

māykā. Mother's house, a woman's natal home (amongst Muslims).

Muharram. The first month of the Muslim year (when Husain's martyrdom is mourned).

munh dykhāī. A ceremony at the bridegroom's house when members of his family make small presents to the bride and lift her veil to see her face: Literally, "the showing of the mouth (or face)."

neg. Honoraria, customary presents (generally cash, jewelry, or clothing) to specified relatives, given on auspicious occasions.

nikāh. A Muslim marriage ceremony.

pājāma. Loose cotton trousers of different designs, in Bijnor worn by Muslim women and Hindu men (not a night-suit).

parāyā dhan. Another's property; used of a daughter who will be married into someone else's house.

purdah. Seclusion or bodily concealment. Literally a curtain; more properly *pardā*.

Qur'ān Sharīf. The Holy Book of Islam.

Ramzān. The ninth month of the Islamic year, when Muslims fast from dawn to dusk.

sārī. Long cloth worn by Hindu women round the lower body with one end pulled over one shoulder (rarely worn in rural Bijnor; see also *dhotī*).

satī. Virtuous or faithful wife; also refers to widow immolation.

sathīyā. An auspicious sign (amongst Hindus).

shādī. Wedding (see also *byāh*).

sharm. Shame, bashfulness, embarrassment.
sīdhā, sīdhī. Plain, straightforward, candid, honest.
Tījo (or *Tīj*). Hindu festival when women fast for the day; worship the goddess Parvati; and request a good husband, prosperity, and children.

Transliteration

We have marked the Hindi long 'a' as 'ā,' the long 'i' as 'ī,' and the long 'u' as 'ū' to distinguish them from the short versions, and '<u>kh</u>' (as in the Scottish 'loch') to distinguish from 'kh', an aspirated 'k'. An 'e' is pronounced like the 'é' in French. We have not distinguished different Hindi 'r,' 't,' and 'd' sounds but in most other respects have followed the transliteration schema in McGregor (1993).

Currency

The Indian Rupee now has 100 paisa. Prior to decimalization, there were sixty-four paisa and sixteen annas in one rupee. There were about thirty-three rupees to the US dollar in 1995, or about fifty rupees to the pound sterling.

Kinship Terminology

Kin terms used in Bijnor by Hindus and Muslims conform to the structure discussed by Vatuk (1969). We have adopted the following notation:

M = Mother	F = Father
W = Wife	H = Husband
D = Daughter	S = Son
Z = Sister	B = Brother
e = elder	y = younger

These can be combined to describe the full range of kin relationships, as in "HeBW" (a woman's husband's elder brother's wife). In north India the "HBW" has very different rights and obligations from the "HZ" (a woman's husband's sister) and from the "BW" (brother's wife), though all three would be translated as "sister-in-law" in English.

Bibliography

Abu-Lughod, Lila. 1990. "The Romance of Resistance: Tracing Transformations of Power Through Bedouin Women." *American Ethnologist* 17:41-55.

———. 1993. *Writing Women's Worlds: Bedouin Stories.* Berkeley: University of California Press.

Agarwal, Bina. 1994a. *A Field of One's Own.* Cambridge: Cambridge University Press.

———. 1994b. "Positioning the Western Feminist Agenda: A Comment." *Indian Journal of Gender Studies* 1:249-55.

Appadorai, Arjun, Frank J. Korom, and Margaret Mills, eds. 1994. *Gender, Genre and Power in South Asian Expressive Traditions.* Delhi: Motilal Banarsidass.

Atiya, Nayra. 1982. *Khul Khaal: Five Egyptian Women Tell Their Stories.* Syracuse: Syracuse University Press.

Balakrishnan, Radhika. 1994. "The Social Context of Sex Selection and the Politics of Abortion in India," in Gita Sen and Rachel Snow, eds, *Power and Decision: The Social Control of Reproduction.* Pp. 267-86. Cambridge, Mass.: Harvard School of Public Health.

Bardhan, Kalpana. 1993. "Social Classes and Gender in India: The Structure of Differences in the Condition of Women," in Alice Clark, ed., *Gender and Political Economy.* Pp. 146-78. Delhi: Oxford University Press.

Basu, Amrita. 1994. "When Local Riots Are Not Merely Local: Bringing the State Back In, Bijnor, 1988-92." *Economic and Political Weekly* 29:2605-21.

Basu, Tapan, Pradip Datta, Sumit Sarkar, Tanika Sarkar, and Sambuddha Sen. 1993. *Khaki Shorts and Saffron Flags.* Delhi: Orient Longman.

Brah, Avtar. 1992. "Questions of Difference and International Feminism," in J. Aaron and Sylvia Walby, eds, *Out of the Margins.* Pp. 168-76. London: Falmer.

Calman, Leslie J. 1992. *Toward Empowerment: Women and Movement Politics in India.* Boulder: Westview Press.

Cassen, Robert H. 1978. *India: Population, Economy, Society.* London: Macmillan.

Chatterjee, Partha. 1989. "Colonialism, Nationalism and the Colonized Woman: The Contest in India." *American Ethnologist* 16:622-33.

Chen, Martha, and Jean Drèze. 1992. "Widows and Health in Rural North India." *Economic and Political Weekly* 27: WS-81 to WS-92.

Daniel, E. Valentine. 1984 *Fluid Signs.* Berkeley: University of California Press.

Das, Veena. 1995. *Critical Events.* Delhi: Oxford University Press.

Datta, S. K. and John B. Nugent. 1984. "Are Old Age Security and the Utility of Children in Rural India Really Unimportant?" *Population Studies* 38:507-12.

Drèze, Jean. 1990. "Widows in Rural India." Development Economics Research Programme Paper 26, London School of Economics, London.

Dube, Leela. 1983. "Misadventures in Amniocentesis." *Economic and Political Weekly* 18:279-80.

————. 1988. "On the Construction of Gender: Hindu Girls in Patrilineal India." *Economic and Political Weekly* 23: WS-11 to WS-19.

Dwyer, Kevin. 1982. *Moroccan Dialogues*. Baltimore: Johns Hopkins University Press.

Dyson, Tim, and Mick Moore. 1983. "On Kinship Structure, Female Autonomy and Demographic Behaviour in India." *Population and Development Review* 9:35-60.

Engineer, Asghar Ali, ed. 1987. *The Shah Bano Controversy*. Bombay: Orient Longman.

————. 1991. "The Bloody Trail: Ramjanmabhoomi and Communal Violence in UP." *Economic and Political Weekly* 26:155-59.

Friedl, Erika. 1989. *Women of Deh Koh: Lives in an Iranian Village*. Washington D.C.: Smithsonian Institution Press.

Gandhi, Nandita, and Nandita Shah. 1992. *The Issues at Stake: Theory and Practice in the Contemporary Women's Movement in India*. New Delhi: Kali for Women.

Geiger, Susan N.G. 1986. "Women's Life Histories: Method and Content." *Signs* 11:334-51.

Gold, Ann. 1988. *Fruitful Journeys*. Berkeley: University of California Press.

Goody, Jack, and Stanley J. Tambiah. 1974. *Bridewealth and Dowry*. London and New York: Cambridge University Press.

Gopal, Sarvepalli, ed. 1991. *Anatomy of a Confrontation*. New Delhi: Penguin.

Guha, Ranajit, ed. 1982-1994. *Subaltern Studies*, vols. 1-9. Delhi: Oxford University Press.

Gupta, Jyotsna A. 1993. "'People Like You Never Agree to Get It': Visit to an Indian Family Planning Clinic." *Reproductive Health Matters* 1:39-43.

Hardiman, David. 1987. *The Coming of the Devi*. Delhi: Oxford University Press.

Hasan, Zoya. 1989. "Minority Identity, Muslim Women Bill Campaign and the Political Process." *Economic and Political Weekly* 24:44-50.

Hasan, Zoya, ed. 1994. *Forging Identities: Gender, Communities and the State*. New Delhi: Kali for Women.

Hastrup, Kirsten. 1992. "Writing Ethnography: The State of the Art," in Judith Okely and Helen Callaway, eds., *Anthropology and Autobiography*. Pp. 116-133. London: Routledge.

Haynes, Douglas, and Gyan Prakash, eds. 1991. *Contesting Power: Resistance and Everyday Social Relations in South Asia*. Delhi: Oxford University Press.

Humphrey, Robin. 1993. "Life Stories and Social Careers: Ageing and Social Life in an Ex-mining Town." *Sociology* 27:166-78.

Jacobson, Doranne. 1976. "Women and Jewelry in Rural India," in Giri Raj Gupta, ed., *Main Currents in Indian Sociology, Vol. ii: Family and Social Change.* Pp. 135-83. New Delhi: Vikas.

Jacobson, Doranne, and Susan Wadley. 1977. *Women in India.* Columbia: South Asia Books.

Jeffery, Patricia. 1979. *Frogs in a Well: Indian Women in Purdah.* London: Zed Press, and Delhi: Vikas.

Jeffery, Patricia, and Roger Jeffery. 1993. "A Woman Belongs to Her Husband: Female Autonomy, Women's Work and Childbearing in Bijnor," in Alice Clark, ed., *Gender and Political Economy.* Pp. 66-114. Delhi: Oxford University Press.

————. 1994 "'Killing My Heart's Desire': On Female Autonomy and Education in Rural North India," in Nita Kumar, ed., *Woman as Subject: Tales and Trials from South Asia.* Pp. 125-71. Calcutta: Stree, and Charlottesville: Virginia University Press.

————. 1996. "What's the Use of Being Educated?" in Roger Jeffery and Alaka Basu, eds., *Girls' Schooling, Women's Autonomy and Fertility Change in South Asia.* New Delhi: Sage.

————. Forthcoming. "Engendering Institutional Communalism: Gender, Community and the Local State in Bijnor," in Patricia Jeffery and Amrita Basu, eds., *Appropriating Gender: Women's Agency and Politicized Religion in South Asia.*

Jeffery, Patricia, Roger Jeffery, and Hazel Johnson. 1994. "A Vulnerable Life," in Tim Allen, Carolyn Baxter, Hazel Johnson, and Eleanor Morris, eds., *Video Notes (Development Studies Study Pack).* Pp. 5-14. Milton Keynes: Open University Press.

Jeffery, Patricia, Roger Jeffery, and Andrew Lyon. 1988. "When Did You Last See Your Mother?" in John C. Caldwell et al., eds., *Advances in Micro-Demography.* Pp. 321-33. London: Kegan Paul International.

————. 1989. *Labour Pains and Labour Power: Women and Childbearing in India.* London: Zed Books, and Delhi: Manohar.

Jeffery, Roger, and Patricia Jeffery. 1993. "Traditional Birth Attendants in Rural North India," in Shirley Lindenbaum and Margaret Lock, eds., *Knowledge, Power and Practice in Medicine and Everyday Life.* Pp. 7-31. Berkeley and London: University of California Press.

————. 1994. "The Bijnor Riots, October 1990: Collapse of a Mythical Special Relationship?" *Economic and Political Weekly* 22:551-58.

————. 1996. *Population and Politics.* Cambridge: Cambridge University Press.

Kabeer, Naila. 1985. "Do Women Gain from High Fertility?" in Haleh Afshar, ed., *Women, Work and Ideology in the Third World.* Pp. 83-106. London: Tavistock.

Kandiyoti, Deniz. 1988. "Bargaining with Patriarchy." *Gender and Society* 2:274-90.

Kishwar, Madhu, and Ruth Vanita, eds. 1984. *In Search of Answers: Indian Women's Voices from Manushi*. London: Zed Books.

Kolenda, Pauline. 1987. "Living the Levirate," in Paul Hockings, ed., *Dimensions of Social Life*. Pp. 45-67. Berlin: de Gruyter.

Kumar, Dharma. 1983. "Male Utopias or Nightmares?" *Economic and Political Weekly* 18:61-64.

Kumar, Nita. 1994. "Introduction," in Nita Kumar, ed., *Woman as Subject: Tales and Trials from South Asia*. Pp. 1-25. Calcutta: Stree, and Charlottesville: Virginia University Press.

Kumar, Radha. 1993. *The History of Doing: An Illustrated Account of Movements for Women's Rights and Feminism in India, 1800-1990*. New Delhi: Kali for Women.

Kumari, Ranjana. 1989. *Brides Are Not for Burning: Dowry Victims in India*. London: Sangam Books.

Mandelbaum, David G. 1988. *Women's Seclusion and Men's Honor: Sex Roles in North India, Bangladesh, and Pakistan*. Tucson: University of Arizona Press.

Mani, Lata. 1990. "Multiple Mediations: Feminist Scholarship in the Age of Multinational Reception." *Feminist Review* 35:24-41.

Marchand, Marianne H., and Jane L. Parpart, eds. 1995. *Feminism/Postmodernism/Development*. London and New York: Routledge.

Marriott, McKim. 1990. "Constructing an Indian Ethnosociology," in McKim Marriott, ed., *India Through Hindu Categories*. Pp. 1-39. New Delhi: Sage.

Mascia-Lees, Frances E., Patricia Sharpe, and Colleen B. Cohen. 1989. "The Postmodernist Turn in Anthropology: Cautions from a Feminist Perspective." *Signs* 15:7-33.

Masselos, Jim. 1994. "The Dis/Appearance of Subalterns: A Reading of a Decade of *Subaltern Studies*." *South Asia* N. S. 15:105-26.

McGregor, R. S. 1993. *The Oxford Hindi-English Dictionary*. Delhi: Oxford University Press.

Miller, Barbara D. 1980. "Female Neglect and the Costs of Marriage in Rural India." *Contributions to Indian Sociology* 14:95-129.

——— . 1981. *The Endangered Sex*. Ithaca: Cornell University Press.

Mills, C. Wright. 1959. *The Sociological Imagination*. New York: Oxford University Press.

Mines, Mattison. 1994. *Public Faces, Private Voices: Community and Individuality in South India*. Berkeley: University of California Press.

Mintz, Sidney W. 1989. "The Sensation of Moving, While Standing Still." *American Ethnologist* 16:786-96.

Mody, N.B. 1987. "The Press in India: Shah Bano Judgment." *Asian Survey* 27:935-53.

Mohanty, Chandra. 1988. "Under Western Eyes: Feminist Scholarship and Colonial Discourses." *Feminist Review* 30:61-88.

Mohanty, Chandra, Ann Russo, and Lourdes Torres, eds. 1991. *Third World Women and the Politics of Feminism.* Bloomington and Indianapolis: Indiana University Press.

Narayan, Kirin. 1986. "Birds on a Branch: Girlfriends and Wedding Songs in Kangra." *Ethos* 14:47-75.

————. 1993. "How Native Is a 'Native' Anthropologist?" *American Anthropologist* 95:671-86.

Narayana, G., and John F. Kantner. 1992. *Doing the Needful: The Dilemmas of India's Population Policy.* Boulder: Westview Press.

Nicholson, Linda J., ed. 1990. *Feminism/Postmodernism.* London: Routledge.

Okely, Judith. 1991. "Defiant Moments: Gender, Resistance and Individuals." *Man* 26:3-22.

Okely, Judith, and Helen Callaway, eds. 1992. *Anthropology and Autobiography.* London: Routledge.

Parashar, Archana. 1992. *Women and Family Law Reform in India.* New Delhi: Sage.

Parry, Jonathan. 1989. "The End of the Body," in Michel Feher, ed., *Fragments for a History of the Human Body, Part 2.* Pp. 490-517. New York: Zone.

Pathak, Zakia, and Rajeswari Sunder Rajan. 1989. "Shahbano." *Signs* 14:558-82.

Raheja, Gloria G. 1988. *The Poison in the Gift.* Chicago: University of Chicago Press.

Raheja, Gloria G., and Ann G. Gold. 1994. *Listen to the Heron's Words: Reimagining Gender and Kinship in North India.* Berkeley: University of California Press.

Rajan, Rajeswari Sunder. 1993. *Real and Imagined Women: Gender, Culture and Postcolonialism.* London: Routledge.

Ramanamma, A. and Usha Bhambawale. 1980. "The Mania for Sons." *Social Science and Medicine* 14B:107-10.

Ramaseshan, R. 1990. "The Press on Ayodhya." *Economic and Political Weekly* 25:2701-05.

Ravindran, T. K. Sundari. 1993. "The Politics of Women, Population and Development in India." *Reproductive Health Matters* 1:26-38.

Sarkar, Tanika. 1991. "The Woman as Communal Subject: Rashtrasevika Samita and Ram Janmabhoomi Movement." *Economic and Political Weekly* 26:2057-62.

Scott, James. C. 1985. *Weapons of the Weak.* New Haven: Yale University Press.

————. 1990. *Domination and the Arts of Resistance: Hidden Transcripts.* New Haven: Yale University Press.

Segal, Lynn. 1987. *Is the Future Female? Troubled Thoughts on Contemporary Feminism.* London: Virago.

Sen, Amartya K. 1990. "Gender and Co-operative Conflicts," in Irene Tinker, ed., *Persistent Inequalities: Women and World Development.* Pp. 123-49. New York: Oxford University Press.

Sharma, Miriam, and Urmila Vanjani. 1993. "Engendering Reproduction: The Political Economy of Reproductive Activities in a Rajasthan Village," in Alice Clark, ed., *Gender and Political Economy.* Pp. 24-65. Delhi: Oxford University Press.

Sharma, Ursula. 1978a. "Women and Their Affines: The Veil as a Symbol of Separation." *Man* 13:218-33.

————. 1978b. "Segregation and Its Consequences for Women," in Patricia Caplan and Janet Bujra, eds., *Women United, Women Divided.* Pp. 259-82. London: Tavistock.

————. 1980. *Women, Work, and Property in North-West India.* London: Tavistock.

————. 1986. *Women's Work, Class, and the Urban Household.* London: Tavistock.

Spivak, Gayatri. 1987. *In Other Worlds.* New York: Methuen.

————. 1988. "Can the Subaltern Speak?" in Cary Nelson and Lawrence Grossberg, eds., *Marxism and the Interpretation of Culture.* Pp. 271-313. Urbana: University of Illinois Press.

Srinivas, Mysore N. 1986. *Dowry.* Delhi: Oxford University Press.

Thompson, Catherine S. 1981. "A Sense of *Sharm*: Its Implications for the Position of Women in Central India." *South Asia Research* 1:39-53.

————. 1984. "Ritual States in the Life-Cycles of Hindu Women in a Village of Central India." Unpublished Ph.D. thesis, London University, School of Oriental and African Studies.

————. 1985. "The Power to Pollute and the Power to Preserve: Perceptions of Female Power in a Hindu Village." *Social Science and Medicine* 21:707-11.

Tonkin, Elizabeth. 1992. *Narrating Our Pasts: The Social Construction of Oral History.* Cambridge: Cambridge University Press.

Vatuk, Sylvia J. 1969. "A Structural Analysis of the Hindi Kinship Terminology." *Contributions to Indian Sociology* 3:94-115.

————. 1972. *Kinship and Urbanization: White Collar Migrants in North India.* Berkeley: University of California Press.

————. 1990. "To Be a Burden on Others: Dependency Anxiety Among the Elderly in India," in Owen M. Lynch, ed., *Divine Passions: The Social Construction of Emotion in India.* Pp. 64-88. Delhi: Oxford University Press.

Visaria, Pravin, and Leela Visaria. 1994. "Demographic Transition: Accelerating Fertility Decline in 1980s." *Economic and Political Weekly* 29:3281-92.

Vishwanath, Snehalata. 1994. "May I Have Some More Milk Pills Please?" *Reproductive Health Matters* 3:46-50.

Vlassoff, Carol. 1990. "The Value of Sons in an Indian Village: How Widows See It." *Population Studies* 44:5-20.

Vlassoff, Michael. 1984. "Old Age Security and the Utility of Children in Rural India: A Rejoinder to Datta and Nugent." *Population Studies* 38:510-12.

Vlassoff, Michael, and Carol Vlassoff. 1980. "Old Age Security and the Utility of Children in Rural India." *Population Studies* 34:487-99.

Wadley, Susan S. 1992. "The Village 'Indira': A Brahman Widow and Political Action in Rural North India," in Patricia Lyons, ed., *Balancing Acts: Women and the Process of Social Change.* Pp. 65-87. Boulder: Westview Press.

———. 1994. *Struggling with Destiny in Karimpur, 1925-84.* Berkeley: University of California Press.

Willis, Paul. 1979. *Learning to Labour.* Farnborough: Saxon House.

About the Book
and Authors

Popular Western images of Indian women range from submissive brides behind their veils to the powerful, active women of Indian politics. In this lively and unique book, Patricia and Roger Jeffery present a different perspective on women's lives. Focusing on the mundane rather than the exotic, they explore the complex interplay between the power of social structures to constrain individuals and the ways women negotiate these constraints to carve out places for themselves.

Based on information collected by the authors during their research in villages in Bijnor District, western Uttar Pradesh, the volume offers eight life histories of Hindu and Muslim women. The women's life histories present a variety of class positions and domestic circumstances, illustrating many aspects of north Indian village life. Interspersed with thematic discussion composed of dialogues, episodes, and songs, the life histories deal with topics of vital concern for women in rural north India: the birth of children, worries about dowry, arranging weddings, sexual politics in marriage, relationships with in-laws, relationships with natal kin, and widowhood.

Patricia Jeffery and **Roger Jeffery** both teach in the Sociology Department at the University of Edinburgh.

Name Index

Adesh (M), b. 1945, married Ashok, 1952, Hindu, Rajput, rich peasant, 110-111, 162-163.

Afrozi (F), b. 1962, married 1977, Muslim, Sheikh, middle peasant, 46-49, 227-228.

Afsana (F), b. 1966, married 1981, Muslim, Sheikh, rich peasant, 159-160.

Ahmed (M), b. 1954, married Asghari 1975 & Anisa, 1987, Muslim, Sheikh, middle peasant, 254-255

Akbar (M), b. 1945, married 1964, Muslim, Sheikh, poor peasant, 196-197, 226

Anisa (F), b. 1957, married 1975 & Ahmed, 1987, Muslim, Sheikh, middle peasant, 254-256

Anjali (F), b. 1933, married 1947, Hindu, Dhimar, middle peasant, 114, 115, 122

Asghari (F), b. 1960, d. 1988, married Ahmed, 1975, Muslim, Sheikh, middle peasant, 254, 262.

Ashok (M), b. 1940, married Adesh, 1952, Hindu, Rajput, rich peasant, 110, 162-163

Bashir (M), b. 1927, married 1946 & Bilquis, 1968, Muslim Sheikh, middle peasant, 259, 265, 266, 272.

Bhagirthi (F), b. 1947, married 1966, Hindu, Rajput, rich peasant, 261-262

Bilquis (F), b. 1946, married 1961 & Bashir, 1968, Muslim, Sheikh, middle peasant, 259, 267

Brijpal (M), b. 1940, married Swati, 1954, Hindu, Jat, middle peasant, 72-74, 137-139, 192-196.

Devinder (M), b. 1951, married Durgi, 1971, Hindu, Sahni, middle peasant, 83-97, 259

Deepa (F), b. 1922, married 1935 & 1941, Hindu, Sahni, poor peasant, 157-158

Dilruba (F), b. 1956, married Dilshad, 1973, Muslim, Sheikh, rich peasant, 142-154, 256

Dilshad (M), b. 1953, married Dilruba, 1973, Muslim, Sheikh, rich peasant, 142-154, 256, 262

Durgi (F), b. 1954, married Devinder, 1971, Hindu, Sahni, middle peasant, 83-97, 197, 198, 238, 259

Farooq (M), b. 1955, married Fatima, 1972, Muslim, Sheikh, middle peasant, 104, 105

Fatima (F), b. 1958, married Farooq, 1972, Muslim, Sheikh, middle peasant, 40, 104-106, 168, 190-192, 262

Firdausi (F), b. 1968, married Khurshid Ahmed, 1985, Muslim, Sheikh, middle peasant, 38, 39, 130-131, 164-165

Furqana (F), b. 1971, married 1988, Muslim, Sheikh, middle peasant, 60, 62, 64-65

Ghazala (F), b. 1963, married Ghulam, 1978, Muslim, Sheikh, middle peasant, 45, 64, 139-140, 168-169